access to history

The Wars of the Roses and Henry VII: Britain 1450–1509

Roger Turvey

HODDER
EDUCATION
AN HACHETTE UK COMPANY

Study Guide authors: Sally Waller (AQA), Angela Leonard (Edexcel),
Geoff Woodward (OCR) and Martin Jones (OCR).

The Publishers would like to thank the following for permission to reproduce
copyright material:
Photo credits: **p.28** The Bridgeman Art Library/English School; **p.35** Mary Evans
Picture Library; **p.41** Getty Images; **p.45** Popperfoto/Getty Images;
p.50 Northampton Museums Service; **p.54** Bibliothèque Nationale, Paris, France/
The Bridgeman Art Library; **p.76** Lebrecht Music and Arts Photo Library/Alamy;
p.91 SuperStock; **p.94** Royal Holloway, University of London/The Bridgeman Art
Library; **p.96** Mary Evans Picture Library; **p.99** The Trustees of the 9th Duke of
Buccleuch's Chattels Fund; **p.109** Getty Images; **p.145** Mary Evans Picture Library;
p.167 Photo © Philip Mould Ltd, London/The Bridgeman Art Library.
Acknowledgements: **p.18** A.J. Pollard, *The Wars of the Roses*, Macmillan Education
(1988); **p.24** J. Warren, *Access to History: The Wars of the Roses and the Yorkist Kings*,
Hodder Arnold (1995); **p.28** R.A. Griffiths, *Henry VI* (New Oxford Dictionary of
National Biography – online edition); **p.30** A.J. Pollard, *John Talbot and the War in
France, 1427–53*, Pen & Sword Books (2005); **p.56** A.J. Pollard, *Warwick the
Kingmaker: Politics, Power and Fame*, Continuum (2007); **p.157** J. Guy, *Tudor
England*, Oxford University Press (1988); **p.167** C. Rogers, *Access to History: Henry
VII*, Hodder Arnold (1992).

Hachette UK's policy is to use papers that are natural, renewable and recyclable
products and made from wood grown in sustainable forests. The logging and
manufacturing processes are expected to conform to the environmental
regulations of the country of origin.

Orders: please contact Bookpoint Ltd, 130 Milton Park, Abingdon,
Oxon OX14 4SB. Telephone: (44) 01235 827720. Fax: (44) 01235 400454.
Lines are open 9.00–5.00, Monday to Saturday, with a 24-hour message
answering service. Visit our website at www.hoddereducation.co.uk

© Roger Turvey
First published in 2010 by
Hodder Education,
An Hachette UK Company
338 Euston Road
London NW1 3BH

Impression number   5
Year   2014

Cover image: Illustration of the Battle of Tewkesbury, 1471 (c.1850),
© Imagestate/Photolibrary.com
Typeset in 10/12pt Baskerville and produced by Gray Publishing, Tunbridge Wells
Printed and bound by CPI Group (UK) Ltd, Croydon, CR0 4YY

A catalogue record for this title is available from the British Library.

ISBN: 978 1444 110074

Contents

Dedication

Keith Randell (1943–2002)

The *Access to History* series was conceived and developed by Keith, who created a series to 'cater for students as they are, not as we might wish them to be'. He leaves a living legacy of a series that for over 20 years has provided a trusted, stimulating and well-loved accompaniment to post-16 study. Our aim with these new editions is to continue to offer students the best possible support for their studies.

1 Fifteenth-century England

POINTS TO CONSIDER

This opening chapter serves to introduce the reader to a very different England to the one we know today. It was a wild, sparsely populated country of peasants ruled by a king supported by his landowning nobility and gentry. It is a period in history which has long fascinated historians because of its drama, intrigue and bloody conflict. Much has been written about the so-called Wars of the Roses, not least how a dynastic civil war involving frequent changes of monarch acquired its title. This introduction provides an essential background by examining three key themes:

- England and Europe in the fifteenth century
- Historians, historiography and the origins of the Wars of the Roses
- Conflict and confrontation: the battles in context 1455–87

Key dates

1399	Henry IV usurped the throne by removing Richard II
1400–10	Glyndŵr rebellion in Wales
1415	Henry V renewed the war against France and won the battle of Agincourt
1455	Wars of the Roses began
1461	Edward IV usurped the throne by removing Henry VI
1469–70	Edward IV was removed and replaced by Henry VI
1471	Edward IV returned as king. Henry VI was killed
1483	Edward V succeeded to the throne but was quickly removed by Richard III
1485	Richard III was killed at the battle of Bosworth. Henry Tudor became King Henry VII
1487	Battle of Stoke marked the end of the Wars of the Roses

1 | England and Europe in the Fifteenth Century

The Kingdom of England

The Kingdom of England embraced the greater part of the British Isles, stretching as far north as Northumberland and Cumberland on the Scottish border, and as far west as the **marcher counties** of Cheshire, Shropshire and Herefordshire bordering Wales. The rest of the kingdom bordered the sea and laid claim to the outlying territories that consisted of the Isle of Wight, the Scilly Isles and the Isle of Man. Beyond the territorial confines of the kingdom, the authority of English kings extended further afield to the whole of Wales, a significant slice of eastern Ireland, the Channel Islands and Calais in France. In fact, until 1453 the English Crown had exercised its authority over great swathes of northern and south-western France.

The struggle against the French and the consequent loss of these continental possessions in the so-called **Hundred Years War** (1338–1453) contributed to a growing sense of Englishness and of nationhood that evolved into an early form of English nationalism. In the opinion of many Tudor historians and writers, the playwright William Shakespeare prominent among them, the key event that defined Englishness was the battle of Agincourt in 1415. Henry V's victory over the French in that battle was used to help create 'a spirit of Agincourt', a feeling of unity within the realm where Englishmen could feel pride in being English.

Yet fifteenth-century England was a divided land, being much more regionalised than it is today. In terms of their customs, culture and mode of life, the north-country people were very different from southern folk. Even as late as the 1530s, John Leland, Henry VIII's librarian, described his visit to Lancashire as if he were entering 'a wild, foreign land'. The west country, too, was thought to be a strange land, especially as it bordered Cornwall, in which more than half the people spoke the Celtic language Cornish, and did not think of themselves as being English. The difference between the English and their Celtic neighbours, the Irish, Scots and Welsh, was more pronounced, with the latter being considered more foreign than even the French. Scotland remained an independent kingdom, but whereas Wales had been conquered and ruled by the English for over 100 years (except for the decade-long Glyndŵr rebellion, 1400–10), Ireland continued to resist complete assimilation, yielding only **the Pale**, a territory with Dublin at its heart, to English rule.

The Kings of England

Between 1399 and 1509 the Kingdom of England was ruled by six monarchs:

- Henry IV   1399–1413
- Henry V   1413–22
- Henry VI   1422–61, 1470–1
- Edward IV   1461–9, 1471–83
- Richard III 1483–5
- Henry VII   1485–1509.

Key question
What was the nature of England's relationship with continental Europe in the fifteenth century?

Key dates

Henry V renewed the war against France and won the battle of Agincourt: 1415

Glyndŵr rebellion in Wales: 1400–10

Key terms

Marcher counties
English counties bordering Wales that were originally intended to defend England from Welsh attack.

Hundred Years War
Historical term used to describe the intermittent conflict between the kings of England and France for possession or control of the French crown and kingdom of France.

The Pale
Territory in eastern Ireland occupied and ruled by English kings since the thirteenth century. The capital of this English-controlled region was Dublin.

By the fifteenth century monarchy had acquired an almost mystical quality. To their subjects, kings were not like ordinary men and claimed God-given power to govern and make laws. This **divine right** to rule enabled the monarch to command the respect of the people, who were constantly reminded of the Crown's privileged status by the Church. The monarchy's strength lay in the combination of traditional respect for its authority and power to dispense patronage and reward. People were expected to abide by the law and for those who disturbed the '**king's peace**' there was arrest by the Crown's officers, trial in the royal courts of justice and punishment by fine, imprisonment or death.

Key terms

Divine right
Belief that monarchs were chosen by God to rule the kingdom and that their word was law. To challenge their right to rule was the same as challenging God's.

King's peace
The idea that, as the king was appointed by God, his law was the highest authority which brought order and protection to the people.

Figure 1.1: Map of fifteenth-century Britain.

However, the fifteenth century witnessed the breakdown of royal authority and an increase in lawlessness and disorder. The frequent breaks in the kingships of Henry VI and Edward IV illustrate the disturbed condition of England during this period. England was a nation seemingly at war with itself; civil war in which nobles fought each other for either possession or control of the crown. The century began with Henry IV's usurpation of the throne when Richard II was forcibly removed and imprisoned. War with France was an added complication that dominated English history for the first half of the century. Failure in the war against the French between 1429 and 1453 did much to cause civil war in England in 1455. For some 30 years thereafter, until 1487, nobles fought each other intermittently in a series of dynastic wars known to history as the Wars of the Roses. In stark contrast to its beginning, the century ended in peace and prosperity due in large part to the leadership, security and stability provided by Henry VII, the first of the Tudor monarchs.

Government and administration

The fifteenth century was a period when personal monarchy stood at the centre of government. The king took a personal interest in the running of the kingdom and in the machinery of government. The most vital cogs in that machine were the **king's council** and departments of state such as the court of Exchequer (finance) and court of Chancery (law) that made up central government. As an aid to government, the monarchy also had **parliament** at its disposal to offer advice, pass laws and raise revenue. Unlike the departments or courts that made up central government, parliament was not a permanent feature of royal rule but it played a vital if occasional role in governing the kingdom. At the very least, the election of representatives from the privileged class in localities across England to sit and meet together in parliament in London had the effect of bringing the kingdom together.

The fifteenth century witnessed the development of central and local government. Local government had long been focused on the county as a unit of administration with its own officials appointed by the Crown. However, by the second half of the century a new tier of administration had developed to sit between central and local government: the regional council. The councils of the North and of Wales (the latter included the western-most counties of England) were established to function as extensions of the king's council. In this way the reach, power and authority of the Crown were beginning to be felt in even the remotest regions of the kingdom. By binding the outlying regions of the kingdom together in partnership with the Crown at the centre, the government of the kingdom became more effective and, in time, more efficient.

Key question
How did government and administration work in fifteenth-century England?

Key terms

King's council
Élite body of councillors, drawn mainly from the nobility, who met the king regularly to frame policy and govern the country.

Parliament
Institution of government representing English landowners consisting of the Houses of Lords and Commons. It had the power to grant taxes and to pass laws.

Key question
How was law and order maintained?

Key terms

Royal proclamations
Royal commands that had the same authority in law as acts of parliament.

Gentry
Class of landowners below the nobility. They were divided into three strata: knight, esquire and gentleman.

Sheriff
Chief law officer in the county who arrested and detained criminals, some of whom were dealt with in the sheriff's court or passed on to the justices of the peace. The sheriff also supervised parliamentary elections.

Justice of the peace
Local law officer and magistrate at county level. He also governed the county by enforcing acts of parliament and acting on decisions taken by the Crown and central government.

The maintenance of law and order

English kings had no police force to maintain and enforce law and order. However, fear of what the Crown, as a God-given institution, could do was a potent weapon in the struggle to uphold the peace. The monarchy communicated its orders by means of **royal proclamations** that were carried by royal messengers to various parts of the kingdom. Although not everyone was able to read these proclamations, word soon spread and thus made the monarch's will known to a great number of people. The monarchy also relied on the unpaid services of the local **gentry** and nobility, who were expected to uphold and enforce the law by means of the powers vested in them through the offices of **sheriff** and **justice of the peace**. The holders of

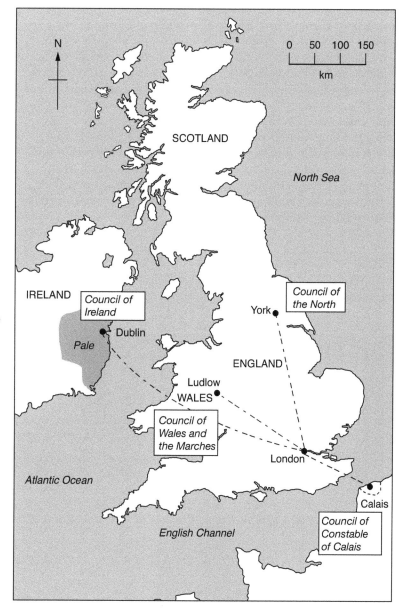

Figure 1.2: A map showing the location and relationship of central government and regional councils.

these offices had no supporting enforcement agencies, but relied on their wealth, status and influence in the community to exert their authority.

Unlike its counterparts on the continent, the English monarchy did not have the financial means to maintain a regular, professional army. Nor, since Edward IV and Henry VII had passed laws to prevent the keeping of private armies, could the Crown rely on the armed retainers maintained by the nobility. This situation was a result of the Crown's experiences in the Wars of the Roses when private armies had been used to defy the law. The only professional forces available to the monarch were the 300 men that garrisoned Berwick to guard the border with Scotland and the 4000 men maintained in the Calais garrison.

The Crown also exercised its authority in more informal but equally effective ways. Royal imagery was used to impress both people and visitors alike. For those wealthy and influential enough to be invited to attend the monarch in one of the many royal palaces, the sheer scale and size of the buildings themselves would have been impressive, let alone the paintings and portraits that hung within. Even the majority of the population who might be fortunate enough to view the palaces from afar would have been impressed. There were also frequent royal progresses in which the king and his **royal court** toured the kingdom. This served to overawe those who witnessed them and to remind the people of the might and majesty of the monarch. But if the people needed reminding of the power of the Crown they had only to reach for their coins, every denomination of which carried pictures of the ruling monarch.

Key term

Royal court
The court acted as a public place for people to come and meet the king. The court was attached to whichever palace the king happened to be living in.

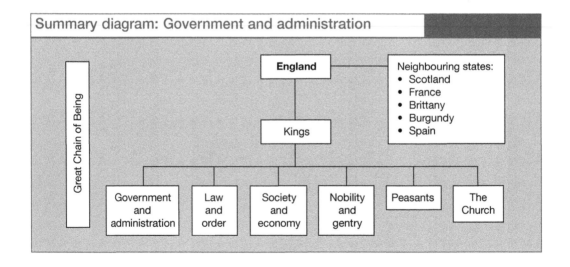

Summary diagram: Government and administration

Great Chain of Being

England — Neighbouring states:
- Scotland
- France
- Brittany
- Burgundy
- Spain

Kings

- Government and administration
- Law and order
- Society and economy
- Nobility and gentry
- Peasants
- The Church

Key question
How were England's society and economy organised?

Key terms

Black Death
Plague that spread across the British Isles between 1347 and 1351 killing up to half of the population.

Bloody flux
Dysentery, an inflammatory disorder of the intestine, that results in severe diarrhoea accompanied by fever and abdominal pain.

French pox
An outbreak of syphilis, a sexually transmitted disease, which spread through the ranks of the French army and also infected the English.

Sweating sickness
A virulent form of influenza.

Infection resistant
Constant exposure to an infection enabled some people to develop a natural immunity.

Society and economy

At the beginning of the fifteenth century, England was a relatively prosperous, if sparsely populated, kingdom of between two and three million people. The population had barely begun to recover from the effects of the **Black Death** in the mid-fourteenth century before it was struck again by disease, pestilence and death. The plague returned in the 1420s and 1430s, killing large numbers of people before it disappeared, only to be replaced by equally deadly outbreaks of the **bloody flux** in 1472 and the so-called **French pox** of 1475. Following another bout of plague in 1479–80 and the **sweating sickness** of 1483, the increasingly **infection-resistant** population first stabilised and then began to rise quite dramatically from the 1490s. Little wonder that the fifteenth century has been described as the 'golden age of bacteria'.

England was a mainly rural kingdom in which the lives of nearly 90 per cent of the population revolved around the cycle of the seasons and the harvesting of the crops. Arable or crop farming went hand in hand with pastoral or animal husbandry, with cattle, pigs and sheep the three most significant livestock in the agricultural economy. Of these, sheep were probably the most important insofar as their wool was the mainstay of England's largest industry – cloth. It has been estimated that the cloth trade employed over 35,000 people, around three per cent of the working population, and accounted for nearly 80 per cent of England's exports. Between 1462 and 1508 the average annual export of bales of cloth had risen from 25,000 to 90,000. This helps explain why nearly half the statutes passed by parliament during the Yorkist period, 1461–85, dealt with commerce and industry.

A society dominated by agriculture depended on the success of the harvest to survive. Harvest failures invariably led to a sharp increase in the death rate and to social unrest, due to deprivation, starvation and disease. W.G. Hoskins, a specialist in social and economic history, calculated that in an average decade around one in every four harvests would be deficient, with one in six being seriously bad. Unfortunately for Edward IV, it is known that England suffered three bad harvests in a row between 1481 and 1483. Nor did it improve much in the following six years, 1484–90, with only one really good harvest in 1485 and the rest merely average. Fortunately for Henry VII, the 1490s were something of a 'golden age', witnessing six plentiful harvests with only one being seriously deficient.

Peasant, priest and parish

If farming dominated the lives of the overwhelmingly peasant population, so did the borders of the parish in which they lived. The local church and parish priest guided and shaped the lives of those who faithfully followed his teachings. The peasants looked to the priest for leadership, advice and comfort, and to satisfy their spiritual needs. The cycle of life was represented by the

Church, in its form of worship, and in the way it regulated baptism, marriage and burial. The Church was an ever-present part of daily life and it served as a reminder of God's plan for man: to work, to worship and to obey. The preacher and the pulpit exerted a powerful influence over all sections of society but they were at their most persuasive with the largely uneducated mass of the population.

Social order and the 'Great Chain of Being'

The Church was able to exert so much authority over the people because of a concept known as the **Great Chain of Being**. This was the belief that every person was born to a specific place in the strict hierarchy of society and had a duty to remain there. It conveyed the contemporary idea of God punishing those who rebelled against their prince – treason – or who questioned the Great Chain of Being – heresy. However, it also emphasised that those in authority held their power for the good of those below them, and were subject to those above them. The concept was clearly expressed in Church doctrine and it was ordered to be taught as a normal part of the church service. Thus, by means of the weekly sermon preached from the pulpit, the Church aided the Crown in its endeavour to govern and control the people.

Nobility and gentry

There had been little structural change by the beginning of the sixteenth century. The three social hierarchies of monarchy, nobility and gentry stayed broadly unaltered in size and in their relationship to each other.

The nobility and gentry made up less than three per cent of the population but they, along with the Crown and Church, possessed over 95 per cent of the wealth of the kingdom. Their wealth came primarily from the ownership of land but the profits of war and the revenue derived from royal service also contributed to their financial power. The maintenance of law and order was as vital to the survival of a medieval king as it was to the survival of the nobility and gentry. Discontent, disorder and rebellion were ever-present threats. To help the Crown maintain the peace and security of the kingdom, the king made use of, and controlled, the richest and most powerful ruling classes in England: the nobility and gentry. The source of their wealth and power, and that of the king, was the ownership of land.

Besides the ownership of land, titles also defined the upper levels of society. For example, a duke was the premier noble title in England followed by a marquis, earl, viscount and baron. The most powerful, the noble élite, were those who could claim a blood relationship with the king or had secured a regular place at court or, more significantly, in the **royal household**. They were men who were well known to the king and who personally served him in government and in war. Although the nobility were comparatively few in number, between 55 and 65, the king relied on them to provide him with the means to govern and police the provinces.

Key terms

Great Chain of Being
The belief that God has ordained that everybody was born into a specific place in the strict hierarchy of society and had a duty to remain there.

Royal household
The retinue and servants who looked after the monarch's personal needs and his financial and political affairs.

The gentry made up the class below the nobility and are sometimes referred to as the lesser nobility because they, too, were landowners and members of a politically and economically privileged élite. Like the nobility, the gentry were also classed according to title but in a less formal sense. For example, the knight occupied the highest rank of gentry but this was a title conferred by the king for life and did not descend to an heir. Below the knights were the esquires and gentlemen, the last rank being adopted in the fifteenth century to take account of the growing numbers of smaller or lesser landowners who had gained their wealth by trade.

The English Church

Key question
How important was the Church in England?

Apart from the king, the Church was by far the largest landowner in the kingdom. The fifteenth-century English Church was part of the Roman Catholic Church and its first allegiance was not to the English Crown but to the Pope in Rome. Although the Pope had no control over the day-to-day running of the Church in England, he had the spiritual authority to determine how the people worshipped and how Church **doctrine** was to be understood. The Pope also had the power to influence a kingdom's domestic and foreign politics by either offering or withholding his support for the ruler.

The Church was a powerful organisation that consisted of the **regular clergy** – some 10,000 strong – and **secular clergy** – numbering around 35,000. It formed a state within a state, with its own system of law courts and privileges available for the clergy, which rivalled the authority of the king. These courts dealt with religious crimes and crimes committed by churchmen. Although this relationship had the potential to be awkward, Crown and Church normally managed to exist side by side in relative harmony.

However, despite its size, power and wealth the Church did have internal problems. The chief abuses were poverty, **pluralism**, non-residence and ignorance. Many parish priests were poorly educated, some were illiterate, and their poverty contrasted with

Key terms

Doctrine
Rules, principles and teachings of the Church.

Regular clergy
Monks and nuns who devoted their lives to prayer and study in monasteries, sheltered from the outside world.

Secular clergy
Parish priests, chaplains and bishops who lived in the outside world. They performed tasks such as marriage, baptism and burial.

Pluralism
The holding of more than one parish by a clergyman.

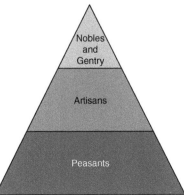

- At the top of this hierarchy were the élite groups: the Lords spiritual and temporal, knights, esquires and gentlemen.

- Next were those distinguished by their occupations: the clergy, lawyers, merchants and master craftsmen.

- Finally came the lowest and the largest group – those with neither wealth nor status: labourers, ordinary soldiers, paupers and vagrants.

Figure 1.3: Social pyramid showing the classes in society from the highest to the lowest.

the wealth of the bishops. For example, by the end of the fifteenth century, 75 per cent of parish priests earned less than £12 per annum (£5500 in today's money) while two-thirds of bishops earned more than £400 (£180,000 in today's money). The average annual wage for unskilled farm labourers at this time was between £2 and £3. In order to survive, many priests tried to serve more than one parish (in the worst cases as many as five), which affected the quality of religious worship. It has been calculated that of the 10,000 parishes in England and Wales a quarter were likely to be without a resident clergyman. Nevertheless, in spite of its flaws, the Church was generally popular with the people, whom it served well.

Summary diagram: The Church and social order

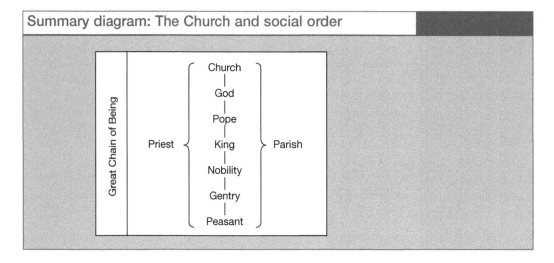

England and its continental neighbours

The people preferred to live in peace; they believed this was the way of life that God had ordained for them. As God's representative on earth, the king was expected to maintain this ordered existence. However, if a ruler were challenged in an aggressive manner by a foreign power, then war was acceptable as a form of defence. In such circumstances, kings were expected to win great victories for the honour of their subjects. Obviously, this was an over-simplified view of the relations between states, which were far more complex in reality, particularly by the late fifteenth century. Diplomacy in this period had become more subtle and wide-ranging than before. This was because communication was swifter, with better roads and faster ships, and decisions were being taken by increasingly powerful and ambitious rulers who, because of better maps, knew much more than their predecessors of the world outside their immediate localities.

France, Burgundy and Brittany

English kings had been gaining and losing territory in France ever since William the Conqueror had first linked England with the Duchy of Normandy in 1066; consequently, a bitter rivalry had existed between them. The latest contest had been the

Hundred Years War (1338–1453), which had resulted in the loss of all English lands in France except Calais. France had finally been able to drive the English out because of the increasing strength of its monarchy that had ended civil conflict and absorbed all but one of the semi-independent **feudatories**, such as Burgundy and Normandy, into a large and prosperous kingdom (see Figure 1.4). Only Brittany remained, but not for long. By the late fifteenth century, France's resources in terms of manpower and revenue were about three times those of its neighbour across the Channel. England could no longer exploit France's weaknesses, nor compete on equal terms with this enlarged kingdom. England's continental ambitions would have to be reassessed by Henry VII.

Key term

Feudatories
Territories with feudal lords who owed allegiance to the King of France.

Figure 1.4: Map of the Kingdom of England and its territorial authority at home and abroad.

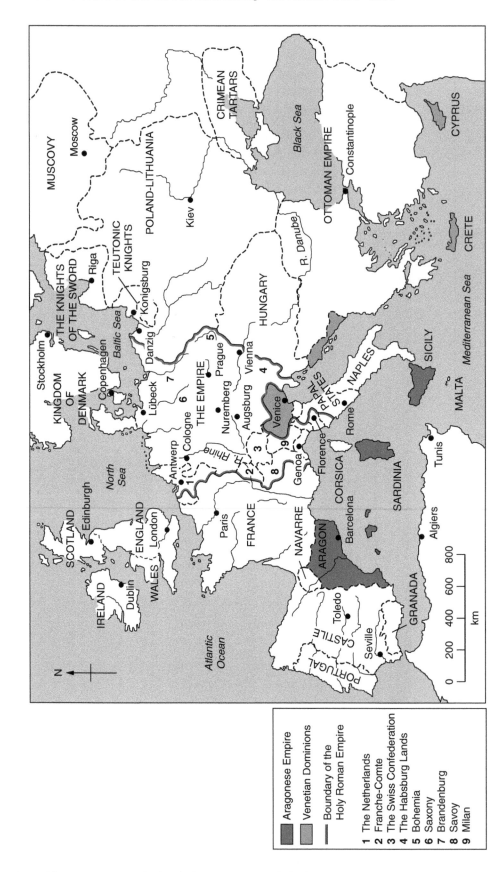

Figure 1.5: A political map of Europe in 1490.

Scotland

Scotland was an independent kingdom but it was smaller and less wealthy than England. As a consequence of this, Scottish kings were often subjected to English pressure to recognise the superior authority of the English king. This occasionally resulted in war but never in conquest. For example, Edward I's failed attempt to conquer Scotland at the beginning of the fourteenth century served as an example to his successors. There were often arguments over where the border between the two states lay but the most pressing point of conflict was the frequent cattle raids into the richer northern counties of England by the poorer Scottish clansmen. To defend themselves, Scottish kings had traditionally allied themselves with the French kings. This 'auld alliance' was a constant source of anxiety for English kings.

Spain and the Holy Roman Empire

Another factor which came to play an important part in influencing the way in which English kings pursued their diplomacy in the second half of the fifteenth century was the unification of Castile and Aragon in 1479 (see Figure 1.5). The marriage between the rulers of Castile and Aragon, Ferdinand and Isabella, led to the creation of Spain, a new power that quickly established itself as a powerful player in international affairs. As the theatre of conflict changed from northern to southern Europe, with England being relegated to the status of a second-rate power, Spain assumed England's traditional position as France's main rival. Not that this deterred the emperors of the Holy Roman Empire (centred mainly on Germany and the Low Countries, see Figure 1.5) from seeking an alliance with the English when the European situation demanded that allies be found in war. England's links with the Empire had grown as a result of trade. This was mainly conducted by way of the **Hanseatic League**, a group of north German port towns that dominated trade in the North Sea and Baltic, sponsored by the emperor. However, as England's trade and commerce grew its kings came into conflict with such commercial monopolies.

Key term

Hanseatic League
Merchants from the mainly German city ports on the Baltic and North Sea who came together to form a trading union and thus dominate trade in northern Europe.

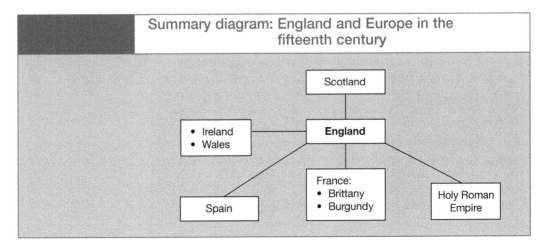

Summary diagram: England and Europe in the fifteenth century

2 | Historians, Historiography and the Origins of the Wars of the Roses

The origins of the Wars of the Roses

The Wars of the Roses were a dynastic struggle between the noble families (and their supporters) of Lancaster and York. Both sides believed that the crown of England rightfully belonged to them. The result of this rivalry was war; between 1455 and 1487 Lancastrians and Yorkists fought a series of pitched battles to secure control of the crown. In seeking reasons to explain why major historical events such as the Wars of the Roses happen, historians tend to classify and categorise their conclusions into long-term and short-term causes. One key area of debate concerning the origins of the Wars of the Roses is how far back historians should look for explanations. The majority of historians believe that the root cause of the later dynastic struggle between Lancaster and York can be found in the reign of Richard II (1377–99). For more immediate or short-term causes of the Wars of the Roses, historians focus on the period from the early to mid-1440s or, more specifically, when Henry VI came of age and became responsible for the war in France and the government of his kingdom.

The long-term causes of the Wars of the Roses

The origins of the dynastic struggle between Lancaster and York can be traced back to the **usurpation** of the Plantagenet king Richard II. The Plantagenets had ruled England more or less unchallenged for around 200 years until 1399, when some members of the aristocracy became unhappy with the arbitrary and authoritarian rule of Richard II. By promoting some noble favourites at the expense of others, some of whom were stripped of their titles and exiled, Richard contributed to a growing sense of discontent and resentment. Chief among the exiled nobility was Richard's cousin, Henry Bolinbroke, Duke of Hereford (1397) and Earl of Derby (1377), who had a distant claim to the throne. Denied his inheritance, the Dukedom of Lancaster, Bolinbroke returned from exile and gathered enough support to win the crown for himself. Richard was **deposed** and imprisoned in Pontefract Castle, where he later died.

Henry IV, as he became, was the son of John of Gaunt, Duke of Lancaster, a younger son of Edward III (see the family tree in Figure 1.6). This royal connection did not protect Henry IV from those who sought to challenge his kingship. Besides complaints from parliament over his extravagant spending, Henry endured a 10-year rebellion (1400–10) by the Welsh under their charismatic leader Owain Glyndŵr. The most serious opposition to his kingship came from a number of powerful noble families who wished to remove him from the throne. The Percy earls of Northumberland and the Mortimer earls of March kept the flame of rebellion alive in England between 1403 and 1408. To add to his troubles, Henry also suffered periodic bouts of ill-health; from

Key question
How has historical opinion of the Wars of the Roses changed?

Key date

Henry IV usurped the throne by removing Richard II: 1399

Key terms

Usurpation
The seizure of the throne without authority or in opposition to the rightful line of succession.

Depose
To rid the kingdom of its reigning monarch by forcing him to abdicate or resign.

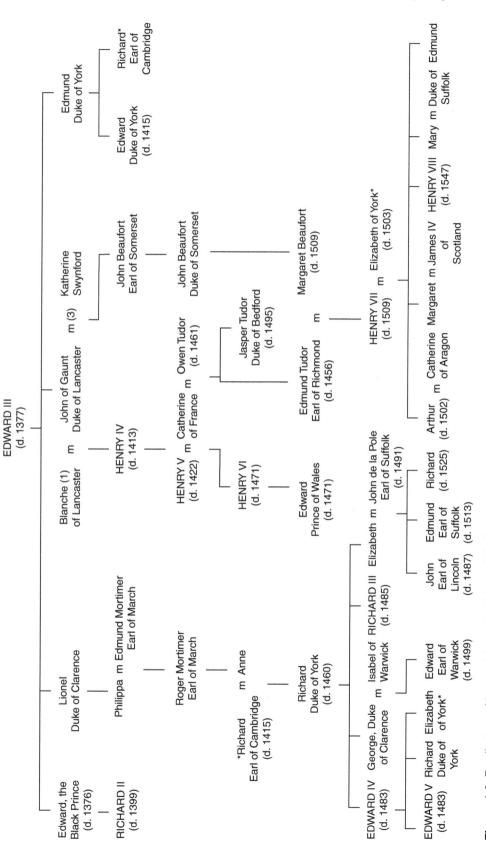

Figure 1.6: Family tree of Lancastrians, Yorkists and Tudors (*people with an asterisk by their name appear twice in the tree).

1410 he ceased to rule effectively after a series of strokes struck him down.

By usurping the throne, Henry had set a dangerous precedent. Other ambitious noblemen might do as he had done and mount a challenge for the crown. Henry's action had led to the throne losing some of its mystique, its majesty and, more importantly, its authority. Henceforth, the power and authority of the Crown would come to rely heavily on the skill, strength and personality of the monarch. During the reign of Henry V there was no problem since he was a man who commanded both respect and fear in equal measure and, apart from the failed rebellion of the Earl of Cambridge in 1415, there was no serious challenge to his kingship. His inspirational leadership, dominant personality and success in war against the French earned the respect and loyalty of the nobility. However, when a weak-willed and indecisive monarch like Henry VI succeeded to the throne, some of the nobility began to grumble while others were stirred into action.

The short-term causes of the Wars of the Roses

In view of Henry VI's weak will and indecision, the majority of historians would agree that, to find the most significant short-term cause of the Wars of the Roses, it is unnecessary to look back further than the personal rule of Henry VI. B.P. Wolffe believes that Henry's incompetence alone explains the dynastic conflict that led to his usurpation. By promoting the rise of a few noble favourites – Edmund Beaufort, Duke of Somerset, Cardinal Henry Beaufort and William de la Pole, Duke of Suffolk – Henry VI alienated some of the most powerful nobles in England. Foremost among them was the king's cousin Richard, Duke of York, a man who could also claim descent from Edward III. Some historians, such as John Watts and Alison Weir, still believe that he, rather than Henry VI, should be blamed for the conflict but others disagree, most notably A.J. Pollard, stating that York had been driven to rebel by the king's mismanagement of him.

Equally serious in the minds of the politically powerful was the king's failure to prosecute the war in France. As the military losses mounted so the Crown's popularity declined. Henry's failure to cure lawlessness and disorder, curb corruption and misgovernment and reduce the burden of taxation added to the monarchy's woes. The result was the popular uprising known as Cade's rebellion (1450), which some historians see as the opening salvo in what was becoming a more volatile and violent period in England's history.

Apart from those few who opted to remain neutral (if they could), the majority of the nobility were faced with the dilemma of who to support should the political struggle turn to military confrontation. Taking sides was no easy choice for the nobility because they had so much to lose. The simmering resentment of the 1440s boiled over into armed conflict in the 1450s and the scene was set for what became known as the Wars of the Roses.

Key question
Why did the term 'Wars of the Roses' come to be used by historians?

Key date

Wars of the Roses began: 1455

The term 'Wars of the Roses'

The term 'Wars of the Roses' was first used in the first half of the nineteenth century to describe the sequence of dynastic plots, rebellions and battles that took place in England between 1455 and 1487. Historians, especially those in the eighteenth and nineteenth centuries, are fond of attaching labels to historical events in order to give them shape and form, and to make them easier to study. Historical events can be defined by date, personality or, as in this case, emblem. It seemed sensible to see the conflict in terms of the badges that each side wore because flags, emblems and uniforms are a distinguishing feature of war even in our own time. However, there is a problem. The warring parties did not use the red and white roses as their badge or emblem. The idea of the 'warring roses' was rooted in Tudor propaganda and was invented by Henry VII after he had secured the throne in 1485. The reasons why Henry adopted the emblems were:

- to make it easier for people to identify with a colourful image or symbol
- to make it easier for people to understand his claim to be the heir of the Lancastrian crown
- to represent his marriage with Elizabeth of York as the union of the red and white roses bringing peace, order and prosperity after decades of anarchy and war.

The popularity and longevity of the symbolism associated with the White Rose of York and Red Rose of Lancaster are due largely to the effective use made of them by William Shakespeare in his history plays *Henry VI, Part 2* and *Richard III*. Written in the 1590s, Shakespeare's plays did much to promote what Henry VII had begun a century before, to mythologise and legitimise the Tudors' claim to power.

In the twentieth century, historians questioned the use of the term 'Wars of the Roses' because it was unknown in the fifteenth and sixteenth centuries. Some historians prefer to call this turbulent period in English history a 'civil war' but it really involved only the nobility, gentry and a minority of peasantry, who had been pressed into war service by their masters. This is why other historians champion the use of the term 'dynastic struggle' because it better describes the conflict for control of the crown by the landowning noble élite. A minority of **revisionist historians** go further by claiming that the use of the term 'Wars of the Roses' makes no sense because, in the words of John Warren, 'they were not wars at all, but scrappy, short-lived and insignificant conflicts that scarcely merit even the name of battles'. The fact that there still exists some disagreement over the use of the term 'Wars of the Roses' means we are stuck with it because it has become such a familiar and convenient label.

Key term

Revisionist historians
Historians who revisit historical events and revise earlier historical interpretations.

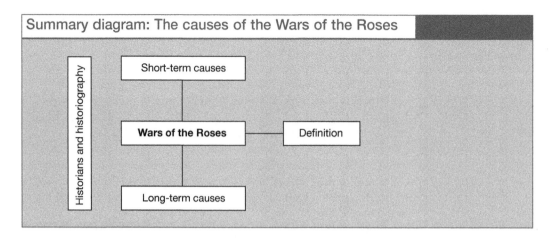

Summary diagram: The causes of the Wars of the Roses

3 | Conflict and Confrontation: The Battles in Context 1455–87

Key question
What were the key battles in the Wars of the Roses?

Ties of kinship, friendship and **clientship** made it almost inevitable that many of England's noble families would be drawn into the conflict between Lancaster and York. In a society dominated by thoughts and images of **chivalry**, heroism and dynasticism, confrontation between nobles was often settled by force of arms. These conflicts might take the form of individual trials of strength, personal duels between one nobleman and another, or larger groupings whereby the nobleman would lead his retainers in combat against his foes.

The scale of the combat is important because some historians have called into question the use of the term 'battle' to describe the character of the fighting that took place during the Wars of the Roses. To some, the skirmishes were so random, scrappy and short-lived that they scarcely merit being called battles. Others challenge this view by arguing that whether they are called battles or skirmishes does not matter because the fact remains that some were so decisive that they paved the way for a change of kingship and dynasty. What can be said with confidence is that some battles were bigger, bloodier and more significant than others.

J.R. Lander's research has concluded that some 35 nobles either sided with or fought for the Lancastrians, while around 20 supported the Yorkists. However, this has been challenged by A.J. Pollard, who believes that:

> one cannot describe the combatants as being irrevocably divided into two parties called Lancastrians and Yorkists; allegiances and alliances were considerably too fluid to enable one to allocate individual lords and gentlemen to one or other side throughout the period.

There were three distinct phases of civil war involving some 18 battles or skirmishes.

Key terms

Clientship
Relationship based on service and support. The majority of the most-powerful nobles led large numbers of followers who served them and who, in turn, were protected by them.

Chivalry
The medieval institution of knighthood. It is usually associated with ideals of knightly virtues, honour and fair play.

Table 1.1: Key players in the Wars of the Roses (*people with an asterisk by their name changed sides at least once)

Yorkists	Lancastrians
Edward IV, Earl of March, later King of England, crowned June 1461. Died April 1483	Henry VI, deposed 1461. Restored 1470–1. Murdered in 1471
Sir Richard Beauchamp	Henry Beaufort, Duke of Somerset
Sir Humphrey Blount and Sir Walter Blount	Henry Holland, Duke of Exeter
William Viscount Bourchier	Jasper Tudor, Earl of Pembroke
William Brandon, Esquire	Thomas Courtenay, Earl of Devon
Edward Brooke, Lord Cobham	James Butler, Earl of Wiltshire
Thomas Lord Stanley*	Henry Percy, Earl of Northumberland*
Sir William Stanley*	Sir John Bigod, Lord Mauley
Richard, Duke of Gloucester	John Lord Audley
Sir Walter Devereaux	Robert Lord Willoughby
William Fiennes, Lord Saye and Sele	Randolph Lord Dacre
Thomas Fitzalan, Lord Maltravers	John Lord Clifford and Sir Roger Clifford
Edmund Lord Grey of Ruthin	John Lord Scrope of Bolton
Reginald Lord Grey of Wilton	Sir Ralph Percy
William Lord Hastings	Sir Richard Tunstall
William Herbert, Earl of Pembroke	Sir John Fortescue*
Richard Woodville, first Earl Rivers,* accompanied Henry VI in flight to Newcastle	Sir Thomas Grey
	Sir John Heron
Anthony Woodville, Lord Scales	Sir Thomas Hervey
Sir William Catesby	Sir James Luttrell
John Mowbray, third Duke of Norfolk	
Edward Neville, Lord Abergavenny	
Richard Neville, Earl of Warwick*	
William Neville, Lord Fauconberg, created Earl of Kent	
Henry Stafford, Duke of Buckingham	
Sir Roger Vaughan	
Sir Thomas Vaughan	

The first phase 1455–64

What began as a political struggle for control of royal government eventually led to outright war for possession of the crown. Between 1455 and 1464 there were 11 battles or skirmishes fought between Lancastrian and Yorkist armies.

1455

In 1455 the aim of Richard of York and his supporters had been to control the king and his government. York achieved his aim after the first battle of St Albans and the civil war might have ended there had the warring parties agreed to resolve their differences. However, the antagonism and distrust between York and the king's advisers and allies, principally the queen, Margaret of Anjou, ran too deep to be healed. When, four years later, the Lancastrians felt strong enough, they tried again to rid the kingdom of York and so, war flared up again.

The battle of St Albans, May 1455

This skirmish marks the beginning of the civil or dynastic war. By confronting the king, Henry VI, with an armed force the Duke of York had set in motion the means by which the nobility of England would settle their quarrels by fighting.

1459–61

York responded by challenging the king directly for possession of the crown. The battles fought between 1459 and 1461 were aimed at overthrowing Henry VI. York was killed at the battle of Wakefield and was succeeded by his son and heir, Duke Edward of York. The most decisive battle of the period was that fought at Towton, after which Edward deposed Henry VI and took the crown for himself. This period of the civil war was the most intense, bloody and decisive, and resulted in a change of dynasty.

> **Key date**
> Edward IV usurped the throne by removing Henry VI: 1461

The battle of Blore Heath, September 1459

This was a victory for the Yorkists, who killed the Lancastrian commander Lord Audley.

The 'rout' of Ludford, October 1459

This marked a defeat for the Yorkists, who fled Ludford when Henry VI turned up to confront them.

The battle of Northampton, July 1460

The Lancastrians were heavily defeated by the Yorkists. Henry VI was captured and Buckingham, the Lancastrian commander, was executed. Queen Margaret and her son Edward escaped.

The battle of Wakefield, December 1460

The Yorkists were crushed by a much larger Lancastrian force. York was killed and his severed head was stuck on the walls of York wearing a paper crown.

The second battle of St Albans, February 1461

The Yorkists under Warwick suffered another decisive defeat at the second Battle of St Alban's.

The battle of Mortimer's Cross, February 1461

The Lancastrians were routed in a significant Yorkist victory that had been planned and led by the teenage Edward, son and heir of the Duke of York.

The battle of Ferrybridge, March 1461
Ferrybridge was a skirmish that took place a day before the much larger and bloodier battle of Towton.

The battle of Towton, March 1461
Towton was the largest and bloodiest battle of the war, with more than 50,000 men involved. The Lancastrians were routed by the victorious Yorkists.

1464–5
The battles fought in 1464 represent a last ditch attempt by the Lancastrians to restore Henry VI. They failed, and Edward IV remained king until 1469. In 1465 Henry VI was captured and imprisoned by Edward IV. This period, and the later one between 1469 and 1471, witnessed an upsurge in local rivalries where the great magnates such as Percy and Neville in the north and Bonville and Courteney in the south-west took advantage of the chaos of war to strike at each other.

The battle of Hedgeley Moor, April 1464
The Lancastrians were soundly beaten by a tactically better Yorkist army.

The battle of Hexham, May 1464
The Lancastrians were cut to pieces by a ruthless and victorious Yorkist force.

The second phase 1469–71
The period between 1469 and 1471 marks the bitter rivalry between two competing Yorkist factions that led to a civil war within a civil war. The Yorkists were turning on each other rather than fighting the Lancastrians. Edward IV's close friend and ally, Richard Neville, was not satisfied with the position and power the king had given him. Warwick was a rich and powerful nobleman who had used his power to help make Edward king in 1461. He is a good example of what historians have called an 'over-mighty' subject – a nobleman with too much power was a threat to the king. His power was such that Richard Neville earned the nickname 'Warwick the Kingmaker'.

Key date | Edward IV was removed and replaced by Henry VI: 1469–70

1469–70
Warwick's rebellion succeeded in toppling Edward IV and restoring Henry VI. Exiled Lancastrians returned to England in the belief that their cause had triumphed. Henry VI was king in name only, for the real power lay in Warwick's hands. Warwick's triumph was short lived; Edward IV returned from exile in France to challenge for the throne a second time.

The battle of Edgecote, July 1469
Edgecote marks the beginning of the Yorkist feud in which one Yorkist faction turned on another. Warwick and Clarence turned against Edward IV and his chief ally the Earl of Pembroke. Pembroke and his largely Welsh army were heavily defeated at

Edgecote. Pembroke was captured and executed. Edward IV was captured by Warwick.

The battle of Losecoat Field, March 1470
Edward IV succeeded in defeating a rebel force under the command of Sir Robert Welles, an ally of Warwick.

The battle of Nibley Green, March 1470
Nibley Green was caused by a private quarrel between the Berkeleys and Talbots which resulted in armed conflict.

1471
With the support of Burgundy and in spite of the interference of France, Edward IV launched his bid for the throne. Victory at Barnet secured the crown while Tewkesbury put paid to the

Figure 1.7: The different battles of the Wars of the Roses.

Key dates

Edward IV returned as king. Henry VI was killed: 1471

Edward V succeeded to the throne but was quickly removed by Richard III: 1483

Richard III was killed at the battle of Bosworth. Henry Tudor became King Henry VII: 1485

Battle of Stoke marked the end of the Wars of the Roses: 1487

Key term

Coup d'état
A French term used to describe the overthrow of a monarch or government.

remnants of the Lancastrian party, many of whom fled again into exile.

The battle of Barnet, April 1471
This was a Yorkist victory which enabled Edward IV to secure the throne and re-establish himself as king. Warwick was killed.

The battle of Tewkesbury, May 1471
This was a Yorkist victory which resulted in the death of the Lancastrian Prince Edward, the capture of his mother, Margaret of Anjou, and the eventual murder of Henry VI.

The third phase 1483–7

This period began with a *coup d'état* when Richard, Duke of Gloucester, usurped the rightful heir to the throne, his young nephew Edward V. The fact that the king was the son of his brother, Edward IV, who he had pledged to protect, did not deter Richard or his chief ally the Duke of Buckingham in ruthlessly killing off enemies. Buckingham's rebellion in late 1483 was a sign that all was not well with the regime, but Richard III held the crown until 1485. Challenged by a Lancastrian with a distant claim to the throne, Henry Tudor, Earl of Richmond, Richard brought his enemies to battle at Bosworth.

1485
The battle of Bosworth, August 1485
This battle settled the question of who would be king of England. Richard III was defeated and killed; Richmond took the throne and was crowned King Henry VII.

1487
The battle of Stoke, June 1487
Henry VII's tenure of the throne was perilously weak in the first few years and he, like Richard III, was forced to fight for the survival of his regime. Unlike Richard, Henry succeeded and thereby established the Tudor dynasty. Stoke is regarded by many historians as the final battle of the Wars of the Roses.

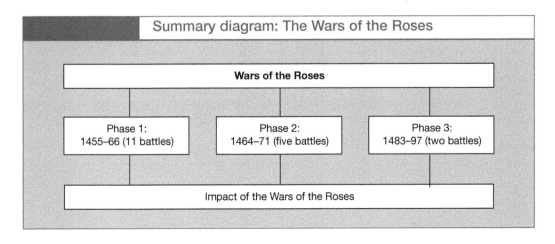

Summary diagram: The Wars of the Roses

The impact of the Wars of the Roses

The death and destruction caused by the Wars of the Roses have been exaggerated by historians. In reality, most of the battles (Towton excepted) were nothing more than skirmishes affecting only a small percentage of the population. The most intense period of fighting was between July 1460 and March 1461 but, as a whole, there was barely more than two years' military activity throughout the 30-year conflict. Civilian casualties and physical destruction to towns and private property were light. Even at its worst, most people were able to go about their everyday affairs.

On the other hand, as John Warren has pointed out:

> this is not to claim that the country was a 'merrie England' of peaceful peasants and bustling towns with the occasional and rather picturesque battle to enliven the dull routine of the workaday world.

Warren claims that 'English society was marked by an undercurrent of violence and disorder' which, in the short term, the wars made worse. There was considerable political upheaval and instability (especially in the years 1459–61 and 1469–71) as the houses of Lancaster and York competed for the throne. There was also a strong element of nobles' feuding and rivalry for local dominance, especially in northern and south-western England. The nobles had seized their opportunity to take control of the provinces, so that it was their orders that were obeyed rather than those of the king. If Edward IV, Richard III and Henry VII were to prove themselves strong kings, they would have to subdue these over-mighty subjects.

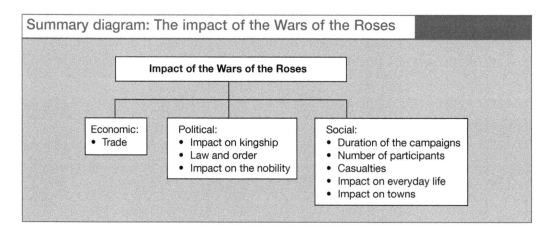

Summary diagram: The impact of the Wars of the Roses

Impact of the Wars of the Roses

Economic:
- Trade

Political:
- Impact on kingship
- Law and order
- Impact on the nobility

Social:
- Duration of the campaigns
- Number of participants
- Casualties
- Impact on everyday life
- Impact on towns

Study Guide: AS Question

In the style of OCR

How strong was kingship in mid-fifteenth century England? Explain your answer.

Exam tips

The cross-references are intended to take you straight to the material that will help you to answer the question.

You might leave this question until the end of the whole study topic because this is a very broad question surveying 'the big picture' so you will need a broad understanding. One way into this question would be to explore the idea that the key problem for monarchy at this time was the contradiction between the theory of kingship, which gave rulers considerable powers, and the practical situation, which saw limitations. Kings were expected to govern in line with divine law and English tradition but this allowed for considerable leeway in interpretation.

Against this, there was an ever-present possibility of a challenge to the throne (remember, the Lancastrians themselves had gained power by overthrowing Richard II in 1399). This meant that royal powers could be threatened by disorder and rebellion. Nobles saw themselves as the natural leaders of society and as the necessary advisers of kings. This situation was heightened during the reign of Henry VI, first by his long minority and then by his natural inadequacies (pages 27–9). The mid-fifteenth century might be seen as the great age of noble power rather than as the age of dominant kingship. From 1461, however, Edward IV began to restore the powers of the Crown and you could assess the progress he had made by the time of his death (page 49).

When measuring the strength of kingship, do not just think of the relationship with the nobility in general and over-mighty subjects in particular (for example, the Duke of Somerset, the Duke of York). You should weigh the strength of the Crown against institutions of administration and government (for example, the council, parliament). You will also need to measure its financial strengths and weaknesses. A strong answer will evaluate clearly a range of factors, offering a more or less balanced discussion of the core issue raised by the question: the strength of kingship in the mid-fifteenth century.

2 Henry VI and the Start of the Wars of the Roses

POINTS TO CONSIDER

A nation's government, security and well-being depend on the character and strength of its ruler. This was particularly evident during the fifteenth century when kings had the power to pass laws, raise revenue and make war. However, Henry VI's weak and irresponsible rule led to noble disaffection, dynastic civil war and royal deposition. These points are examined as four themes:

- Henry VI: personality, war and debt
- 'Under-mighty monarch', 'over-mighty subjects': Henry VI and the nobility
- The Yorkist challenge and Lancastrian response 1450–5
- Triumph and overthrow: the deposition of Henry VI and coronation of Edward IV

Key dates

1413	Henry V succeeded to the throne
1415	Henry V renewed the war against France and won the battle of Agincourt
1421	Henry VI born
1422	Henry VI succeeded to the throne
1431	Henry VI crowned King of France in Paris
1437	Henry VI took control of government
1444	Treaty of Tours
1445	Marriage of Henry VI and Margaret of Anjou
1447	Death of Humphrey, Duke of Gloucester
1450	Normandy lost to the French
	Duke of Suffolk executed
	Cade's rebellion
1451	Loss of Gascony
1453	Henry VI suffered mental breakdown. Duke of York appointed protector
1455	Wars of the Roses began with the battle of St Albans

1455–6		York served second term as protector
1458		The Loveday
1459	September	Battle of Blore Heath
	October	'Rout' of Ludford
	November	Parliament of Devils
1460	July	Battle of Northampton
	December	Battle of Wakefield
	December	Richard, Duke of York, killed at Wakefield
1461	February	Second battle of St Albans
	February	Battle of Mortimer's Cross
	March	Battle of Ferrybridge
	March	Battle of Towton
	March	Edward IV usurped the throne by removing Henry VI

1 | Henry VI: Personality, War and Debt

Key question
To what extent did Henry VI contribute to the problems facing the monarchy in the 1450s?

If the primary long-term cause of the Wars of the Roses was the dangerous precedent set by Henry IV's usurpation of the throne in 1399, the more immediate or short-term cause almost inevitably centres on Henry VI. The character and personality of Henry VI have been examined closely by historians, as has his failure to manage the royal debt and prosecute the war in France.

Personality
In the opinion of John Warren, 'the king's personality touched and affected every facet of power and authority in the kingdom'. To a large extent this is true since the king was expected to:

- defend the kingdom through force of arms
- ensure the stability and security of the kingdom
- provide peace, law and order within the kingdom
- rule wisely, fairly and effectively by means of what was called at the time 'good governance'.

Education
To deliver on all these points was a tall order even for a talented or competent individual, but in Henry VI some or all of these elements were lacking. This was not through want of upbringing or education, for Henry received the best tuition available at that time. During his minority he learnt the art of kingship and war from no less a person than his late father's companion-in-arms, the well-travelled Richard Beauchamp, Earl of Warwick. For nine years (1428–37) Henry was schooled in the crafts of good governance, patronage and military leadership, but the lessons learnt seemed not to have had the desired effect.

HENRICVS.

VI.

A portrait of Henry VI. What does this portrait reveal about Henry VI?

Governance

Contemporary chroniclers were scathing in their assessment of Henry VI. For example, in 1446 John Capgrave reported that the naval and coastal security of the kingdom were neglected. By drawing attention to civil unrest and local injustice, John Hardyng criticised the king for failing to establish peace and effective law and order. One anonymous writer even noted Henry's 'habitual dilatoriness', that is being indecisive or slow to act, while another, writing in the mid-1460s, stated that 'the realm of England was out of all good governance'.

Military leadership

Nor did Henry 'cut a dash in war', being the first English king never to command an army against a foreign enemy. As Henry VI's modern biographer, Ralph Griffiths, noted:

> He never visited France after 1432: the projected visit in 1445–7 to discuss peace with Charles VII never took place. He never fought in Scotland or crossed to Ireland, and he rarely set foot in Wales – perhaps only once, in August 1452, when he visited Monmouth.

The king left the kingdom's military leadership in the hands of others, principally his uncles John, Duke of Bedford, and Humphrey, Duke of Gloucester, and courtiers such as Edmund Beaufort, Duke of Somerset, William de la Pole, Duke of Suffolk and Richard, Duke of York. Even Henry VI's wife, Margaret of Anjou (they married in 1445), showed a greater inclination to employ military means to achieve her aims of securing control of both the Crown and the government.

It was Henry's failure to live up to the military reputation of his father, Henry V, on the battlefields of France that attracted most criticism. Kings were expected to lead their men in war but the only occasion when his subjects saw Henry in battle array before the civil war was in 1450 (and possibly again in 1452) when he rode through London with his nobles against his own people. This was the occasion of the Cade rebellion (see pages 38–9), an armed insurrection by the people of Kent who were intent on removing the king's closest advisers, who they blamed for corruption and misgovernment in south-east England.

Advisers

The king's advisers are significant because they link with what Abbot John Whethamstede of St Albans had to say about Henry VI in 1456, that he could 'not resist those who led him to unwise decisions'. This is key to understanding Henry VI since he was a man of weak character who relied too much on the advice of those around him, the majority of whom he had personally chosen or appointed. He was clearly not a good judge of character and it is evident that those around him knew how to manipulate him. Their manipulation of Henry became decisive when the king began to suffer mental health problems that eventually led to his temporary lapse into insanity in 1453. According to the king's own chaplain and contemporary biographer, John Blacman, Henry VI was a good man but a bad king who became a '**fool of God**'.

Assessments of Henry

We must remember that judgements on Henry VI in fifteenth-century chronicles may be distorted by the propaganda of civil war, and later Yorkist or Tudor opinions of his reign. For example, in c.1512, Polydore Vergil, the respected Italian scholar and author of *Anglia Historia* (*History of England*), wrote:

> King Henry was a man of mild and plain-dealing disposition, who preferred peace before wars, quietness before troubles ... and leisure before business; and, to be short, there was not in this world a more pure, honest and more holy creature.

Henry was certainly a pious man who delighted in learning and religious patronage. According to one of his modern biographers, Bertram Wolffe, it is a measure of Henry's personality that he should choose to mark his accession to the throne with a massive scheme of religious rather than military building. The castle and

Key term

Fool of God
A contemporary term used to describe someone who is far too religious for his own good.

machines of war, such as siege engines and catapults, were set aside for churches, cathedrals and colleges such as those at Eton and Cambridge. Surprisingly, Henry VI's piety did not win him the respect of the Pope, Pius II, who described the king as 'a man more timorous than a woman, utterly devoid of wit or spirit, who left everything in his wife's hands'. Clearly, Henry's queen, Margaret of Anjou, cut more of a dash in politics and war.

It can be said that, at best, contemporary estimates of Henry VI hint at a monarch who, although possessed of worthy personal qualities, neglected some of his kingly duties. At worst, they depict Henry as tragically and spectacularly incompetent.

Modern historians have been even less flattering in their assessment of Henry VI. J.R. Lander said of Henry that although he was an intelligent and precocious child, he 'developed or degenerated into a man who could hardly have been worse equipped to meet the stresses' of governing a kingdom'. His mental breakdown suggests that there is some truth in this assessment. Perhaps the most devastating assessment of Henry VI is that by A.J. Pollard:

> Henry VI proved to be improvident, malleable, vacillating, partisan, uninterested in the arts of government, and, above all, antipathetic [opposite] to the chivalric world his ancestors had adorned.

War

War is an expensive business and the wars in France, a continuation of the Hundred Years War, proved to be a massive drain on England's financial resources. The war proved costly in other ways also; not least in the damage it did to the image and prestige of the English Crown. Kings were expected to be warriors, but Henry was no warrior and his failure to lead his subjects in war did much to harm his reputation and that of the English Crown. Henry was unfortunate to be the son of a great man with a mighty reputation. The weight of expectation on Henry to be like his father was too much for him to bear. This may, in part, explain why Henry VI suffered a mental breakdown in the early 1450s. He recovered his physical health but his mental health remained impaired for the rest of his life. Not surprisingly perhaps, when contemporaries came to compare father and son there could only be one winner and it was not Henry VI.

Henry's father, Henry V, had proven himself to be a strong character, a great soldier and an inspirational leader of men in war. His success in battle, such as at Agincourt in 1415, and in conquering large areas of northern France, brought the French king to the negotiating table. They agreed that Henry V should marry the French king's daughter and that their son, Henry VI, would succeed to the French crown. Unfortunately, Henry V died less than two years after making the agreement, leaving a nine-month-old son to succeed him. Taking advantage of the opportunity afforded by the king's death and his son's minority, the French resumed their war with the English.

Key question
To what extent did Henry VI's failure in war affect his kingship?

Key dates

Henry V succeeded to the throne: 1413

Henry V renewed the war against France and won the battle of Agincourt: 1415

Henry VI born: 1421

Henry VI succeeded to the throne: 1422

During Henry VI's minority the war was conducted with some success under the direction of his uncle John, Duke of Bedford. There was no repeat of the famous victory at Agincourt, but the English managed to hold the French at bay by denying them victory in a succession of decisive battles. To deny the enemy victory is not the same as winning it. The English were becoming adept at holding out against increasingly impossible odds. As a mark of English success in this respect, the 10-year-old king was able to travel to Paris to be crowned King of France in December 1431. However, even before the coronation, the military situation had begun to turn against the English partly as a result of the inspirational leadership displayed by the teenage Joan of Arc and partly as a result of growing French military strength. Gradually the war turned into one of attrition; with vastly superior resources

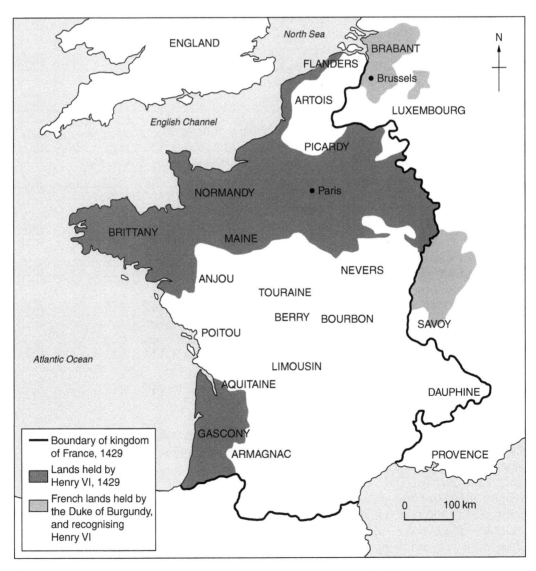

Figure 2.1: Map of France showing the extent of English territory in 1429.

in men and money it would only be a matter of time before the French prevailed. What the English needed was a king of exceptional ability and the kind of decisive victory in battle that Agincourt had provided in 1415. Under Henry VI they were to get neither.

The Treaty of Tours

Henry VI's greatest achievement was the Treaty of Tours in 1444, which established a fragile peace that lasted until 1449. The truce of Tours was opposed by the king's uncle, Humphrey, Duke of Gloucester, who argued that it favoured the French because it gave them time to regroup, re-equip and return to the field of battle stronger than before. Tours also marked the marriage between Henry VI and Margaret of Anjou, the daughter of the French queen's sister. The marriage was not popular in England because Margaret was dowerless (the promised **dowry** of 20,000 francs was never paid) and, as part of the truce, Henry agreed to hand the French the strategically vital territory of Maine. When war resumed in 1449 it was the fault not of the French but of the English. Foolishly following the advice of the Duke of Suffolk, Henry VI backed the attack and capture of the Breton town of Fougères.

Key dates

Treaty of Tours: 1444

Marriage of Henry VI and Margaret of Anjou: 1445

Normandy lost to the French: 1450

Loss of Gascony: 1451

Debt

The longer the war went on the greater the burden of taxes at home. The noble and gentry taxpayers of England may not have minded paying for success but they were reluctant to fund failure. Nor could the king win them over by persuasion and example when it was clear to all that his heart was not in the fight. Defeat and failure in France – principally the loss of Normandy in 1450 and Gascony in 1451 – affected not only morale at home but the incomes of a large number of noble families. A war of conquest enables the victor to reward his followers with grants of land, and under Henry V the English nobility had been well provided for. However, under the faltering kingship of Henry VI, England lost its right to rule those French territories that had been granted to, and settled by, those same English nobles. A disillusioned nobility were not about to pledge their loyalty to a king who, in their eyes, had failed in his primary duty to ensure stability, security and victory in war.

Equally unsettling for a king, denied the opportunity to reward loyalty with grants of land in France, was the fact the Crown was in serious debt. The royal debt spiralled out of control and it has been calculated that, by 1450, the Crown owed in the region of £370,000 (over £168 million in today's money). One of those to whom the king owed money, in excess of £38,000 (£17 million today), was Richard, Duke of York. To make matters worse, the regular annual income enjoyed by the Crown had fallen from a high of £120,000 (£55 million today) in the reign of Henry IV to as little as £45,000 (£21 million today) for Henry VI. This sharp drop in income and rising level of debt were due to a number of factors:

Key question
What effect did debt have on Henry VI's kingship?

Dowry
The sum of money or property a father provided to his daughter to give to her husband on marriage.

Key term

- a reduction in income from customs and taxes resulting from a general trade depression
- a reduction in income from Crown lands due to inflation and rising arrears in payments of rent
- an increase in spending on the war in France
- an increase in loans, and interest payments from Italian bankers and merchants.

Henry was unable to offer the kind of cash incentives that his nobility might have accepted in lieu of land in France. Not that this deterred Henry from spending money he did not have or from granting away Crown lands in England he could ill-afford to lose. This led to a collapse in royal finances which handicapped the Crown because it increased its dependence on the nobility and the growing financial potential of parliament. By 1455, the Lancastrian dynasty was virtually bankrupt.

The king's favourites

With so little to go around, anger and jealousy increased against those who seemed to be unaffected by the reduction in **royal patronage**. Indeed, some of the king's favourites – principally Edmund Beaufort, Duke of Somerset, Cardinal Henry Beaufort and William de la Pole, Duke of Suffolk – appeared to be doing rather well as a result of the king's generosity. Consequently, these royal favourites bore the brunt of the hatred and resentment that was increasingly being directed towards the Crown. Opposition to the king's favourites or '**evil councillors**', as critics came to describe them, soon turned into a demand for their removal. People were more willing to join an opposition group if it could be shown that the aim was not to attack the king but simply to remove those who would damage both him and the country.

Key terms

Royal patronage
Rewards given by the Crown for faithful service. The rewards were often given in the form of property, money, title or office.

Evil councillors
A useful and often-used contemporary label to brand those around the king as the enemies of sound advice and good government.

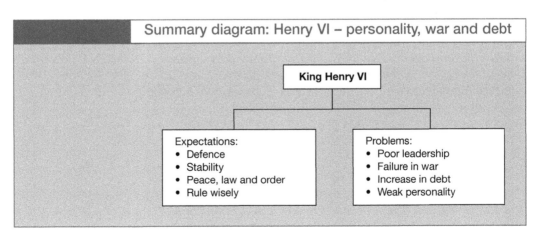

Summary diagram: Henry VI – personality, war and debt

King Henry VI

Expectations:
- Defence
- Stability
- Peace, law and order
- Rule wisely

Problems:
- Poor leadership
- Failure in war
- Increase in debt
- Weak personality

2 | 'Under-mighty Monarch', 'Over-mighty Subjects': Henry VI and the Nobility

Key question
How weak was Henry VI and how strong was his nobility?

It is important to remember that the king was not solely responsible for the Wars of the Roses. The Duke of York and others of the nobility, both Yorkist and Lancastrian, must also shoulder some of the blame for the conflict. The 'good governance' of the kingdom depended as much on the ruled as on the ruler so that the relationship between the monarch and his nobility was crucial if peace, prosperity and political stability were to be maintained. The king could not rule the kingdom alone. Lacking a civil service and police force, he needed the advice, co-operation, experience and local knowledge of the nobility to help him govern every corner of the realm. If the relationship between the ruler and his leading subjects broke down, then chaos and perhaps even civil war might ensue. Thus, an '**under-mighty monarch**' was as much a cause of the Wars of the Roses as the '**over-mighty subject**'.

Key terms

Under-mighty monarch
A weak king.

Over-mighty subject
A strong noble who was very wealthy, powerful and often over-ambitious.

'Under-mighty monarch'

It is perhaps fair to say that Henry VI comes closest to defining what it was to be a 'under-mighty monarch'. For the first 16 years of his reign the king was a minor under the control of a select group of nobles tasked with the government of the kingdom and the prosecution of the war in France. Henry VI had no say on what must be done, when it ought be done and who should do it. When he reached his majority in 1437, Henry came under the influence of favourites such as Edmund Beaufort, Duke of Somerset, and William de la Pole, Duke of Suffolk. Henry may have been king but the effective running of government remained in the hands of noble ministers. This led to tension and rivalry at court between powerful and ambitious nobles, which the king seemed unable to manage or control.

Unchecked political rivalry could turn into personal animosity with fateful consequences. In 1447, Henry VI's uncle Humphrey, Duke of Gloucester, was brought down by his bitter rival at court, the Duke of Somerset's uncle, Cardinal Henry Beaufort. The king did nothing to help his uncle, who died in mysterious circumstances before he could be tried for treason. Henry VI seemed incapable of judging people or situations. It can be argued that:

Key date

Death of Humphrey, Duke of Gloucester: 1447

- Henry mistook Cardinal Beaufort's offer to lend him substantial sums of money as friendship rather than as a means to control him. By 1444, Beaufort had lent the Crown various sums totalling in excess of £200,000, only part of which had been repaid.
- He misunderstood the seriousness of the bitter rivalry that grew between and divided Richard, Duke of York, and Edmund Beaufort, Duke of Somerset. His failure to heal the rift and pacify the two warring dukes contributed to the outbreak of civil war.

- Henry mishandled the war in France by resuming the conflict in 1449 that resulted in the loss of Normandy and the fall of the Crown's chief adviser, William de la Pole, Duke of Suffolk, who shouldered the blame for the disaster.

Margaret of Anjou too was a factor in promoting the impression of an 'under-mighty monarch'. She was a formidable woman and her strong will and domineering personality made the king appear even weaker and indecisive. As their marriage wore on Margaret came to exercise a greater degree of influence over her husband. Some nobles like Richard, Duke of York, and John Mowbray, Duke of Norfolk, resented the queen's meddling in affairs of state. They were particularly unhappy with Margaret's close relationship with, and promotion of, William de la Pole, who was created Duke of Suffolk in 1448, partly as a reward for arranging the marriage between her and Henry VI. In consequence of Margaret's increasing influence at court, the king sought advice from an ever-decreasing circle of nobles. The excluded became increasingly resentful, but Margaret brushed them aside. Her political skill came to the fore during her husband's mental incapacity.

Wedding of Henry VI and Margaret of Anjou. How are the couple portrayed by the artist?

'Over-mighty subjects'

If Henry VI comes closest to defining what it was to be an 'under-mighty monarch' then it can be argued that Richard, Duke of York, comes equally close to defining what it was to be an 'over-mighty subject'. York was a blood relation of the royal family, a descendant of King Edward III and the owner of a vast, landed estate that stretched across England as well as English-controlled northern France. He seemed to be everything that Henry VI was not: a capable politician, a warrior of distinction and a father of healthy sons. His strength of personality matched his ambition, which, by the 1450s, had come to embrace the crown of England.

However, York was not alone in aspiring to even greater land, wealth and power; these aims were shared by almost all his noble compatriots. Where he and they differed was in his over-reaching ambition, which included the kingship itself. In the opinion of some historians, this is what marks out the 'over-mighty subject', but this may be too narrow a definition because it would exclude men like Edmund Beaufort, Duke of Somerset, William de la Pole, Duke of Suffolk, and Humphrey, Duke of Gloucester. They too may be described as 'over-mighty subjects' but unlike York they did not covet the crown; they only sought to control it.

That this period saw the rise of the 'over-mighty subject' says as much about the king and his relationship with his nobles as it does about the nobility itself. In his relations with the nobles, the monarch had numerous advantages over them, not the least of which was the power of patronage and reward. The distribution of royal favour stood at the heart of the relationship between the Crown and the nobility and took the form of titles, estates, offices and **wardships**. Even marriage was within the power of the Crown to control; no nobleman or woman could normally be wed without the king's knowledge and approval.

The competition for royal patronage should have worked to the advantage of the monarch, who was in a unique position either to bestow or to withhold rewards. This policy is traditionally referred to as 'divide and rule' since a divided nobility would be too preoccupied with their own quarrels and rivalries to trouble, let alone challenge, the king. The monarch was able to act as a referee with the power to arbitrate in disputes between competing nobles. The key to success lay in not allowing these rivalries and quarrels to get out of hand. Under a strong and decisive king, this policy worked well, but Henry was weak and indecisive, which enabled some of the more ambitious nobles to become too powerful. The outbreak of the Wars of the Roses showed that Henry was no longer in control of his nobility and that they, in turn, had allowed their political rivalry to spill over into armed conflict. This suggests that the Wars of the Roses may be regarded as much as a war between nobles as one between the nobility and the monarchy.

Key term

Wardship
The practice whereby the king took control of the estates of minors (those who were too young to be legally responsible for their inheritance) and received most of the profits from their estates.

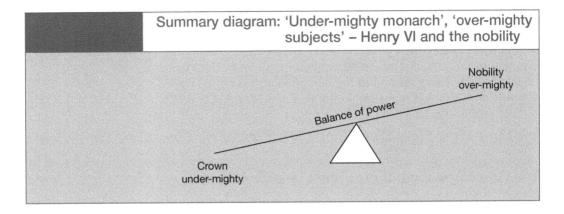

Summary diagram: 'Under-mighty monarch', 'over-mighty subjects' – Henry VI and the nobility

Key question
What was the Yorkist challenge and how did the Lancastrians respond?

3 | The Yorkist Challenge and Lancastrian Response 1450–5

The exclusion and resentment of Richard, Duke of York

As the king's closest living male relative, Richard, Duke of York, expected to be one of the power brokers at court. The fact that he was excluded from the centre of power became a burning source of resentment for him. His exclusion was due to three factors:

- The opposition of the king's chief advisers, William de la Pole, Duke of Suffolk, and Edmund Beaufort, Duke of Somerset. These men created and led a household or court faction that enabled them to monopolise royal patronage. They were not prepared to share power by admitting York into this 'charmed circle', nor were they prepared to tolerate his leadership.
- The queen, Margaret of Anjou, did not like or trust York because of his forcefulness, his blood relationship with the king and his claim to the throne. Her suspicions of York deepened when, with the death of Henry VI's uncle, the Duke of Gloucester, in 1447, he became heir-presumptive. This meant that, if Henry VI should die childless, York and his heirs would succeed to the throne. Margaret succeeded in keeping York at arm's length from both the king and court.
- York was his own worst enemy in that he was too arrogant, stubborn and demanding. Instead of exercising patience and cultivating friendships he preferred confrontation and challenge. He had little time or respect for those whom he considered his inferiors in title, intellect and military skill.

Having served twice (1436–7 and 1440–5) with some distinction as the king's military commander in France, York was mortified when he was removed and replaced by Somerset. Thus began a bitter feud with Somerset, who York suspected of having 'kingly ambitions' on account of his being a grandson of John of Gaunt, son of King Edward III. York's suspicion intensified the longer that Henry VI remained childless. York's complaints to the king and Suffolk that Somerset was ill-equipped to command English armies in France fell on deaf ears. Angry at being owed over £38,000 by the Crown for his service in France, York pressed the king to settle at least part of the debt or employ him in some meaningful role. In an effort to silence him and remove him from England, York was appointed to the lieutenancy of Ireland. This was not what York had in mind, but he reluctantly accepted the post. His debts remained unpaid and it was only with the financial assistance of his friends and the sale of some his properties that York was able to survive.

The fall and execution of Suffolk, and the act of resumption

Key question
Did the fall of Suffolk have any impact on events in the late 1440s?

York's complaint about Somerset and the conduct of the war in France was proved valid when, after the resumption of hostilities in 1449, English forces suffered catastrophic defeats, resulting in the loss of Normandy and Gascony. In an effort to restore England's declining military fortunes in France, Henry VI twice called on parliament, in February and November 1449, to provide funds for the war. However, after reluctantly granting only half of what the king had expected, parliament was dissolved. The fact that Suffolk had been instrumental in renewing the war meant that he, too, alongside Somerset, was blamed for the defeats. When Henry VI again called on parliament to raise money to finance the war, they, the **Commons**, not only refused but charged Suffolk with treason. Suffolk was accused of misgovernment, mismanaging the war and financial corruption. Imprisoned in the Tower of London, he was saved by the intervention of Henry VI, who banished him for five years. To ensure his safety, the king provided Suffolk with a ship to take him to France. Unfortunately for Suffolk, his ship was intercepted in the Channel and he was captured by his enemies. In a public snub to the king's authority, Suffolk was executed by the crew of the *Nicholas of the Tower* on behalf of the 'community of the realm'.

Key dates
Duke of Suffolk executed: 1450

Cade's rebellion: 1450

Key terms
Commons
One of the two houses of parliament staffed by elected representatives, mainly gentry landowners, to assist in the business of government.

Act of resumption
An act of parliament intended to recover Crown lands given away as reward for service.

As the price of any further grants of taxation, the Commons demanded that the king approve the passing of an **act of resumption**. The passing of this act made it possible to recover most, if not all, of the grants of land with which the king had rewarded his favourites over the previous decade. This was a humiliation for the king since it undermined his authority and his ability to offer rewards for faithful service. The discontent expressed by the Commons in parliament was matched by the social class who usually played little part in matters of state – the peasants. The Cade rebellion, with its epicentre in Kent, was a serious blow to the Crown's authority and prestige.

Cade's rebellion and the return of York

Key question
How did York take advantage of Cade's rebellion?

Cade's rebellion simply made matters worse for the king and his principal adviser, Somerset. Described by John Warren as 'a kind of armed petition to the king', these people from Kent regarded themselves not as rebels but as members of the wider

Key term	**Commonweal** The common good or common wealth of the people and the nation.

'**commonweal**' supporting the demands of parliament. In the opinion of David Cook, 'Political reform was their desire, not revolution.' To the Crown, of course, they were rebels, led by a man, Jack Cade, who the government claimed was nothing more than a murderous criminal. The rebels pledged their loyalty to the king but demanded:

- The removal and punishment of royal officials found guilty of corruption and misgovernment in Kent.
- Fair and impartial justice, and the restoration of law and order.
- The removal of the king's 'evil councillors'.
- The appointment of the Dukes of York, Buckingham and Exeter to the royal council.

The rebellion eventually collapsed but not before it had taken London and captured a number of courtiers, some of whom, including Lord Saye, the king's treasurer, were executed.

In spite of rumours to the contrary, there is no evidence to suggest that York had anything to do with the rebellion. Taking advantage of the growing dissatisfaction with the Crown, he left Ireland without permission and, in September 1450, returned to London. York's return was greeted with enormous public support. Emboldened by the popular reaction to his return from Ireland, York presented the king with a list of grievances which were contained in two bills of complaint:

- *First bill*: a list of personal grievances concerned with York's position as heir, his debts and the fact that his advice had been ignored.
- *Second bill*: a list of general grievances that echoed what Cade's rebels had drawn up; namely, the increase in lawlessness and disorder, the corruption of royal officials and the king's 'evil councillors' and the demise of 'good governance'.

Backed by a force of 3000 armed retainers, York succeeded in persuading the king to meet some of his demands. He was appointed to the royal council, a more effective act of resumption was passed and the king promised to re-establish law and order throughout the kingdom. However, Somerset still dominated the king's council, monies owed to York were not paid and his position as heir-presumptive was not legally recognised. In fact, when Thomas Yonge, one of York's councillors, proposed a bill in parliament recognising the duke as heir of the king the MP for Bristol was arrested and put in the Tower. To make matters worse, Somerset was made Captain of Calais, giving him command of the largest army at the Crown's disposal.

A frustrated attempt was made by York to impeach Somerset in parliament, but when this failed he decided that force of arms was the only alternative left to him. In February 1452, York's army met the king's forces at Dartford, but the duke had miscalculated. Apart from the Earl of Devon and Lord Cobham, the most powerful nobles in the kingdom, including the Duke of Buckingham and the Neville Earls of Salisbury and Warwick, remained loyal to the king. York was outnumbered and forced to submit. The tide was turning against York for, not long after being compelled to make a public apology in St Paul's Cathedral and take a solemn oath to remain faithful to the king, it was announced that the queen was pregnant. This was a serious blow to York's position as heir-presumptive.

Henry VI's insanity and York's protectorate

In August 1453, on hearing the news of devastating defeats in France that all but ended English hopes of victory in the Hundred Years War, Henry VI suffered a mental breakdown. His pregnant wife, Margaret of Anjou, assumed a more active role in politics. Working closely with Somerset, she hoped to exclude York from power and set herself up as **regent** until such time as her husband recovered. This appalled the nobility, who promptly rejected the idea. The noble élite turned on Somerset and supported York. In an effort to conciliate her enemies, Margaret ruthlessly abandoned Somerset and imprisoned him in the Tower. Dissatisfied by the turn of events, one of the most powerful noble families in England, the Nevilles, threw in their lot with York. One reason for this change of allegiance was the Neville feud with the Percy earls of Northumberland, who the king had favoured and Margaret continued to support. Margaret could not prevent York, made more powerful by the support of the Nevilles, from assuming the powers and authority of **protector** and defender of the realm in March 1454. In effect, York had become king in all but name.

York's protectorate was short lived, but in his 12 months of power he did succeed in reducing the size and expenditure of the royal household and in restoring greater law and order, particularly in the north. On the other hand, he failed to have Somerset put on trial for treason and fell short of enlisting all but a handful of nobles to serve in his government. In spite of York's attempts to present himself as the champion of justice and enemy of corruption, the majority of England's noble families stopped short of openly supporting him, preferring instead to remain aloof and cautious.

When Margaret gave birth to a healthy son, Edward, in October 1453, she became convinced that York posed a threat to his inheritance. After the return to health of her husband, in December 1454, Margaret retained her political power and tightened her grip on the court. Margaret was determined to destroy York, but apart from having him stripped of his powers as protector, she failed at first to have him banished from the court. In fact, after the king had shown that he had recovered sufficiently to rule again he publicly recognised York's importance by declaring him to be his principal royal adviser. This act of conciliation was short lived. Margaret persuaded Henry VI to exclude York from the decision-making process on important matters of state. In addition, Somerset was released from the

Key question
How did the king's insanity benefit York?

Key date

Henry VI suffered mental breakdown. Duke of York appointed protector: 1453

Key terms

Regent
Someone who governs the kingdom on behalf of a king.

Protector
Another word for regent.

Profile: Richard Plantagenet, Duke of York 1411–60

1411	– Only son of Richard, Earl of Cambridge. Paternal grandson of Edmund, fifth son of King Edward III
1415	– Succeeded his uncle, Edward Plantagenet, as third Duke of York
1425	– Inherited the possessions of his uncle, Edmund de Mortimer, fifth Earl of March
1436–7	– Served as a soldier in France
1438	– Married Cicely, daughter of Ralph Neville, first Earl of Westmorland
1440–5	– Served as Henry VI's lieutenant in France
1447–50	– Served as Henry VI's lieutenant in Ireland
1452	– Retired from politics after failing to remove the king's chief adviser, Duke of Somerset
1453–4	– Returned to politics and became Lord Protector during the king's first bout of mental illness
1455	– Removed from position when the king recovered and forced out of power. Responded with an armed rising to defeat royal forces at St Albans
1456	– Lord Protector during the king's second bout of mental illness
1457	– Removed again when the king recovered
1458–9	– Driven out of government and took refuge in Wales. Left Wales for Ireland and returned with an army to claim the crown
1460	– Killed in battle at Wakefield

Richard of York did much to influence politics and the way in which the Wars of the Roses began. He was ambitious and after first trying, and failing, to control and rule through the king, he turned eventually to claim the crown for himself. York was a good soldier but he lacked political judgement. Queen Margaret of Anjou did not trust York and she became his most implacable enemy. On his death his cause was taken up by his son and heir Edward of York.

Tower and reappointed to the king's council and to the post of Captain of Calais. It can be argued that, thereafter, Henry VI became little more than a puppet in the hands of his more politically astute wife. This was all too much for York, who fled north to raise an army. With the support of the Nevilles, York intended to impose his will on the king and his council.

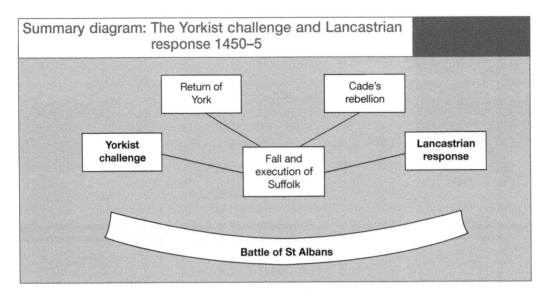

Summary diagram: The Yorkist challenge and Lancastrian response 1450–5

4 | Triumph and Overthrow: The Deposition of Henry VI and Coronation of Edward IV

The fighting begins: St Albans

What began as a political struggle for control of the king and royal government eventually led to outright war for possession of the crown. In 1455, Richard, Duke of York, led his supporters, principally the Neville Earls of Salisbury and Warwick, into rebellion against Henry VI. Their aim was the destruction of Somerset, the elimination of Margaret's influence and the control of the king. At this point, York had no intention of taking the crown for himself. Aware that the birth of Prince Edward had rendered his position as heir-presumptive redundant, York was determined to carve out a new career as the king's chief councillor; to become the power behind the throne. Somerset and the queen had other ideas and they convinced the king that York was plotting treason.

Henry VI summoned York to Leicester to explain himself. York surprised the king by attending the meeting backed by a force of over 3000 men. The king had fewer than 2000 troops so he was forced to negotiate; the failure of these talks led to the so-called battle of St Albans. Although the 'battle' was little more than a skirmish in which some 60 or 70 men were killed, Henry VI was wounded by an arrow and among the dead lay the king's principal adviser, Somerset, and Henry Percy, Earl of Northumberland.

York had prevailed but he lacked the noble support necessary to control the king and his government. A compromise was reached whereby York was reappointed to the council and became the king's principal adviser. In addition, York had his ally Warwick appointed Captain of Calais. The strain proved too much for the king, who again lapsed into insanity. Between November 1455 and February 1456 York served a second term as

Key question
How and why was Henry VI overthrown?

Key dates

Wars of the Roses began with the battle of St Albans: 1455

York served second term as protector: 1455–6

protector. In the opinion of David Cook, 'the remarkable aspect of the years 1456–9 is that civil war did not break out again before 1459'.

The Loveday

Peace between the warring parties was fragile and, ultimately, short lived. In spite of Henry VI's attempts at reconciliation in March 1458, the so-called 'Loveday', distrust and suspicion lingered and eventually turned into bloody conflict. The Loveday was the name given to the elaborately staged ritual reconciliation that saw members of the rival factions march arm-in-arm into St Paul's Cathedral and which sought to heal the divisions between the victims and victors at the battle of St Albans. It was a superficial act of unity that fooled no one. While York was away dealing with problems in Ireland, a bitter feud developed between Margaret and Warwick. The queen tried to have Warwick arrested on charges of piracy and riot, but failed.

The fighting resumes: Blore Heath and the 'rout' of Ludford

Convinced that York was plotting to take the throne, Queen Margaret and her principal ally, Humphrey Stafford, Duke of Buckingham, raised an army to destroy the Yorkists. To defend themselves, York and his supporters, Salisbury and Warwick, each raised an army. To prevent the three Yorkist armies joining together, the Lancastrians under Lord Audley intercepted Salisbury at Blore Heath. Audley was defeated and killed. The Yorkists merged their armies and awaited the Lancastrians at Ludford. When Henry VI himself turned up to lead the royal forces a substantial part of the Yorkist forces defected to the Lancastrians. After a brief but bloody skirmish York, Salisbury and Warwick fled, leaving their troops to surrender. Not long afterwards the Yorkist leaders left England; York took refuge in Ireland while Salisbury, Warwick and York's heir, Edward, took shelter in Calais.

The Parliament of Devils

Having seen off the Yorkists, Margaret persuaded the king to call a parliament in Coventry in order to disgrace publicly York and his adherents. Meeting in November 1459, parliament branded York, Salisbury and Warwick as traitors, sentenced them to death and ordered their lands and goods to be seized. In a gross violation of long-held custom that protected the rights of innocent offspring, parliament also disinherited the Yorkist leaders' heirs. This last act shocked the nobility, turning some against the Crown. This parliament became notorious and earned the nickname 'Parliament of Devils'. The harsh treatment meted out to the Yorkists backfired since it only stiffened their resolve to seek revenge.

Northampton and Wakefield: the death of York

The opportunity for revenge presented itself in June 1460 in the so-called '**Yorkist invasion**', when Warwick, Salisbury and York's heir Edward, Earl of March, returned to England, landing on the south coast with an army of 2000 Calais veterans. Having returned from exile, the Yorkists set about taking London, which they did with ease, and recruiting more troops to take on the Lancastrians. A Yorkist army under Warwick encountered Henry VI's army near Northampton. Led by the Duke of Buckingham, the Lancastrians were heavily defeated owing to the treachery of Lord Grey of Ruthin, who changed sides and joined the Yorkists. Henry VI and Buckingham were captured and the latter was executed. Margaret and her son Edward escaped.

Control of the government was no longer enough for York and, three months after the Yorkist victory at Northampton, he all but claimed the throne for himself by forcing Henry VI to agree to the **act of accord**. According to the terms of the act:

- Henry VI was to remain king for the rest of his life.
- Henry VI's son, Prince Edward, was disinherited.
- Henry VI's wife, Queen Margaret, was banished for life.
- The succession was entrusted to Richard of York, and his offspring, who was recognised in law as heir-proper.

Queen Margaret refused to accept this and raised troops in the north. York, his son Edmund, Earl of Rutland, and Salisbury marched to Yorkshire to meet her in battle. However, at Wakefield the Yorkists were crushed by a much larger Lancastrian force. York and Rutland were killed and Salisbury was captured and later executed. York's severed head, with a paper crown on it, was stuck on the walls of York. He was succeeded by his eldest son and heir, the 19-year-old Edward, Earl of March.

Yorkists triumphant: Henry deposed, Edward proclaimed

To exploit her victory at Wakefield, Margaret hurried south to rescue her husband, who was in Warwick's custody. The Yorkists, under Warwick, suffered another decisive defeat, at the second battle of St Alban's. Henry VI was released from captivity and reunited with his wife. Margaret failed to follow up her victory by not taking London. Warwick fled to the Welsh border to join up with York's son and heir, Edward.

Edward, Duke of York and Earl of March, was determined to avenge the defeat and death of his father at Wakefield. He marched north from Gloucester to intercept a Lancastrian army under James Butler, Earl of Wiltshire and Lieutenant of Ireland, and Jasper Tudor, Earl of Pembroke. The Lancastrians were routed in a significant victory at Mortimer's Cross that had been planned and led by the teenage Edward. Within a month of his victory, Edward was in London, where he was proclaimed King Edward IV on 4 March 1461. However, before he could be crowned he had to march north to confront the Lancastrians.

Key dates

Battle of Northampton: July 1460

Battle of Wakefield: December 1460

Richard, Duke of York, killed at Wakefield: December 1460

Second battle of St Albans: February 1461

Battle of Mortimer's Cross: February 1461

Battle of Ferrybridge: March 1461

Battle of Towton: March 1461

Edward IV usurped the throne by removing Henry VI: March 1461

Key terms

Yorkist invasion
Used by historians to describe the return of armed Yorkists to England from exile abroad.

Act of accord
An act of parliament responsible for determining the line of succession to the throne.

Portrait of Edward IV. Why do you think Edward IV commissioned an artist to paint his portrait?

Ferrybridge was a skirmish that took place a day before the much larger and bloodier battle of Towton. A small force of Lancastrians under Lord Clifford attempted to stop Yorkist troops under Warwick from using a river crossing at Ferrybridge. In the ensuing fight, Clifford was killed, Warwick was wounded and the Lancastrians fled. Fought in a snowstorm the following day, the battle of Towton witnessed the largest armies ever assembled in the kingdom, with more than 50,000 men involved. The slaughter was great and the Lancastrians were routed. Towton was the decisive engagement that both sides had been seeking since the renewal of war in 1459. Henry VI, Queen Margaret and their young son Edward fled to Scotland while Edward returned to London to be crowned. The Yorkists had triumphed.

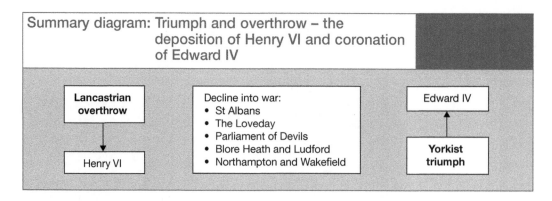

Study Guide: AS Questions

In the style of Edexcel

To what extent were the ambitions of Richard of York responsible for the outbreak of conflict in England in 1455?

> **Exam tips**
>
> *The cross-references are intended to take you straight to the material that will help you to answer the question.*
>
> When you plan, keep the focus on the question. Resist the temptation to provide a narrative of the events of 1455. This question is essentially asking you why the Wars of the Roses began. In answering a question of this type, you should expect to deal with several factors: three or four at least. But where a particular reason is given to you in the question, you should plan to give substantial attention to this factor – probably about one-third of your answer – and you should make sure you deal with this factor in your conclusion, even if you are going to say that other factors are more important.
>
> Below is a list of other factors you could include in your response. In what order will you use them? What information will you select to develop them?
>
> - The personality of Henry VI (pages 27–8).
> - The role of Margaret of Anjou (page 35).
> - The impact of defeat in France (page 40).
> - The financial weakness of the Crown (pages 32–3).
> - Neville resentment of Somerset's influence (pages 40–2).
>
> And what is your conclusion? You should show in the body of your answer that these factors interacted and culminated in outright rebellion in 1455, and you must make a judgement about whether the ambitions of the Duke of York primarily were responsible for conflict. You should take into account the other factors which promoted discontent and which prompted the challenge to King Henry VI.

In the style of OCR

'The ambitions of Richard Duke of York were the main reason why England was unstable during the years 1450–60.' How far do you agree?

Exam tips

The cross-references are intended to take you straight to the material that will help you to answer the question.

The focus here is on the beginning and early years of the Wars of the Roses and, in particular, the role of the Duke of York in the growing conflict. York played a central role in events between 1453 and 1460, and may have had links to Cade's rebellion (1450) (pages 38–9). He had some success in restoring order in the north during his first protectorate in 1454, but after his removal he came in force to the royal court at Leicester. He defeated royal troops in the first battle of the war (St Albans) in 1455, and by the end of the year he was protector once more. Over the next few years, both sides built up their forces until in 1459 the Yorkists were defeated at Ludford Bridge and York was attainted as a traitor (page 44). He fled to Ireland but returned in 1460 after Yorkist forces defeated the king at Northampton (page 44). York's claim to the throne was rejected and he had to accept the act of accord. Finally, in December 1460 he was defeated and killed at Wakefield (page 44).

Do not write a simple descriptive outline of events as has been done above or you will score a very low mark. To do better, you must use the knowledge you have to investigate why these things were happening. One focus of your causal analysis must look at York and his ambitions (which may extend from York himself to the aims of his supporters and members of his family). To score very well you must, however, go further still and weigh York's ambitions against other causal factors that help to explain the instability of the period, for example:

- the king's incapacity (pages 40–1)
- the Crown's financial weakness (pages 32–3)
- defeat in France (page 40)
- local rivalries among the nobility (pages 36–7)
- the role of Queen Margaret of Anjou (page 35).

It might be argued that Henry's 'madness' made him an incapable king. This gave room for the ambitions of great nobles such as the Beauforts and York to jostle for position in the power vacuum. On the other hand, you might argue that Henry was weakened by grave financial problems that were not his personal responsibility. The expectation of many that England should pursue the old war with France was unrealistic, but Henry's peaceful character and interests undermined his position.

Alternatively, you might argue that Henry, willingly or unwillingly, gave too much influence to Margaret of Anjou and it was her stubborn inflexibility and narrow patronage of the Beauforts that drove York and his allies to war. Wherever you decide the key to this problem lies, be sure to evaluate a range of factors and weigh them against each other – the phrase 'the main reason' in the question demands nothing less.

3

The First Reign of Edward IV 1461–70

POINTS TO CONSIDER

The accession of Edward IV seemed to have brought stability and security to England but this was not so in reality. In spite of efforts to consolidate his power, Edward IV struggled to impose his authority on the kingdom. Noble disaffection, laced with jealousy over Edward's promotion, combined to threaten his throne. Nor could he look to those closest to him for support, for once steadfast allies turned into vengeful enemies. These issues are examined as four themes:

- Edward IV: consolidation of Yorkist power and the restoration of order
- Edward IV and the nobility
- The king and 'the kingmaker': Edward IV and the Earl of Warwick
- Warwick's rebellion and the restoration of Henry VI 1469–71

Key dates

1461	Reign of Edward IV began
1464	Edward IV married Elizabeth Woodville
	Battles of Hedgeley Moor and Hexham
1465	Henry VI captured and imprisoned in the Tower
1468	Edward IV's sister Margaret married Duke Charles of Burgundy
1469	Warwick and Clarence rebelled against Edward IV
	Battle of Edgecote
1470	Henry VI restored to the throne by Warwick. Edward IV and his brother Richard forced into exile in Burgundy
	Battles of Losecoat Field and Nibley Green
1471	Edward IV restored to the throne after victory at the battle of Barnet, in which Warwick was killed
	Henry VI murdered in the Tower, his son Edward, Prince of Wales, killed in battle of Tewkesbury

Key question
How successful was Edward in consolidating his power and restoring law and order?

Key dates

Reign of Edward IV began: 1461

Battles of Hedgeley Moor and Hexham: 1464

Henry VI captured and imprisoned in the Tower: 1465

1 | Edward IV: Consolidation of Yorkist Power and the Restoration of Order

The fighting continues: 1461–5

If Edward thought his coronation in June 1461 as Edward IV would bring an end to the civil wars he was sadly mistaken. It took him over three years to eliminate his Lancastrian enemies, who concentrated their power in Northumberland and were sustained by Scottish and French help. A number of Lancastrian plots were unearthed, there were invasion scares on the south coast and disturbances occurred in several parts of the kingdom. In Wales the Lancastrians lost a skirmish in the Tywi valley near Dryslwyn but they had better success in the north, where Harlech Castle was besieged but held by them for nearly seven years until it finally fell in 1468. In Northumberland the castles of Alnwick, Bamburgh and Dunstanburgh became the focal point of Lancastrian resistance in the north. Twice these castles were besieged and taken by the Yorkists and twice they were recaptured by the Lancastrians.

Early in 1464, Henry VI and Margaret returned to England to rally the substantial support they still enjoyed in the north. Their principal support came from the Percy earls of Northumberland. It was to Sir Ralph Percy that Henry VI and Margaret marched with a largely French-financed army consisting mainly of Scottish and French mercenaries. They were joined by troops raised by Henry Beaufort, Duke of Somerset (son and heir of the king's principal adviser, killed at St Albans in 1455). Edward IV responded by sending a Yorkist army north under the command of Warwick's younger brother, John Neville, Lord Montagu. At Hedgeley Moor, in April 1464, the Lancastrians were soundly beaten, with Percy among the casualties. Somerset escaped and offered battle three weeks later at Hexham. This time Montagu made no mistake when he cut the Lancastrians to pieces, captured Somerset and executed him. Margaret and her son escaped and sought refuge in France while her husband went on the run. Henry VI was eventually captured in Lancashire in 1465 and imprisoned in the Tower.

Key question
How did Edward IV secure and consolidate his position as king?

Security and consolidation

In order to secure the crown and consolidate his power, Edward IV realised that he had to deal with threats and problems both external and internal.

External threats and problems

Concerned by the scale of support the Lancastrians had obtained from both Scotland and France, Edward was determined to establish better foreign relations. He successfully negotiated truces with James III of Scotland and Louis XI of France. Edward hoped this would be enough to deny the Lancastrians any aid abroad, be it political, financial or military. The king also opened negotiations with the powerful Duke of Burgundy to exploit trading opportunities and to secure an ally should the French

Wedding of Edward IV and Elizabeth Woodville. When Elizabeth Woodville married Edward IV she was not pregnant but the artist has shown her to be so. Why do you think this was done?

renege on their truce. In an effort to turn the truce with France into something more lasting, Warwick tried to persuade Edward IV to marry the French king's daughter. However, his attempt to cement an Anglo-French alliance through marriage failed when Edward ignored his advice and secretly married Elizabeth Woodville instead. This was a serious miscalculation on Edward's part for it alienated the French. Equally significant was Edward's failure to persuade the influential Hanseatic League (see page 180), an organisation of German merchants, to agree to his request for trading concessions. These concessions had the potential to increase trade and customs revenue for the king.

> Edward IV married Elizabeth Woodville: 1464
>
> **Key date**

Internal threats and problems

Fearful of further fighting, Edward adopted a policy of conciliation. Lancastrians were offered pardons and encouraged to serve the Crown. Henry VI was imprisoned in the Tower but was well treated. Lawlessness and disorder were tackled alongside

National debt
Money owed by the Crown to members of the English nobility and continental bankers and financiers. The Crown borrowed the money to help pay for the costs of the court, the royal household and the government.

the **national debt** and the economy. Edward tried to improve the efficiency and authority of the agencies of government, particularly in the farthest reaches of the kingdom. Unfortunately, Edward's successes were few. Law and order were restored in some regions, and government was improved, mainly in the professionalisation of its personnel, but its effectiveness remained questionable. The Crown's finances were well on the way to recovery but the national debt remained high. Perhaps the most glaring failure was Edward's tendency to over-reward close family and a small circle of noble supporters. This bred resentment, not just among Lancastrians but among some Yorkists, too.

In the final analysis, the fact that Edward was deposed with what appeared to be relative ease in 1469 shows that he had failed not only to restore law and order but also to secure and consolidate his power.

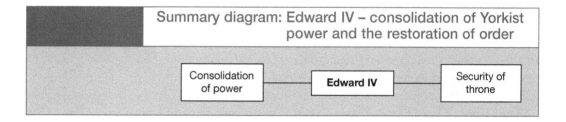

Summary diagram: Edward IV – consolidation of Yorkist power and the restoration of order

Consolidation of power — **Edward IV** — Security of throne

2 | Edward IV and the Nobility

Key question
How successful was Edward's relationship with the nobility?

Edward was well aware that the success of his kingship depended largely on his relationship with the nobility. He wished to avoid the problems encountered by Henry VI by widening the circle of patronage but, as a result of the war, the nobility were more bitterly divided than ever. Thus, the task of managing and satisfying them would be a difficult one. His policy was based on two general principles:

- pardon and reconciliation for Lancastrians
- employment, patronage and reward for nobles of both factions.

Edward therefore began his reign with the best of intentions, but his laudable aims fell well short of their target. Almost from the beginning he encountered difficulties, not the least of which was that some Lancastrians were reluctant to accept his offers of reconciliation and employment in the service of the Crown. Indeed, Edward did not have the financial or material resources to reward them if they had sought it. Owing in part to his inexperience of kingship, he had badly miscalculated the resources available to him. In fact, he was hard pressed to recompense his own Yorkist supporters, many of whom waited impatiently for their rewards in land and office. Then there were the demands made on him by his closest allies and family, such as Warwick and the Woodvilles.

In order to meet the demands of his Yorkist supporters, Edward turned to exploiting his defeated Lancastrian enemies. He set in motion a large-scale redistribution of titles, offices and estates that he had confiscated from at least 13 Lancastrian peers and from almost 100 well-off gentry. **Attainted** for **treason** in the parliament of 1461, the dispossessed Lancastrians had no choice but to accept their fate. The fact that some of them had been killed in battle meant that their families bore the brunt of the confiscations. Naturally, this bred resentment and it was not long before some of them began to plot Edward's downfall.

In the 22 years of Edward IV's reign he created or revived at least 37 noble titles, 22 of which were bestowed during his first reign, 1461–9. This apparent generosity was intended to bolster a depleted peerage, many peers having been killed in the wars, and to provide him with a wide circle of grateful supporters. The policy failed because the bestowal of a title did not necessarily bring with it any land. For all his promises, many of the confiscated estates ended up in the hands of a privileged few. The principal beneficiaries were:

- *Edward's brothers*. George and Richard were created Dukes of Clarence and Gloucester, respectively. Clarence was endowed with lands to the value of some £3660 (£1.78 million in today's money) annually and offices with a combined annual salary of just over £650 (£305,000 today).
- *The Nevilles*. William, Lord Fauconberg, was made Earl of Kent; John, Lord Montagu, was given the Earldom of Northumberland, while George was appointed Archbishop of York. The most favoured of the family was Richard Neville, Earl of Warwick. The gifts in land and money bestowed on him were on a scale that dwarfed that given to any other courtier. Even more significantly, he was given unparalleled power in the north of England, ruling it virtually as king's **viceroy**.
- *The Woodvilles*. Edward IV's wife, Elizabeth, was keen to see her family benefit from her marriage. Her father Richard was created Earl Rivers and her brother Anthony, Lord Scales, was entrusted with considerable influence at court.
- *Favoured individuals*. Men such as Sir William Herbert and William Lord Hastings benefited from Edward's largesse. Hastings became the king's closest friend and was appointed Chamberlain of the Royal Household. Herbert was advanced to the peerage as Earl of Pembroke. He was virtually given Wales to rule as viceroy of the king, a position of power comparable to Warwick's authority in the north of England.

In practice, Edward IV relied on a comparatively small group of nobles to help him exercise his royal authority. They are estimated to have been no more than a dozen strong and were created by the king. This favoured clique bears comparison with the inner ring of noble councillors on whom Henry VI relied to govern his kingdom. Very little, it seems, had changed. The resentment that led to civil war in 1455 was as much a factor in the renewal of civil war in 1469.

Key terms

Attainted
The process by which nobles who broke the law were condemned and then punished. This law enabled the king to seize the law-breaker's estates so that he could benefit from the profits.

Treason
Betrayal of one's country and its ruler.

Viceroy
A title given to a nobleman entrusted with royal authority to rule as the king's deputy in some part of the realm.

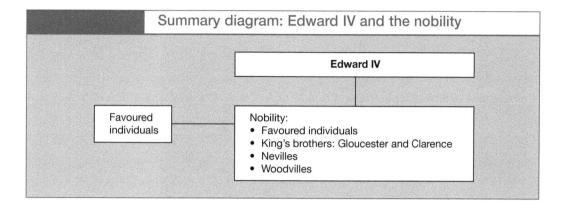

Summary diagram: Edward IV and the nobility

Edward IV

Favoured individuals

Nobility:
- Favoured individuals
- King's brothers: Gloucester and Clarence
- Nevilles
- Woodvilles

Key question
Why did Edward IV and the Earl of Warwick quarrel?

3 | The King and 'the Kingmaker': Edward IV and the Earl of Warwick

Warwick the man

The life, character and career of Richard Neville, Earl of Warwick, have long fascinated historians. Known as 'the kingmaker', a nickname first applied in the sixteenth century, Warwick was, in the opinion of modern historian, A.J. Pollard, 'the mightiest of over-mighty subjects', who was instrumental in putting Edward IV on the throne in 1461. Equally significant is the fact that he played a pivotal role in deposing Edward IV in 1469 and restoring Henry VI in 1470. Warwick was certainly mightier than Richard, Duke of York, but he, too, fell from power, being cut down in bloody battle in 1471. As far as the man is concerned, we know comparatively little about him. No effigy or painting survives nor do we have a contemporary description of him. He seems not to have been a patron of the arts but devoted himself to politics and war. The most potent example of his fame in history is his reputation.

Warwick's career began in 1449 when, aged 21 he succeeded to the wealthy earldom of Warwick in right of his wife, the heiress Anne Beauchamp. Anne's father, Richard Beauchamp, Earl of Warwick, was among the richest nobles in England and when he died without sons to succeed him all his wealth and possessions passed to his daughter. Through her, and with the king's approval, Richard Neville successfully claimed the title and earldom of his deceased father-in-law. When Richard, Duke of York, claimed the regency in 1453, Warwick offered his support and took up arms with him at the battle of St Albans in 1455. His reward was the prestigious and powerful post of Captain of Calais. He took part in the Loveday procession of 1458 (see page 43) and became a popular hero soon afterwards as a result of his successful attack on a fleet of Spanish ships off Calais. He defended Calais from Somerset who, on being appointed Captain by Margaret of Anjou, tried to take up his post but found the gates closed against him. Warwick returned to England in 1460, gaining an easy victory at Northampton and bringing the captive Henry VI to London.

Family portrait showing Richard Neville and his 12 children. Why did Richard Neville commission this painting?

After the death of the Duke of York, Warwick transferred his allegiance to Richard's son and heir, Edward, Earl of March. After the victories at Mortimer's Cross and Towton, Warwick smoothed the path to Edward's declaration as king and assisted in organising the coronation. Warwick's power owed much to the fact that he possessed vast estates that stretched across the length and breadth of England and Wales. He held the title to four earldoms to which were added offices of state, many of which were bestowed on him by a grateful Edward IV. It is this, his position as Edward IV's right-hand man, his most trusted adviser and most generously rewarded favourite, that marks Warwick out as a figure of enormous interest to contemporaries and modern historians alike. However, his favoured position is also the source of much debate regarding the extent of his influence and power.

Kingmaker or kingserver?

The key issue is the extent to which Warwick deserves the title of kingmaker; did he make and unmake kings or did he merely serve them? It is accepted that Warwick was a rich and powerful man and there is general agreement that by putting his vast

Key question
Did Warwick make kings or simply serve them?

resources at the disposal of the Yorkist cause he contributed to Edward's triumph in 1461. More debatable is the extent to which Edward relied on Warwick and his wealth and whether without them he could have become king and maintained his hold on the crown. Equally debatable is the nature of the relationship between Warwick and the king and the extent to which one was subject to the authority of the other. In short, who actually ruled England? There are two schools of thought:

- Warwick not only 'made' King Edward (and unmade him) but also ruled England in his name.
- Warwick's influence has been exaggerated and he was merely a servant of the king, albeit a powerful and favoured one.

Kingmaker

In the opinion of one contemporary, James Kennedy, Bishop of St Andrews, Warwick was 'governor of the realm of England beneath King Edward'. This statement, from a man who was the most influential politician in Scotland, has been taken to imply the Scotsman's contempt for the authority of the young King Edward. However, it should be noted that Kennedy's sympathies lay with the Lancastrians, as shown by the protection he offered Henry VI and Margaret when they fled to Scotland.

More damning is the witty remark of the governor of Abbeville, who reported to his king, Louis XI of France, in May 1464, that in England 'they have but two rulers – M. de Warwick and another, whose name I have forgotten'. From across the English Channel, Warwick may well have appeared to be all-powerful, especially as he was better known to the French because he was entrusted with conducting the king's foreign policy. This miscalculation of Edward's position and power by the French would come back to haunt King Louis.

Even as far afield as Italy, the perception appeared to be that Warwick was the real power behind the throne. In a letter to the Duke of Milan, written in April 1461, the Papal Legate, Francesco Coppini, wrote, 'My lord of Warwick … has made a new king of the son of the duke of York.'

Some modern historians agree with this image of an all-powerful Warwick. At the turn of the twentieth century the *Dictionary of National Biography* stated with confidence that Warwick 'was the real ruler of England during the first three years of Edward's reign'. In 1955, P.M. Kendall had no doubt that Edward's usurpation of the throne in 1461 was the first true example of Warwick's 'kingmaking', after which 'Warwick governed in the saddle from the periphery of the realm'. Another popular pithy turn of phrase is that coined by the Victorian historian J.A. Froude, 'Warwick ruled while Edward reigned.'

Kingserver

However, more recently, historians have been inclined to play down the extent of Warwick's kingmaking. In the opinion of Edward IV's modern biographer, Charles Ross, 'the whole pattern of Edward's activities in these years [1461–9] suggest[s] that he was very much king in fact as well as in name'. Andrew Pickering stated emphatically that 'Edward was neither "made" by Warwick nor controlled by him.' David Cook expressed his view that the relationship between Warwick and Edward IV was 'an alliance of mutual interests which triumphed in 1461, not a puppet and puppeteer'. The last word should be left to A.J. Pollard:

> It was largely to foreign observers that Warwick appeared all-powerful. In reality the relationship between the two was more a partnership between mighty subject and insecure king, and it would be entirely wrong to suppose that Warwick was the sole author of royal policy during these early years.

The alienation of Warwick

It may have come as something of a shock to Edward IV to discover that his close friend and ally was not satisfied with the position and power he had been given. Nor was he sufficiently grateful for the freedom accorded him in the conduct of national affairs. Among the most important offices showered on Warwick were the following:

Key question
Why did Warwick turn against Edward IV?

- Captainship of Calais
- Constableship of Dover Castle
- Wardenship of the Cinque Ports
- Admiralship of England and Ireland
- Wardenship of the eastern and western Marches on the Scottish border.

Short of monopolising royal patronage and alienating the other Yorkist nobility there was not much more that Edward could do or give the earl. Warwick was evidently greedy and grasping, and it was his desire to add the whole of Wales and the Marches (see page 77) to his portfolio of authority that brought him into conflict with William Herbert, Earl of Pembroke. Pembroke believed that his contribution to putting Edward on the throne was equally deserving of reward. The two men, Pembroke and Warwick, would quarrel and eventually become the deadliest of enemies.

Edward's inexperience of kingship added to Warwick's ambition was a recipe for disaster. For the first three years of Edward IV's reign all seemed well between them, probably because they still faced a common and very real threat in the Lancastrians. However, this changed after 1465 with the defeat in battle and subsequent exile of the Lancastrian leaders, and the capture of Henry VI. The first sign that all may not have been well occurred in May 1464 when Edward IV secretly married Elizabeth Woodville. The fact that Warwick did not know of and was not consulted about the union is telling. In fact, Edward shocked and angered members of his own family with his decision to marry a widow with children whose family had, until recently, been staunch Lancastrians. In the opinion of Charles Ross this was 'the first major blunder of his political career'.

Warwick was left embarrassed by this marriage because he had been working hard to cement an alliance with the French by proposing a match between Edward IV and Louis XI's sister-in-law. It was, in part, their disagreement over the conduct of foreign policy that led to a rift between Warwick and Edward. Warwick favoured an alliance with France but Edward preferred a treaty with the Duchy of Burgundy. Burgundy had been England's ally during the Hundred Years War and although that war had ended in 1453, the Duchy had remained an enemy of France. Louis XI feared an Anglo-Burgundian alliance as he thought it might persuade the English to renew the war for control of France. While Louis XI was also keen to destroy Burgundy's trade and end its commercial power, Edward IV was equally keen to exploit it. Since Burgundy's rulers, Phillip and his successor Charles the Bold, wished to maintain their independence from the French Crown, an alliance with England suited their purposes.

Key date
Edward IV's sister Margaret married Duke Charles of Burgundy: 1468

Unhappy with having to negotiate with foreign powers according to the dictates of the increasingly influential Woodvilles, Warwick withdrew from the court in 1467. The final straw came in 1468, when Edward arranged the marriage of his sister, Margaret, to Duke Charles of Burgundy. This ended any hope of a French alliance and turned Louis XI into a dangerous enemy. As Woodville influence increased, Warwick's declined. Over time, the earl's advice either was not sought or was ignored. Warwick's role as the king's chief councillor appeared to be all but over. Whether Warwick's young protégé, the king, had, in the words of David Cook, 'hurt his grossly inflated ego', we have no way of knowing, but it may have occurred to 'the kingmaker' that in order to retain his power and influence he might have to contemplate removing Edward from the throne.

The alienation of Clarence

Key question
Why did Clarence turn against his brother, King Edward IV?

Warwick was not the only one with grievances, real or imagined, against Edward IV. The king's unstable and over-ambitious brother, George, Duke of Clarence, had opposed Edward's marriage and he resented the Woodville influence at court. Clarence shared Warwick's irritation at the way the Woodvilles were cornering the marriage market. By the beginning of 1467, the queen's siblings had contracted marriages with the Duke of Buckingham and the heirs of the Earls of Arundel, Essex, Kent and Pembroke (William Herbert was elevated to the peerage in 1468). In addition, the queen's eldest son from her first marriage, Thomas Grey, took as his wife the heiress of the Duke of Exeter, while her 20-year-old brother, John Woodville, married the 65-year-old Duchess of Norfolk. Described by a contemporary chronicler as a *maritagium diabolicum* (a diabolical marriage), this union is taken as evidence of Woodville greed and ambition.

Fearful of losing his privileged status at court, Clarence turned to Warwick for support. It was agreed that Clarence should marry Warwick's eldest daughter, Isabel, but the king refused to sanction the match. This was a serious blow to Clarence and Warwick, who blamed the queen and her brother Anthony, Lord Scales, for influencing the king against the marriage. Neither Clarence nor Warwick was prepared to tolerate this public humiliation, so together they plotted the destruction of the Woodvilles and the downfall of the king. They were sustained in their plotting by the knowledge that while Warwick was generally popular in the kingdom, the Woodvilles were not. Warwick was a politician with a talent for propaganda and the cultivation of friendships. Unfortunately for him, it became clear that his 'popularity' was not as widespread as he had thought, for while the Commons supported him, the majority of the nobility did not.

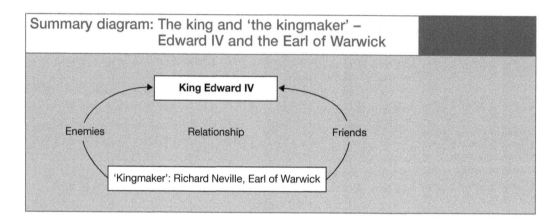

Summary diagram: The king and 'the kingmaker' – Edward IV and the Earl of Warwick

4 | Warwick's Rebellion and the Restoration of Henry VI 1469–71

Political upheaval and instability

Jealousy, bitterness and greed lay at the root of the renewal of civil war in 1469. Unlike previous conflicts, this was a war not between two sides – the Lancastrians and Yorkists – but between two halves of the same side. Warwick's rebellion split the Yorkists and forced Edward on to the defensive. Trouble began in April 1469 in the north of England when two separate Warwick-inspired risings led by '**Robin of Redesdale**' and '**Robin of Holderness**' broke out. Taking advantage of the growing economic crisis due to a series of bad harvests, general discontent and slide into disorder that was gripping the country from mid-1468, Warwick hoped to keep Edward busy in the north while he and Clarence slipped over to Calais to plot the king's usurpation.

In Calais, they took command of the garrison of veteran troops and issued a manifesto outlining their grievances and stating their intention to rid the kingdom of the Crown's 'evil councillors'. To seal their alliance, Clarence was married to Warwick's daughter. Warwick and Clarence's public declaration and return to England in July 1469 alarmed Edward, who called on his principal supporters, the Earls of Pembroke and Devon, to bring their forces to join his. However, Warwick and Clarence

Key question
Why did Warwick rebel in 1469 and why was Henry VI restored?

Warwick and Clarence rebelled against Edward IV: 1469

Battle of Edgecote: 1469

Key dates

Robin of Redesdale and Robin of Holderness
Pseudonyms used to mask the true identities of the rebel leaders.

Key term

managed to intercept Pembroke, and his largely Welsh army was heavily defeated at Edgecote. Pembroke was captured and executed. On hearing the news, Edward IV's troops deserted and he fled but was soon captured by Warwick.

Warwick's attempt to govern the kingdom failed. The economic crisis and increased disorder that had served his purpose earlier in the year now threatened to topple him. The nobility remained cautious and aloof to the extent that they did not support him in the face of a Lancastrian rising in the north-west. To help him put down this rising and to quell other significant pockets of unrest, Warwick released Edward IV from custody. The relationship between the two men was strained and it soon became clear to Warwick that he would never again regain his former position as the king's principal adviser. With peace restored in much of the kingdom, Warwick began a new plot to oust the king. In an effort to dispose of Edward, in March 1470, Warwick secretly encouraged a rebellion under Sir Robert Welles in Lincolnshire. At the battle of Losecoat Field the rebels were defeated by Edward, who pursued them as they tore off their incriminating coats and badges. Welles was captured and executed.

As events nationally spiralled out of control, some members of the nobility took advantage of the chaos and confusion to pursue bitter family feuds. The battle at Nibley Green in March 1470 was one such private quarrel between the Berkeleys and Talbots. There were numerous other private quarrels settled by combat, although most did not result in pitched battles. For example, in the autumn of 1470, Lord Stanley besieged the Harringtons in Hornby Castle.

France and Burgundy

As England descended into civil war, the rulers of France and Burgundy looked on with great interest. They hoped to use the situation to their advantage by backing one side against the other. In fact, France and Burgundy were to play a crucial role in this phase of the Wars of the Roses.

As relations between the king and Warwick deteriorated, the latter, in the company of Clarence, fled to France. Louis XI intended to use them as a diplomatic tool in his conflict with Burgundy. In an often tense and hostile round of negotiations, Louis managed to persuade Warwick, Clarence and Margaret of Anjou to set aside their differences and join forces. The French king had long hoped to arrange a Neville–Lancastrian alliance in order to restore Henry VI to the English throne. In return, Louis expected the English to break their treaty with Burgundy and help him in his conflict with Duke Charles. To seal this alliance it was agreed that Margaret's son, Prince Edward, should marry Warwick's youngest daughter, Anne.

In September 1470 Warwick returned to England. With French financial assistance and a group of mercenaries at his disposal, Warwick set about recruiting an army. He was able to do this almost unmolested because Edward IV was in the north putting

Key dates

Battles of Losecoat Field and Nibley Green: 1470

Henry VI restored to the throne by Warwick. Edward IV and his brother Richard forced into exile in Burgundy: 1470

Key question
Why did France and Burgundy play such a significant part in English affairs?

down a rebellion led by Lord FitzHugh, Warwick's brother-in-law. At about the same time, in what may have been part of a co-ordinated plan, Warwick's brother John, Lord Montagu, betrayed the king by switching his allegiance. To avoid being caught in a pincer movement, King Edward, together with his brother Richard, Duke of Gloucester, Lord Hastings and Earl Rivers, was forced to flee and seek shelter in Burgundy. Charles the Bold now played host to a group of exiled English nobles and, like Louis of France, he intended to use them in his conflict with the French.

As part of Warwick's agreement with Queen Margaret, Henry VI was released from prison and restored to the throne. The **readeption** of Henry VI brought England into conflict with Burgundy. True to their word, Warwick and Margaret of Anjou supported Louis XI when he attacked Burgundy. This proved disastrous for Warwick because he lost the support of parliament, which had not been consulted about the declaration of war, and the powerful merchant community, who feared the damage this conflict would do to the kingdom's chief export, wool. Duke Charles responded by gifting Edward IV 50,000 crowns, helping him plan his return to England and putting at his disposal a bodyguard of Burgundian troops.

It may be argued that in providing a safe haven for exiles, together with financial, military and diplomatic assistance, France and Burgundy had done much to determine the course of English political history in the latter half of the fifteenth century. Of course, they did so not because it mattered to them what happened in England so long as it kept the English weak and distracted by civil war. The bargains the French and Burgundians struck with individuals such as Edward IV, Margaret of Anjou and Warwick, and later with Jasper and Henry Tudor, were only ever intended to be advantageous in the short term.

The defection of Clarence and the murder of Henry VI

Edward returned from Burgundy in March 1470 and hastily set about recruiting an army. On his march to London, Edward was joined by his brother Clarence, who he forgave for betraying him. Clarence's defection was caused by his disappointment at Warwick's failure to consider, let alone support, his candidature for the crown. His opposition to the restoration of Henry VI inevitably brought him into conflict with Warwick. Warwick condemned Clarence's duplicity and resolved either to kill him in battle or to execute him should he be captured. Warwick never got that chance for in April he was defeated and killed at the battle of Barnet. 'False, fleeting, perjur'd Clarence', as Shakespeare referred to him in his play *Henry VI*, survived to betray another day.

Within weeks of his crushing victory at Barnet, Edward IV scored another success at the battle of Tewkesbury. A number of Lancastrian magnates were killed including the Duke of Somerset

Battle of Tewkesbury 1471. Why has a tradition grown up suggesting that the man in black pulled from his horse and killed in the centre of the picture was Prince Edward, son of Henry VI?

Key dates

Edward IV restored to the throne after victory at the battle of Barnet, in which Warwick was killed: 1471

Henry VI murdered in the Tower, his son Edward, Prince of Wales, killed in battle of Tewkesbury: 1471

and, crucially, Margaret of Anjou's son, Prince Edward. The queen herself made good her escape, only to be captured a few days later. It is widely believed that, in an effort to end the wars once and for all, Edward IV ordered the execution of Henry VI. The constable of the Tower, where Henry VI was incarcerated, was Edward's brother, Richard, Duke of York, and it is thought that he may have been responsible for carrying out the deed.

Following the destruction of the Lancastrians at Tewkesbury, Henry VI's half-brother, Jasper Tudor, fled to France, taking his 14-year-old nephew, Henry, Earl of Richmond, with him. Created Earl of Pembroke by Henry VI in 1452, Jasper Tudor was one of the few die-hard Lancastrians who refused to come to terms with Edward IV. After the death in 1456 of his elder brother Edmund, Earl of Richmond, Jasper Tudor had been entrusted with the government of Wales. Under him, the principality of Wales was well governed and it remained solidly behind Henry VI. Although Henry VI trusted his half-brother he never promoted him to the ministerial front bench. This may have saved Jasper Tudor's life since he never became a major figure at court and, therefore, never became a target for his Yorkist enemies. This was to change after 1471.

The devastating losses suffered by the Lancastrian nobility, together with the murder of Henry VI and death of his son, Prince Edward, meant that the Tudors were one of the few families who could reasonably lay claim to the throne. This elevated their status from renegade exiles into serious political opponents. However, Edward IV's crushing triumph in 1471 meant that the futures of Jasper and Henry Tudor looked bleak. Edward IV seemed secure on the throne and the Wars of the Roses appeared to be over. Nevertheless, in time, these Lancastrian exiles in France would become a convenient rallying-point for dissidents in England.

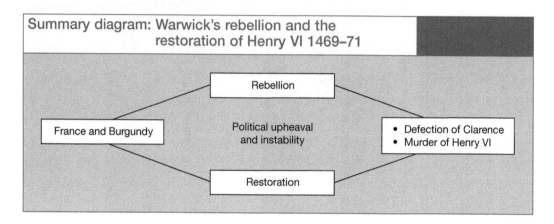

Summary diagram: Warwick's rebellion and the restoration of Henry VI 1469–71

Study Guide: AS Questions

In the style of Edexcel

Why did Edward IV find it so difficult to consolidate his power in the years 1461–9?

Exam tips

The cross-references are intended to take you straight to the material that will help you to answer the question.

Always take a little while to think about the structure of examination questions. Questions will never simply ask you for information, so falling for the temptation to narrate the events of the period will not get you very far here. Usually questions will begin 'how far' or 'to what extent' and ask you for a judgement. But occasionally you will see a question in this form which begins 'why'; this is asking you to provide an explanation. The emphasis in your answer in this case should be on showing the significance of each factor you introduce and on showing the interaction of causes. Although the question does not require a judgement about the primary cause, you can offer one if you choose, but there is not the same requirement you saw in Chapter 2 to place a substantial emphasis on one stated factor in your answer. Note the focus of this question, and the emphasis on 'so difficult' in 'so difficult to consolidate power'. You could show your appreciation of the issue in an introduction which notes Edward's strengths compared to the character and position of the deposed Henry VI, but that he was a king whose debt to Warwick carried a heavy price.

You will have time to develop only four or five points, so selection of key factors will be important to your answer. You could consider:

- The problems of reconciling Lancastrians and rewarding Yorkists at the beginning of the reign, and how far Edward's initial decisions stoked up resentment (pages 49–52).
- The significance of Edward's continued reliance on a 'favoured clique' (page 51) of noble advisers and how far this was significant in stoking up resentment.
- The political instability provoked by the position in court and treatment of the Woodville faction (page 52).
- The contribution of Edward's pro-Burgundian foreign policy in adding to his difficulties (pages 59–60).
- The pivotal role played by Neville, Earl of Warwick, in Edward's deposition in 1469. In assessing the overall significance of Warwick's role, you could acknowledge the debate over the extent of his role as kingmaker (pages 54–6).

In coming to a conclusion you should focus on the root cause of Edward's difficulties. Your answer should have shown that the challenge of reconciling the ambitions of powerful and competing noble families lay at the heart of Edward's difficulties.

In the style of OCR

Assess the claim that his handling of the royal finances was Edward IV's most important achievement as king during his first reign.

Exam tips

The cross-references are intended to take you straight to the material that will help you to answer the question.

The question asks you to assess the relative importance of the achievements of Edward's first reign. To do this, you must establish a clear rank order of importance between the factors you examine. One cause is given in the question. You must, therefore, examine seriously the importance of the recovery of the royal finances, even if you are going to reject it in favour of an achievement that you believe to have been more important. You might divide your answer into separate sections looking at middle-term and short-term achievements. Alternatively, you might decide from the start your rank order and examine the relative significance of individual factors throughout your essay. However you structure your answer, point out instances where different factors linked together, influencing each other.

What else has Edward had to deal with? A high-scoring answer will examine Edward's:

- relations with the nobility (pages 51–2)
- handling of royal administration and the royal finances (pages 49–51)
- problems with Clarence and Warwick (pages 56–8)
- trade and foreign policies (pages 59–60).

Edward took care to restore the Crown's weak financial position. He benefited from the considerable resources that the Yorkists brought to the Crown, and he secured money from various additional sources. In administration, Edward was notable for his use of able servants, including knights, lawyers and clerics, to supplement the nobility. Edward took a personal interest in the administration of justice and lived up to contemporary expectations by associating himself closely with good government.

Alternatively, you might claim that Edward IV lacked any important achievements during his first reign. He was young and personable but spent too much time on pleasure. He handled powerful nobles poorly (notably Warwick, pages 56–7). His marriage proved unpopular and was foolish politically (page 50). The Lancastrians, effectively led by Margaret of Anjou, were a constant threat, leading to Edward's defeat and Henry's redemption (page 60). For success, your answer will be judged not on what it says but how well you argue the case that you are making. Weigh achievements against each other and come to a clear decision on the most important.

4

The Second Reign of Edward IV 1471–83

POINTS TO CONSIDER

During his first reign Edward was never fully secure on the throne. He began his second reign determined to establish his dynasty and revive the power of the Crown. In a period spanning 12 years, Edward largely succeeded in restoring peace and prosperity to England. He strengthened royal government, restored the kingdom's finances and managed parliament. He made war on France and ruthlessly cut down his enemies at home. The Wars of the Roses seemed to be at an end. These developments are examined as four themes:

- Edward IV restored: establishing the Yorkist dynasty 1471–83
- The politics of rivalry: Clarence and Gloucester
- Government and administration
- Parliament and finance

Key dates

1471   Edward IV restored to the throne
1472   Edward's brother, Richard, made Duke of Gloucester
1473   Edward signed treaty with King James of Scotland Parliament passed an act of resumption
1475   Edward IV invaded France. Signed Treaty of Picquigny
1478   Clarence executed in the Tower after being found guilty of treason

Key question
How was Edward able to restore the Yorkist dynasty?

1 | Edward IV Restored: Establishing the Yorkist Dynasty 1471–83

The contemporary chronicler John Warkworth had no doubt why Edward's first reign as king had ended so disastrously in 1469:

> The [Yorkists] had expected prosperity and peace from Edward IV, but it was not to be. One battle followed another, and there was widespread disorder, and the common people lost much of their money and goods [mainly through heavy taxation]. England had been reduced to the direst poverty. Many people thought that King

> Edward was to blame for harming the reputation and esteem of the merchants, for, at that time, both in England and abroad, these were not as great as they had been in times past.

Edward had learnt his lesson. There were to be no more 'over-mighty' subjects and no alternative kings, either free or in prison. The battle of Barnet had destroyed the Nevilles as Tewkesbury had ruined the Lancastrians. Henry VI was murdered, his son was slain and Margaret of Anjou was imprisoned. To hide the truth of what he had done, Edward made it known that Henry VI had died of 'melancholy' (sadness) on hearing the news of his son's death. Edward had come to realise how powerful **propaganda** could be when managed effectively. One method Edward used to ensure his message was heard and understood was by the issuing of royal proclamations. Proclamations were royal commands that had the force of law and they had to be obeyed. Edward's second reign would be cast in a different light where his successes would be magnified, his failures buried and rumours scotched.

Key term

Propaganda
The method by which ideas are spread to support a particular point of view.

The restoration of law and order

The personal activity and support of the king was a vital element in the process of restoring law and order. Edward was determined that he should be obeyed and for those who were slow to bend to his will there was only one outcome: punishment. When Sir John Paston, a troublesome knight from Norfolk, failed to answer two royal summons to appear before the king, Edward angrily announced:

Key date

Edward IV restored to the throne: 1471

> We will send him another tomorrow and by God's mercy, if he come not then he shall die for it. We will make all other men beware by him how they shall disobey our writings.

When Paston finally did appear before the king he was flung into prison alongside the county sheriff, Sir John Howard, for his inability to execute efficiently the king's command. Royal agents were keen to cultivate an image of a well-informed king who took a personal interest in all matters connected with law and order within his realm.

Rebellion in Kent

Opposition was crushed and rebellion, where it broke out, was ruthlessly put down. The first victim of this policy was Thomas, the Bastard of Fauconberg, who stirred up rebellion in Kent. In an echo of Cade's rebellion (see pages 38–9), Fauconberg issued a call to arms to the people of Kent to resist the usurper Edward IV and demand reform of the government. The rebellion failed and a little later Fauconberg was executed. The fact that Fauconberg had been supported by the pro-Neville governor of Calais meant that Edward would need to stamp his authority on this important English outpost.

Rebellion in Wales

The most serious threat to the new Yorkist regime came from Wales. Here the Lancastrians continued to defy Edward and they scored a notable success when they captured and executed a die-hard Yorkist, Roger Vaughan of Tretower. However, by October 1471, the last Lancastrian strongholds in Wales, Pembroke and Tenby surrendered. Edward used parliament to issue acts of attainder (see page 52) against those who had dared defy him. As the representative body of the king's subjects (the landowning and politically active, at least), parliament offered the Crown a means of claiming that it had the support and consent of the people.

Key figures

Sir John Fortescue
Fortescue (c.1394–c.1480) was an English lawyer recommended for his wisdom, gravity and uprightness. He is said to have been favoured by Henry VI, who appointed him chief justice of the king's bench. He held office during the reign of Henry VI but was attainted for treason in the first parliament of Edward IV. He was later pardoned.

William Neville
William Neville (c.1410–63), Earl of Kent and Baron Fauconberg was an English nobleman and soldier. The second son of Ralph Neville, first Earl of Westmorland, he was made a member of Edward IV's council, and appointed Lieutenant of the North, Steward of the Royal Household and Lord Admiral. Edward IV relied on him for both land and naval warfare. He was the father of Thomas Neville (d.1471), the Bastard of Fauconberg.

Sir Richard Tunstall
Tunstall (1427–92) was a Lancashire landowner and soldier who fought with distinction for Henry VI in the Wars of the Roses. He fought at Wakefield, St Albans and Towton. After Towton he escaped with Margaret of Anjou to Scotland. He led an army of Scots across the border and was with the Lancastrians at Hedgeley Moor. He went on the run with Henry VI, but when the king was captured Tunstall fled to Harlech and continued the fight from there. He eventually surrendered in 1468 and was sent to the Tower. After a year in custody he was pardoned. When Henry VI returned to the throne in 1470–1 Tunstall was taken back into royal service. Following Henry VI's deposition and murder, Tunstall was again arrested and imprisoned. In 1472 he was pardoned for a second time and taken into Edward IV's service. He served the Yorkist kings, Edward IV and Richard III, loyally thereafter. He was pardoned in 1485 and employed by Henry VII as Sheriff of Yorkshire until his death.

For those Lancastrians who submitted, such as the lawyer Sir John Fortescue, the cleric John Morton and former die-hards like Sir Richard Tunstall, Edward offered pardon and the possibility of future reward if they remained loyal. For the remainder, those Lancastrians considered too dangerous to negotiate with such as Jasper Tudor, Earl of Pembroke, and John de Vere, Earl of Oxford, there was no pardon, only persecution and exile. So, by these means, a combination of reward and punishment, Edward secured his throne, established his dynasty and restored law and order. There were to be no more serious plots or rebellions during his reign.

Profile: John Morton c.1420–1500

c.1420	– Born in Dorset, the son of a minor landowner
Early 1440s	– Educated at Balliol College, Oxford. Graduated with a doctorate in canon (Church) law
c.1440s/50s	– Worked as a canon lawyer in Church courts
1461	– Joined the Lancastrians and was forced to flee abroad after the battle of Towton
1470	– Returned to England and made peace with the Yorkist king, Edward IV
1473	– Appointed to government office as Master of the Rolls (responsible for government records)
1474	– Selected by Edward IV to go on a mission to Hungary
1475	– Appointed to negotiate the Treaty of Picquigny with France
1479	– Promoted and appointed Bishop of Ely. He also became tutor to Edward IV's son, Prince Edward
1483	– Arrested and imprisoned by Richard III
1484	– Escaped to Flanders. Joined Henry Tudor and the Lancastrians in exile
1485	– Appointed to Henry VII's ruling council
1486	– Promoted to Archbishop of Canterbury
1487	– Appointed Lord Chancellor and took charge of Henry VII's government
1493	– Promoted to Cardinal by Pope Alexander VI of Rome

Morton had served Edward IV loyally but he was especially trusted by Henry VII and, as a result, was able to exert a great deal of influence over the king and government policy. He was an experienced administrator and possessed the leadership qualities Henry VII needed to run his government. Morton's control and management of the Church ensured that it and its senior clerics remained loyal to the king.

Livery and maintenance

One of the most serious problems that Edward IV had to contend with was that of illegal **retaining**, often referred to as **livery** and **maintenance**. This was a common practice whereby great lords recruited those of lesser status as their servants or followers to help advance their ambitions (by force of arms if necessary) and to increase their prestige. They were given a uniform on which was emblazoned their master's crest or coat of arms showing whom they served.

Kings had permitted this practice to exist because it could help the **magnate** control his particular locality and provided a quick and efficient way of raising an army, both of which were important to the king. Apart from these obvious uses, it was felt to be only natural that a nobleman should be attended by a retinue of men of respectable social status. However, the Wars of the Roses had shown that these retainers could also create lawlessness at both local and national levels, and could be used as an effective force against the king.

Retainers could also be used as armed forces to threaten those who opposed their master. Such behaviour occurred to settle not just the lord's disputes but also those of his servants. This was because the lords had obligations to their followers, the **indenture** of retainder requiring them to be good lords to their men. However, it was originally meant to be based on principles of honour and mutual respect, with a lord accepting the responsibility of advancing and protecting the interests of his servant, but not where they clashed with the law. Thus maintenance was now all too often abused, with nobles frequently going beyond the bounds of 'good lordship'.

In order to control the nobles and restrict their ability to raise and employ armed servants, Edward attempted to pass legislation to deal with this practice. The parliament of 1468 had passed a statute prohibiting retaining except for domestic servants, estate officials and legal advisers. However, this law was largely ineffectual because it allowed the continuance of retaining for 'lawful service'. Therefore, during Edward's reign nobles continued to maintain their retinues, using the excuse that they were doing so within the existing framework of the law. Indeed, as many as 64 new indentures of retainder for one nobleman were recorded for the years 1469–82 alone. Historians now believe that Edward intended this statute merely as a public relations exercise and passed it to soothe the fears of the House of Commons but with no intention of strictly adhering to it.

Foreign policy

Foreign policy was a major concern for Edward. The intervention of both France and Burgundy, and to a lesser extent Scotland, in the Wars of the Roses convinced the king that a coherent policy was necessary if only to prevent future foreign interference in English affairs.

Key terms

Retaining
Employing or maintaining armed servants and/or private armies.

Livery
The giving of a uniform or badge to a follower.

Maintenance
The protection of a follower's interests.

Magnate
A greater or more powerful nobleman.

Indenture
Agreement or contract between a master and his servant.

Key question
Why was foreign policy a major concern for Edward?

France

Edward sought to revenge himself on Louis XI because the French king had supported both Warwick and Margaret of Anjou. This would be neither forgotten nor forgiven by Edward. Indeed, Edward had cause to complain to Louis over more recent events when the French king had given refuge to Jasper and Henry Tudor in 1471. However, Edward's more immediate concern was the defence of England's final continental possession, Calais. In Edward's military mind, the best form of defence was attack and for the next four years, 1471–5, he planned his invasion of France and prepared his armed forces for war.

Scotland

Before he could go to war, Edward had to ensure that England was free from the threat of a Scottish invasion. So, in October 1473, he negotiated a treaty with James III of Scotland. By the terms of the treaty, Edward agreed to offer his four-year-old daughter, Cecily, in marriage to James's six-month-old son. To sweeten the deal, Edward also offered a cash sum of 20,000 crowns (just over £4000, £2 million in today's money) to the cash-strapped Scottish king. The betrothal would last until both parties were of marriageable age – 14 years old – so that Edward could be reasonably assured of peace for at least a decade.

Edward signed treaty with King James of Scotland: 1473

Key date

In the event, the truce lasted until 1481, when Edward determined to invade Scotland after the Scots had broken the terms of the truce by raiding the border towns of northern England. The honour of leading the English army into Scotland was given to Edward's brother Gloucester. The invasion was a spectacular success. Edinburgh was captured and the Scottish army retreated rather than fight. Having made his point, and to avoid a costly occupation, Gloucester withdrew his army and the Scottish king came to terms with Edward.

Burgundy and Brittany

Prior to his invasion, Edward also tried hard to make alliances with Burgundy and Brittany. He hoped to exploit their fear and hatred of the French and persuade them to join him as allies in a war against France. He met with only limited success. The Dukes of Burgundy and Brittany were reluctant to stir up the French against them. They were well aware of how wealthy and mighty the French had become since their defeat of England in the Hundred Years War. Only when the French threatened them did they turn to Edward IV for support. For example, in 1472, Edward sent 3000 archers to aid Brittany when the French invaded. When the French invasion failed, a grateful Francis II, Duke of Brittany, signed a treaty with Edward promising 8000 troops if the English should invade France. Duke Charles of Burgundy, Edward's brother-in-law, proved less willing to support the English but he did all he could to avoid confrontation. The result was the Treaty of London, which was ratified in 1474, in which it was agreed that, if either nation was attacked by the French, the other would go to its aid.

Invasion of France

Key dates

Edward IV invaded France. Signed the Treaty of Picquigny: 1475

Edward's brother, Richard, made Duke of Gloucester: 1472

By 1475, Edward IV was ready to invade. Leading an army of over 12,000 well-trained and well-armed men, Edward made his way from Calais into the heart of northern France. However, it was not long before Edward's triumphal invasion began to go wrong. The troops promised by Duke Francis of Brittany did not turn up and the French army kept its distance, hoping to draw the English further away from their supply lines. Frustrated by his failure to force the French into a decisive battle, Edward sued for peace. Louis XI was relieved since he wanted to avoid a prolonged war, and so the two kings met at Picquigny on the Somme, where they signed a treaty in August 1475. Edward did rather well out of the treaty. Besides agreeing a seven-year truce, Louis paid Edward £15,000 immediately, to be followed by an annual pension of £10,000. Thereafter, Edward had little to fear from the French or any other of his continental neighbours.

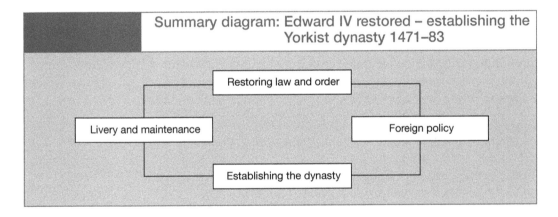

Summary diagram: Edward IV restored – establishing the Yorkist dynasty 1471–83

2 | The Politics of Rivalry: Clarence and Gloucester

Key question
Why did Clarence and Gloucester quarrel?

The most serious problem Edward faced during his second period as king was the political rivalry that flared up between his brothers. After his restoration, Edward was determined to control royal patronage.

The main beneficiaries were members of his own family, especially Richard, Duke of Gloucester. Gloucester was given all of Warwick's confiscated properties in northern England and was entrusted with the government and defence of that region. His wealth and power were thereby considerably enhanced by the generosity of the king.

Clarence, too, was treated generously by the king and, in spite of his earlier betrayal, he was restored to all of his properties (including Warwick's estates in southern England) and was even given substantial additional lands confiscated from the Courtenay earls of Devon. All Edward asked of his brother in return was that he give up the Percy properties, which he had been granted during the first reign, so that they could be restored to the family. However, rather than being grateful for his good fortune, Clarence resented the favour shown to his younger brother, Richard. Aware of Clarence's resentment, Edward hoped to satisfy his brother by granting him the lands of the earldom of Richmond (the earl, Henry Tudor, was in exile), which he had originally given to Gloucester.

Gloucester and Clarence's quarrel

With Clarence satisfied, Edward now had the task of compensating Gloucester. When Gloucester requested the king's permission to marry Anne Neville, Warwick's daughter, Edward agreed. This angered Clarence, who feared that the couple, once married, might lay claim to his Warwick properties. Clarence tried to prevent the marriage but failed. The quarrel had become so bitter and public that the king summoned the dukes to put their case before the king's council. The matter was settled when Clarence was assured that his Neville properties were safe and, as if to reinforce this fact, the king agreed to his creation as Earl of Warwick and Salisbury. Not content with his victory, Clarence also pressed the king for a royal appointment at court, which Edward granted by bestowing on him the office of Great Chamberlain of England in May 1472. The man forced to part with this office and make way for the appointment of the Duke of Clarence was none other than Gloucester.

The row rumbled on and Edward was forced to intervene in November 1473 when parliament passed an act of resumption, under whose terms both Clarence and Gloucester were deprived of all the estates they held by royal grant. This was clearly designed to remind the feuding dukes of the power and authority of the Crown. The estates were not restored until a further act of parliament was passed in May 1474.

Parliament passed an act of resumption: 1473

Key date

Clarence and the Woodvilles' quarrel

Clarence failed to heed the lesson. He temporarily set aside his feud with Gloucester and turned his attention to the Woodvilles. He made known his resentment at the growing power of Anthony, Earl Rivers, in Wales and the queen's increasing influence at court. Clarence's feud with the queen surfaced when his wife died in 1476 and he looked to secure a foreign bride. Clarence's choice was Mary, daughter of Charles the Bold, Duke of Burgundy, but Edward refused to agree to the match. The king feared becoming drawn into Burgundy's continental problems if the marriage went ahead. Edward also felt the marriage of an English nobleman with the daughter of a foreign ruler might set a dangerous precedent. Clarence's ambition knew no bounds. Thwarted in his Burgundian adventure, for which he blamed the queen, he now looked to the daughter of the King of Scotland. Edward again refused to sanction the marriage.

Clarence's trial and execution

It was becoming clear to Edward that Clarence's aspirations were verging on the 'over-mighty' and he had to be stopped. It has been claimed that Gloucester was mainly to blame for persuading his brother to arrest and convict Clarence of treason but the queen, Elizabeth Woodville, also bears some responsibility. She was convinced that Clarence was conspiring against the succession of her son, Prince Edward. In February 1478, Clarence was tried for high treason, found guilty and executed. The ultimate responsibility for his death rested with Edward IV.

Key date

Clarence executed in the Tower after being found guilty of treason: 1478

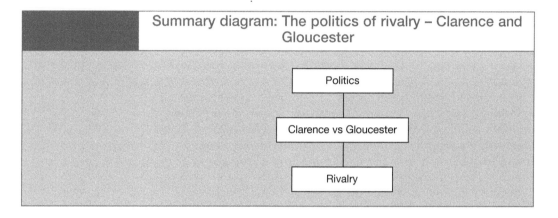

Summary diagram: The politics of rivalry – Clarence and Gloucester

3 | Government and Administration

Governing the kingdom

Key question
How effective was Edward IV's government of the kingdom?

Edward IV had found that governing the kingdom was no easy task. War, lawlessness and disorder had combined to make the task of government that much harder. Edward was determined to re-establish the rule of law and 'good governance' after the dislocation and strife caused by the Wars of the Roses. Fortunately for Edward, he had one huge advantage in that the Crown continued to command respect. This reverence for the institution of monarchy had survived the war but, in order to ensure its continuance, Edward enlisted the aid of the Church. In an age without a police force, the Church was the only organisation with the means and the authority to reach every community in the realm. England and Wales were divided into parishes and every parish had a church and every church a priest. The Church and the majority of its clergy were respected and it preached peace and obedience. To disobey the king was the same as disobeying God. By careful use of parliament, proclamation and pulpit Edward strove to make the Crown's authority felt in all parts of his kingdom.

The Church as an instrument of control

Key question
Why did the Crown use the Church to control the people?

Rulers were seen as God's deputies on earth acting as guardians of his people. Therefore, any threat to the ruler or to the internal peace and security of the nation was interpreted as a challenge to

God. By the same reasoning, when a ruler like Richard III lost his life in battle it was thought to be an indication of God's displeasure with his deputy whose authority had rightly been challenged. Rebellion or any type of civil unrest was abhorrent to most people from nobleman to peasant because, as Sir Thomas Elyot wrote, 'Where there is any lack of order needs must be perpetual conflict.' This meant that the worst fear for most people was an outbreak of general anarchy.

The late Middle Ages were littered with examples of this type of unrest: the Peasants' Revolt in 1381 against the poll tax, the conflict over the crown in the middle of the fifteenth century, and Cade's rebellion in 1450, stemming mainly from the ill-feeling caused by what was regarded to be an unfair or unjust rule. On all these occasions resentment built up slowly and people took up arms only as a last resort. There was little violence for the sake of violence.

The fate of Henry IV and Henry VI (see pages 14–16) acted as a warning to Edward IV of how an unscrupulous or incompetent monarch could be overthrown. The Wars of the Roses showed him that, with the support of the Church, his subjects would quickly return to obedience if he and his bishops proved capable of asserting the right degree of authority. In the absence of a police force and standing army, Edward recognised the Church's important role in maintaining social stability and in ensuring people's loyalty.

Council and councillors

Unlike Henry VI, Edward was an energetic king determined to establish strong government at the heart of his kingdom. The structure and machinery of central government did not change but Edward brought a new dynamism to its operation.

The centre of medieval English government was the king himself and the men he chose to sit on his council. Therefore, the king's council remained the key co-ordinating body and was staffed by the monarch's most trusted advisers. The primary functions of the council were the same under Edward IV as they had been under Henry VI:

Key question
How effective were the council and its councillors in governing the kingdom?

- to advise the king on matters of state
- to administer law and order
- to dispense justice
- to draw up and issue letters, warrants and proclamations.

The composition of the council was not fixed and, in times of crisis, might include upwards of 125 members but, in practice, Edward relied on a core group of between 10 and 15 men.

These royal councillors included a mix of Yorkists and former Lancastrians, the latter including men like John Morton and Sir Richard Tunstall. In fact, Morton, promoted to Bishop of Ely by the king, came to earn Edward's 'secret trust and special favour'. In the opinion of Richard III's modern biographer, the historian Charles Ross, Morton's 'rapid rise in the royal service is a good example of Edward's political realism in making use of talent wherever he found it'. Edward was not afraid to promote men of humble backgrounds so long as they had the administrative and bureaucratic talent to serve him. Some of the most prominent members of the king's government, and household, were loyal Yorkists such as John Fogge, John Scott, William Parr and Thomas Vaughan.

Edward did not neglect the nobility and higher clergy, many of whom filled the chief offices of state such as chancellor, treasurer and keeper of the **privy seal**. For example, when the king was absent he appointed his treasurer, Henry Bourchier, Earl of Essex, to chair meetings of the royal council. The key difference between Edward IV and previous kings is that he was not prepared to appoint members of the nobility to serve him on his council simply because of their status and title. Unless they possessed some skill or particular talent, they were unlikely to be summoned to serve on the king's council. For example, Edward's cousin, the Duke of Norfolk, and his brother-in-law, the Duke of Suffolk, were never appointed to the council.

Besides offering the king advice and helping to shape and direct policy, the councillors were responsible for law and order, finance, trade and a host of other duties that occurred on a daily basis. While the king concentrated on making decisions, his councillors could focus on carrying them out.

Privy seal
The king's personal seal was a substitute for his signature and was used to authenticate documents.

Key question
How was regional government organised?

Regional or provincial councils

There was no radical difference between Edward's two reigns in the way he governed the outlying regions of the kingdom. The policies that had served him reasonably well in his first reign were pursued in the second. In the 1460s Edward entrusted the government of the regions to powerful men, like Neville in the north and Herbert in Wales. Edward still relied on a core group of powerful men but they were more closely tied to him through blood rather than by title. The regional councils are a good example of how Edward extended the authority of central government into the provinces. By relying on trusted servants and members of his own family to enforce his will in the outlying areas, Edward was ensuring that personal government was felt in even the remotest parts of his realm.

The north

The Council of the North was based in the city of York. Its primary function was to ensure the good governance of a lawless and undisciplined region that was too remote from London to be effectively controlled from there. In addition, it was given responsibility to oversee the defence of the northern counties of England which were vulnerable to attack from a potentially hostile Scotland. This northern council was closely linked to the king's council, enjoying similar administrative and judicial power to enable the law to be enforced swiftly and efficiently, and it was ultimately subordinate to the king. Control of the north and the council that governed it was given over to Edward's trusted younger brother, Richard, Duke of Gloucester.

An illustration of Ludlow Castle, seat of the Council of Wales. Why was the seat of the Welsh government located in an English border town?

Wales

Wales consisted of the Principality (made up of what later became the counties of Anglesey, Caernarfon, Merioneth, Cardigan and Carmarthen) and the Marcher Lordships (made up of some 50 semi-independent lordships located either side of the modern boundary between England and Wales). Ruled since 1301 by the king's eldest son, the Principality was acknowledged to be separate from England, in consequence of which, its shires did not return members to parliament. The lordships of the March were relics of the piecemeal Norman/English conquest of Wales in the two centuries between 1066 and 1282. These had their own systems of government, different from each other and from that of England. Both the Principality and the lordships owed allegiance to the King of England and he had ultimate control over them, but the absence of continuous effective rule from London had resulted in frequent outbreaks of disorder caused by criminals. This disorder was particularly marked during the Wars of the Roses, when it was famously said that, 'the king's writ [written orders] did not run' in the March.

With the freedom to raise troops for war, the Marcher lords were drawn into the dynastic conflict on the side of both Yorkists and Lancastrians. Until Edward IV established a council to govern Wales in 1471, no attempt had been made to weld together into a single system the counties and lordships of the Principality and the March, or to abolish the privileges of the individual Marchers lords. Although Edward never succeeded in either respect, his council had improved the situation in Wales by restraining, what one contemporary called, 'the wild Welshmen

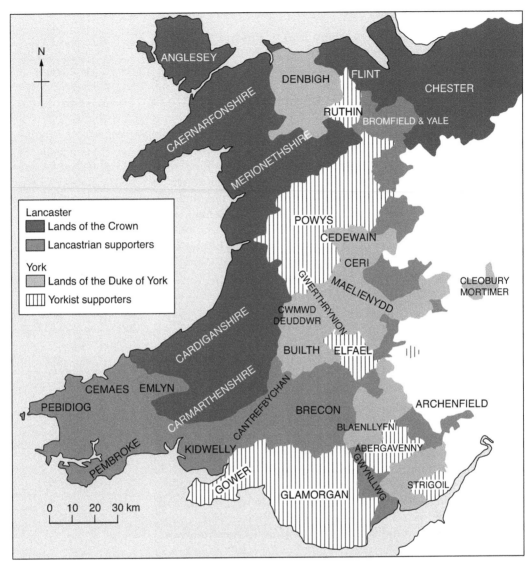

Figure 4.1: Map showing the complex division of Wales into Marcher and Crown Lordships, and the counties of the Principality. Why did English kings find Wales so difficult to govern?

and the evil disposed persons from their accustomed murders and outrages'.

In 1471 Edward entrusted the government of Wales and the Marches to his wife's family the Woodvilles, with Anthony, Earl Rivers, at their head. This angered William Herbert's son and heir, the second Earl of Pembroke, who expected to succeed his father (killed in 1469) as ruler of Wales. In fact, Edward went further for he also forced the younger Herbert to give up his lands in Wales and exchange the Earldom of Pembroke for the less significant (and less wealthy) Earldom of Huntingdon. Apart from Ireland, it seems the king was determined not to allow any magnate to establish a hereditary title to any office or region of his realm.

Ireland

As King of England, Edward was also Lord of Ireland. However, the island was not ruled in a conciliar way like Wales and the north. The king appointed a **Lord Lieutenant** (George, Duke of Clarence, held the post between 1472 and 1478), but this was an honorary position. The actual work of governing Ireland was carried out by a **Lord Deputy**.

Ireland presented a far more difficult problem to Edward than any of the other outlying areas of the kingdom. Only in the English Pale (see page 5), a narrow band of territory about 80 km long to the north and west of Dublin, was the king's authority really felt. In the rest of the island, the effective rulers were the Anglo-Irish lords (descendants of English settlers who had come over earlier in the Middle Ages) and Irish chieftains, who held power by exploiting and controlling family loyalties. Of these the most important families were the Geraldines, Earls of Desmond and Kildare, and the Butlers, Earls of Ormond.

No English king had been able to dominate these lords, not even Richard, Duke of York, in the 1450s, and so Ireland remained very much a law unto itself. At the beginning of Edward's reign, the Geraldine family held the most important offices, those of Lord Deputy and Chancellor of Ireland. Edward found that in order to avoid conflict it was easier to bestow these positions on the Irish leaders. Thus Gerald FitzGerald, eighth Earl of Kildare, succeeded his father, a prominent Yorkist, as Lord Deputy of Ireland in 1477, a post he held until 1513.

The Midlands and south-west of England

William Lord Hastings was given charge of the Midlands, and the queen's son from her first marriage, Thomas Grey, Marquis of Dorset, was entrusted with the care of the south-west of England. There was room for local magnates like the Percy earls of Northumberland and the Stanleys of Cheshire to exercise royal authority but not everyone was included in Edward's attempt to share out power in the localities. The second Earl of Pembroke, the Duke of Buckingham and the king's brother, Clarence, were left largely on the sidelines.

The most frequent problems in the regions that Edward had to face were the disputes between members of the nobility. His favoured method of dealing with this was to travel around the country intervening in disputes and personally hearing cases in the common law courts. Owing to his energy and efficiency this system proved quite successful until his death in 1483.

Local government

While great magnates dominated regional government at local or county level, the gentry ran the local administration. During the Wars of the Roses the system of local government had almost completely collapsed and Edward IV had no choice but to attempt to rebuild this structure almost from scratch. He tried to do this in three ways:

Lord Lieutenant
In times of peace the office had no function beyond the ceremonial, such as the state opening of the Irish parliament, but in times of war it was responsible for raising and leading the Crown's forces in Ireland. Between 1472 and 1478 Ireland was at peace so Clarence played no effective part in Irish affairs.

Lord Deputy
The effective ruler of Ireland invested with the power and authority to govern the Irish on behalf of the Crown.

Key question
How was local government organised?

- He appointed Crown commissioners to travel the country to support local law enforcement.
- He appointed only the most trusted gentry to serve as justices of the peace and sheriffs.
- He appointed powerful local magnates to control particular regions or areas.

In order to increase his authority throughout his kingdom, Edward increased the size of his household. This enabled him to draw on a larger pool of servants from whom he appointed Crown commissioners, justices of the peace and sheriffs. In effect, he created a two-tier system whereby his household was divided into those servants who attended him at court on a daily basis and those who could do so only on an occasional basis. The fact that the latter could not attend the king on a regular basis at court did not matter to Edward. His aim was to mark these men out as servants of the Crown and thereby extend the reach and influence of the royal household into the localities.

The sheriffs

Local government was carried out in each of the 50 or so counties of England by a complex network of local officials who were directly responsible to the king. He communicated with them through written orders known as writs, and their work was checked by senior judges or **justices of assize** and **commissioners of 'oyer et terminer'** at regular intervals. The two most important royal officials in each county were the sheriff and the justice of the peace. The sheriff was appointed annually from among the local landowners in each county and was the closest thing fifteenth-century England had to a police officer. He kept the king's peace and was responsible for the arrest, detention and prosecution of criminals.

The sheriff was as much a judge as a law officer and he had his own court where he administered the king's laws. He also organised and supervised elections to parliament, and MPs could only take their seats if they had the sheriff's writ to confirm their election. The sheriff also had a military role, being responsible for supervising the **muster of the militia**. Although sheriffs continued to play an important role in local justice and administration they gradually gave way to the justices of the peace. For example, as early as 1461 Edward IV had transferred the criminal jurisdiction of the sheriff to the justice of the peace.

The justices of the peace

The justices of the peace (JPs) were appointed annually from among the local landowners, the average number commissioned for a county being about 18. The local bishop would usually head the list of those appointed, with the lay landowners following in strict order of social precedence (see Figure 4.2). Although some of the largest landowners were sometimes chosen to be JPs, it was the knights and squires who carried out the majority of the commission's duties on a daily basis. JPs were responsible for the

Key terms

Justices of assize
Senior judges who dealt with serious crimes and dispensed justice in the king's courts, which were held twice a year in each county.

Commissioners of 'oyer et terminer'
Literally meaning to 'hear and determine', these commissions were given the power to investigate any crime or disturbance thought serious enough for the Crown to become involved.

Muster of the militia
The muster was a method by which local representatives of the Crown called up fit and able men to serve in the army. The militia was an army of conscripts raised to serve the king for a set period.

Th., Lord Audley of Walden, Chancellor; D. of Norfolk, Treasurer; D. of Suffolk, President of Council; J. Russell, kt., Keeper of Privy Seal; B. of Coventry & Lichfield, President of Council in the Marches of Wales; B. of St. Davids; Walter, Lord Ferrers; Nich. Hare, Ed. Croft, Rice Mansel, J. Vernon, kts.; J. Pakington; Th. Holte; David Brooke; J. ap Rice; Rich. Hassall; p. Rich. Devereux; Th. Jones; J. Phillip; W. Morgan of Kidwelly; Jenkin Lloyd of Kidwelly; Jas. Williams; Walter Vaughan; Griffith Dwnn; J. Lloyd senior; W. Morgan of Llangathen; Th. Bryne; Howel ap Rither; Th. Hancock; David Vaughan.

Figure 4.2: Example of a royal commission with a list of those appointed by the Crown. This example is for Carmarthen, dated 12 March 1543.

maintenance of public order and for implementing the various statutes of a social and economic nature, such as those concerned with the regulation of wages and the guilds. They also acted as judges ready to dispense justice to deal with the criminals brought before them by the sheriffs. Four times a year they were required to meet in Quarter Sessions so that they could try those accused of the more serious crimes – except treason, which was left to the council to investigate.

Although justices of the peace had the authority to pass judgement on all other crimes, more difficult cases were traditionally passed to the assize courts. The assizes were sessions held twice a year in each county in England by professional judges acting under special commission from the Crown. The position of justice of the peace did not carry with it any form of payment, because, as property owners, it was also in their own self-interest. In fact, it had always been felt that to offer rewards for such work would be inappropriate as it was thought to be a natural part of the landowning classes' responsibility to ensure an effective system of law enforcement.

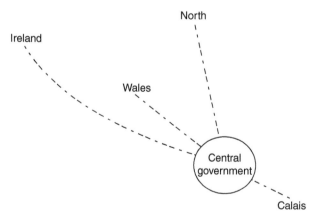

Figure 4.3: Plan showing links between central and regional government.

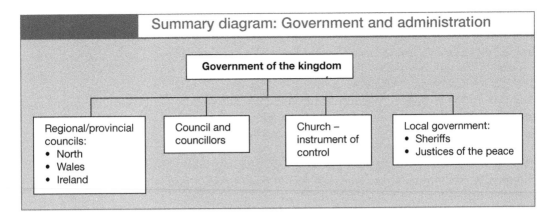

Summary diagram: Government and administration

Government of the kingdom

Regional/provincial councils:
- North
- Wales
- Ireland

Council and councillors

Church – instrument of control

Local government:
- Sheriffs
- Justices of the peace

4 | Parliament and Finance

King, Lords and Commons

In the fifteenth century the government of England was clearly the responsibility of the king and his council. Parliament played no regular part in the maintenance of law and order. It met only to grant taxes and to pass laws, and it was in this latter role that it was of use to the king in controlling his subjects. Parliament was the meeting of the two Houses of Lords and Commons. The importance of the Lords can be gauged by where they met: the Lords were invited to meet in a room in the royal palace of Westminster, while the Commons were denied access to the palace and were instead summoned to meet in the nearby, and more humble, chapter house of Westminster Abbey.

The Lords

The House of Lords was made up of two groups: the Lords spiritual (the archbishops, bishops and abbots, the heads of the more important monasteries) and the Lords temporal (the peers). Tradition gave the Lords greater authority than the Commons, which is why important legislation had first to be introduced in the House of Lords.

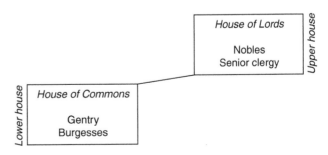

House of Lords

Nobles
Senior clergy

Upper house

House of Commons

Gentry
Burgesses

Lower house

Figure 4.4: Diagram showing the working relationship between the Houses of Parliament.

The Commons

The House of Commons was composed of MPs chosen by a very limited electorate made up of those who possessed considerable property. Two members were elected to represent each county and borough. The men sitting in the lower house were typically drawn from the local gentry representing the **counties**, while merchants and lawyers represented the **boroughs**. In practice, parliament was the meeting of the king, his councillors and the Lords. The Commons met while the king discussed issues with the Lords, but he only spoke to them, and they with him, through the speaker. Although the speaker was elected from among the membership of the Commons, in reality he was almost always a royal nominee. Parliament was summoned only when there was a special need, and when it met the meeting normally lasted only a few weeks.

Parliaments

The parliaments of Edward IV's reign were both pliant and compliant to the king's wishes. They were summoned on only six occasions during his reign, meeting for little more than 84 weeks in total. In order to enact legislation dealing with lawlessness and disorder, parliament was summoned to help unify the kingdom by crushing those who challenged the authority of the Crown. For example, the parliament of 1478 was summoned to secure the attainder of the king's brother Clarence. In all, parliament issued 113 attainders on the king's enemies. However, the majority of the statutes passed by Edward's parliaments were concerned mainly with finance and the economy. In fact, one of the key features of Edward's use of parliament was the passing of acts of resumption. Four such acts were passed, bringing back into the hands of the Crown estates that had been granted out to favourites by previous monarchs. The accumulation of estates added greatly to the regular income of the king.

Finance

A major limitation facing Edward in the management of his financial affairs was that throughout the Middle Ages English kings had been expected to '**live of their own**'. They formally swore to do so at their coronation. This meant that they had to manage on the regular income that came to them annually as monarchs and as landowners. It has been calculated that in order to govern the kingdom effectively the Crown had to spend in the region of £50,000 per annum (£25 million in today's money). The income Edward IV inherited from his predecessors did not match this expenditure. To make up the difference, Henry VI had borrowed money, but Edward now had to pay off these debts, settle the interest and raise enough money to help pay for the cost of governing the realm.

The king knew that any proposal to raise money from new sources would arouse suspicion and probably provoke opposition. The king could not ask parliament for a grant (additional taxation) except in unusual circumstances, such as war. There was

Key terms

Counties
The key units of administration in England. The kingdom was divided up into counties, very much like today, to make the government of England easier. Each county elected representatives to sit in parliament.

Boroughs
Towns with a royal charter granting privileges for services rendered, usually dating well back into the Middle Ages.

Live of their own
A contemporary term meaning monarchs should pay their own way using money from their own pockets rather than burden the state with taxes.

always the fear that, if additional direct taxes were demanded frequently, rebellion might follow. This might explain why, in 1467, Edward told the Commons that: 'I purpose [intend] to live upon my own, and not to charge my subjects but in great and urgent causes concerning … the defence of them, and of this my realm.' He was determined to prove that the existing sources of income available to the Crown could be expanded sufficiently to give him the financial strength he needed.

Key question
What sources of income were available to medieval English kings?

Sources of income

It is possible to make a distinction between two separate types of revenue that rulers received at this time. These were 'ordinary' and 'extraordinary' revenue. It is important to clarify what is meant by both these terms:

- Ordinary revenue came in every year, although in different amounts, from Crown lands and custom duties, but also included the profits of justice (fines) and feudal dues on lands held in return for military service. It was largely on the income from ordinary revenue that kings were expected to 'live of their own'.
- Extraordinary revenue came from the subject's obligation to help the king in time of need. By the fifteenth century this usually meant taxation levied in parliament, which came in the form of a 'grant' that the king had to request from his subjects. Less frequently it could also be money which came to the king as feudal overlord, a right which belonged to any feudal lord; this was known as a 'feudal aid' and was levied on specific occasions. For example, if the king was captured and held to ransom, he could demand an aid to raise the money necessary to obtain his release. It could also be money raised by borrowing from his richer subjects in an emergency, or gifts from other rulers, often granted as part of a favourable peace treaty. The Church too was asked to contribute, in the form of clerical taxes, towards the financial well-being of the kingdom.

Ordinary revenue

As far as ordinary revenue is concerned there were three principal sources of income available to Edward IV:

- *Crown lands*. The most important way in which Edward increased his ordinary revenue was by maximising the income from Crown lands. This was partly because they were collected more efficiently. These lands included Edward's own personal estates as Duke of York, the lands of the Duchy of Lancaster and all properties confiscated or forfeited for treason such as those owned by Clarence. It has been estimated that by 1482–3 Edward was enjoying an annual income of £30,000 (£15 million in today's money).
- *Customs duties*. At the beginning of Edward's reign customs duties on imported goods made up the largest part of the king's income. The principal duties or taxes levied were on wool, leather, cloth and wine, but many of these (such as the

duties on cloth) had not changed since 1347. Under Edward IV, the average annual yield had increased from £25,000 to a little over £35,000 (£12.5 million to £17.5 million in today's money) owing to his encouragement of trade and a tighter administration, which cut down on fraud and embezzlement.

- *Profits of justice.* Like monarchs before him, Edward was head of the judicial system and was, therefore, entitled to its profits. The law courts yielded income in two ways:
  - The fees paid by those involved in a court case for the legal writ or summons necessary for any case to begin. This provided the king with a continuous and not inconsiderable income that varied between £300 and £800 per annum (£150,000–400,000 in today's money).
  - The fines levied by the courts as punishment. The amount raised by fines was irregular because it depended on the number of cases heard in court, but the sums involved were often considerable.

- *Feudal dues.* Another part of the Crown's income was the feudal dues, paid by those who held land from the king. As the greatest feudal lord, the king was owed certain obligations by his tenants-in-chief (those holding their land directly from the king), just as they in turn were owed the same duties by their tenants. These included wardship, **marriage**, livery and the fine known as **relief**. It is thought that Edward collected around £550 per annum (£275,000 in today's money) from this source of income.

Extraordinary revenue

In terms of extraordinary revenue, there were three principal sources of income available to Edward IV:

- *Parliamentary grants.* By the later Middle Ages the main form of extraordinary revenue was a sum of money granted by parliament for emergencies, such as war or defence. Edward was aware that his subjects were prepared to help him when the national interest was threatened and he was careful not misuse this right. He was reluctant to tax unless absolutely necessary. This was because the Lancastrian kings had encountered difficulties with parliament which, realising it had a bargaining position, had demanded restrictions on the king's power in exchange for grants of money. The usual type of tax levied was a **national assessment**. This was a fifteenth (in the countryside) and a tenth (in the towns) of the value of a subject's income. Several of these grants could be levied in one session of parliament, depending on how much the king needed. In 1473, the fifteenth and tenth brought in £30,000 (£15 million in today's money).

  This was not really satisfactory as it was based on town and county assessments that were centuries out of date, and which, therefore, did not tap anything approaching all the available taxable wealth of the country. So when he needed money to finance the French war, in 1472–3, Edward tried another

Key terms

Marriage
The royal right to arrange the marriage, for a fee, of heirs and heiresses.

Relief
A payment the king received on the transfer of lands through inheritance.

National assessment
A country-wide system of assessing people's wealth for purposes of taxation.

Key terms

Subsidy
Voluntary grants of money to the king by his subjects.

Benevolence
A type of forced loan which would not normally be repaid to the loanee.

Convocation
The clerical equivalent of parliament in which the upper house of bishops and lower house of ordinary clergy met to discuss Church business.

Receivers
Officials who collected and stored money on behalf of the king.

Auditors
Officials who counted and wrote down the figures in an account book.

method – a form of income tax. Unfortunately for him, it failed. Only half of the expected £60,000 (£30 million in today's money) was collected. This directly assessed **subsidy** was viewed with suspicion and hostility in parliament, which insisted that no precedents were to be set and no returns were to be recorded.

- *Loans and benevolences*. The king could also rely on loans from his richer subjects in times of emergency. However, if these were not forthcoming, Edward turned to a different method called the **benevolence**, a kind of forced loan. Introduced in 1475, when he was preparing to invade France, the benevolence was a general tax more far-reaching than the fifteenth and tenth. Subjects were asked to contribute to the king's expenses as a sign of their goodwill towards him at a time of crisis. If not over used, it was an effective way of raising money. Edward collected nearly £22,000 (£11 million in today's money) by this method.
- *French pension*. The Treaty of Picquigny brought the Crown an annual pension of £10,000 (£5 million in today's money).
- *Clerical taxes*. The king was entitled to tax the Church but Edward did not fully exploit this source of income. In an effort to keep the Church on his side, he made no demands other than that **convocation** collect and pay the usual clerical tenths. Between 1472 and 1475 the Church paid Edward £48,000 (£24 million in today's money).

Financial administration
In order to manage the collection of money more efficiently, Edward turned his mind to reform of the financial institutions.

Exchequer and Chamber
Since the twelfth century the centre of the Crown's financial administration had been the Exchequer. This had two functions:

- to receive, store and pay out money
- to audit the accounts.

To organise this department and prevent fraud and embezzlement, there was a complex hierarchy of officials. Although it worked in an honest and reliable fashion, it did have flaws. The system was slow and cumbersome, outstanding sums often taking years to collect, and audits being equally behind time. It was because of this that Edward developed the Chamber as his chief financial department.

The Chamber was a more informal and flexible system, partly because it had not been involved in royal finance for so long. It had originated from the accounting system used on the estates of the great nobles, who appointed officials called **receivers** and **auditors** from within their household to run certain groups of their estates in their absence. Edward IV had been familiar with this practice on the Yorkist estates, so, when he became king in 1461, he applied it to the royal estates. He had chosen to use the king's chamber, the innermost part of the king's household, to handle his finances in an attempt to exert more personal control over what happened. The result was that money now went directly to the king and not through an inefficient bureaucracy.

There is no doubt that Edward deserves credit for the way he made the financial system more flexible. As a result of the more efficient methods of identification and collection of revenue, the Crown's income rose to just under £70,000 per annum (£35 million in today's money). Although still under-funded when compared with some of the wealthier European monarchies, Edward had succeeded in restoring the Crown's finances to the extent that he could now act independently of both parliament and the nobility. His greatest achievement was that he died solvent, the first monarch to do so for more than a century.

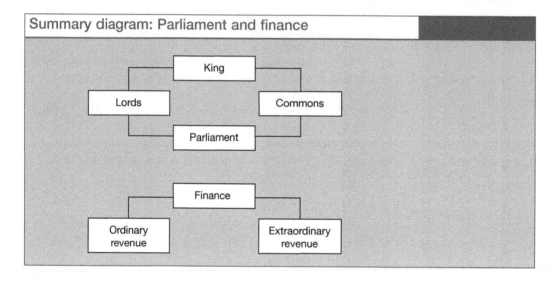

Summary diagram: Parliament and finance

Study Guide: AS Questions

In the style of Edexcel

To what extent did Edward strengthen royal authority in the years 1471–83?

Exam tips

The cross-references are intended to take you straight to the material that will help you to answer the question.

This question has a different focus from those at the end of Chapters 2 and 3. Here you are being asked not to explore causes, but to think about the extent of change. You will construct a good answer if you avoid description and instead use criteria to show 'strengthen royal authority'. You should also use well-chosen evidence to support your points.

You can also cover the 'to what extent' aspect of the question by considering previous weaknesses and also by indicating areas which were not strengthened, or where royal authority was still fragile.

To show 'strengthen' you could explore:

- The range of methods used to restore law and order in the first months of Edward's reign: use of punishment and rewards (page 66).
- Strengthening personal authority of the king: new dynamism to government; use of proclamations; personal intervention to resolve disputes between nobility; ruthlessness in dealing with challenge, containment of the political rivalry of Gloucester and Clarence (pages 66–8).
- Improvement in royal finances: more efficient identification and collection of revenues (pages 82–6).
- The reforming of local government, allied to an increase in the size of the royal household (pages 78–80).

To assess 'how far' these measures increased royal authority you could consider:

- The absence of serious plots or rebellions after 1471.
- Financial recovery sufficient to allow Edward to act independently of parliament and the nobility (pages 81–6).

However, also consider the limitations of reductions in the power of the nobility:

- There was limited success in tacking illegal retaining (page 69).
- Great magnates dominated government at regional and county level (pages 75–8).

In coming to your conclusion, you could distinguish between those measures which had significantly strengthened royal authority (for example, the financial reforms), and those which indicated that the challenge of the over-mighty subject had been contained, but only by the force of personality of this monarch.

In the style of OCR

Assess the claim that Edward IV's only problem at the end of his second reign was his relationship with the nobility.

Exam tips

The cross-references are intended to take you straight to the material that will help you to answer the question.

This question asks you to evaluate problems. 'Assess' does not mean look at each problem in isolation. Events happen because of the combined influence of factors, so aim to explain how one influenced another. Work out which factor you think was most important and justify your choice with evidence.

Edward seemed secure during his second reign. He did not face serious rebellion. Warwick was dead. Clarence, another inveterate plotter, had been tried and executed. Edward had built up his supporters, especially relying on men like Hastings and his brother Gloucester (who held the north, a vital area, for the house of York). Although Edward spent lavishly on his court, officials and gifts to the nobility, he generally managed his finances effectively. Responsibility was given to the Chamber from the Exchequer (pages 85–6), allowing the king more personal control. The succession was not a problem until Edward's early death, because his heir was only 13 years of age.

You might want to argue that there were other problems, particularly with the nobility. Did Edward IV give them too much leeway? Although he curbed the nobility, he did not destroy the power of nobles. You might claim that the strength of Edward's monarchy depended too much on his personality and that political stability could not survive his death. However you decide this question should best be answered, your essay must be driven by the instruction to 'assess the claim'. That means judging problems against each other, putting them in rank order of significance and giving a clear verdict that relations with the nobility were or were not the only problem Edward faced in 1483.

5 Richard III and the End of the Wars of the Roses 1483–5

POINTS TO CONSIDER

If Henry VI's weak and irresponsible rule resulted in civil war, Richard III's seizure of the throne led to rebellion, battle and ultimately his own death. Richard had the potential to be a good, if not a great, king but his unpopularity encouraged claimants like Henry Tudor to challenge him for the crown. These developments are examined as four themes:

- Richard, Duke of Gloucester, and the overthrow of Edward V
- 'Uneasy lies the head that wears the crown': challenges to Richard's rule
- Politics and government in the reign of Richard III
- Bosworth and the overthrow of Richard III

Key dates

1483	April 9	Death of Edward IV and succession of Edward V
	April 30	Richard and Buckingham took custody of Edward V
	June 16	Edward V's brother handed to Richard and Buckingham
	June 20	Lord Hastings executed
	June 26	Parliament petitioned Richard to take the throne
	July 6	Richard III crowned king
	November 2	Buckingham rebelled and was executed
1484	January	Parliament met
1485	August 22	Battle of Bosworth. Richard killed

1 | Richard, Duke of Gloucester, and the Overthrow of Edward V

Key question
Why was Richard able to seize the throne?

Richard, Duke of Gloucester

Richard is, arguably, one of England's most controversial monarchs who history has seen fit to label a monstrous villain. History's assessment of Richard owes much to the pen of the Tudor playwright William Shakespeare, whose play, *Richard III*, portrayed him as evil personified. 'The royal Satan', as historian

Roger Lockyer so memorably described him, has that rare distinction of being the only monarch with, what some have described, a modern-day 'fan club' – the Richard III Society – dedicated to clearing his name.

The primary reason why the Richard III Society believes his name needs clearing is because of his supposed involvement in the murder of his young nephews, Edward and Richard, the 'Princes in the Tower'. Their disappearance and disposal during his seizure of power have cast a shadow over his short reign ever since. Indeed, so dark has that shadow become that he is credited with being involved in the murders of others: Prince Edward, the 17-year-old son of Henry VI, his brother Duke of Clarence, Henry VI himself and even his own wife, Anne Neville, Countess of Warwick. Yet on each count there is insufficient evidence to accuse him, let alone convict him. In the opinion of A.J. Pollard, 'It is almost impossible to get to the bottom of all these controversies' because:

- Insufficient evidence has survived.
- Tudor propaganda has influenced our perception of him.
- He divided opinion even in his own day.
- In the 500 years since his death some of the stories surrounding him have solidified into apparent fact.

Upbringing

Richard's birth and upbringing were entirely conventional and give no hint of the controversies to come. He was the youngest of the three sons of Richard, Duke of York, and was still a child when his elder brother Edward seized the throne in 1461. There is no evidence to suggest that he was the deformed hunchback portrayed by Tudor historians and Shakespeare; if anything he was as fit and as healthy as his brothers. It is now generally agreed that these descriptions – 'little of stature, ill-featured of limbs, crooked back' – were simply literary inventions to signify evil. While he may not have been kind-hearted or unambitious there is nothing to suggest that he was anything like the 'malicious, wrathful, envious' creation of Shakespeare.

Political influences

Richard entered the political world in 1469 in the midst of national crisis. The 17-year-old duke witnessed at first hand Warwick's betrayal and the deposition of his brother Edward. These episodes may have affected him deeply and influenced his thinking. They may have taught him to strike first rather than be struck down by his enemies. This may help to explain why he was complicit in the judicial murder of Henry VI (1471) and execution of Clarence (1478). It may be argued that these acts were pragmatic and necessary solutions to problems that threatened him and his brother's security. Yet it should be remembered that Richard did not act on his own initiative (see pages 72–3) but was following the instructions issued by his brother, the king.

A portrait of Richard III. Shakespeare portrayed Richard as a deformed hunchback, with one leg shorter than the other and two fingers missing from his right hand. The playwright also states that his face had the look of evil. How far does this portrait of Richard III match Shakespeare's description?

Key question
Why did Richard act so aggressively in seizing the throne from his nephew, Edward V?

Edward and Richard: king and protector

Historians have long debated the reasons why Richard acted so aggressively in seizing the throne from his nephew. Having been so loyal to Edward IV throughout his reign, Richard's behaviour and actions in the months following his brother's death seem all the more puzzling. When Edward IV's brother, George, Duke of Clarence, joined the Earl of Warwick in rebellion against the Crown, Richard remained loyal. He distinguished himself at the battle of Barnet in 1471, led the war against the Scots in 1480 and recovered the city of Berwick from Scotland in 1482. Richard was handsomely rewarded by Edward, who granted him vast estates and royal offices in the north of England.

Edward had virtually set his brother up as a prince of the north by granting him, in January 1483, a great **palatine** comprising the counties of Cumberland and Westmorland. In a gesture of generosity rarely displayed by English kings, including even the profligate Henry VI, Edward invested his brother with the power and freedom to conquer Scottish territory to add to his palatinate. Without realising it, Edward had elevated Richard to a position of power that warrants the description of an 'over-mighty subject'. Arguably, Richard's power and influence were greater than those enjoyed by Warwick back in the early 1460s.

Key term

Palatine
A territory ruled by a person invested with princely or royal authority.

Richard's claim to the role of protector

Clearly, Richard was a man in whom the king had complete trust but this caused resentment at court where the queen's family, the Woodvilles, became jealous and fearful of his growing power. Richard probably distrusted, if not hated, them also and it is notable that he rarely ventured to court in the final four years of his brother's reign. Nevertheless, so long as Edward remained alive to keep the peace between them, the balance of power within the political establishment could be maintained. However, Edward's sudden and unexpected death in April 1483 upset the balance of power and put Richard's future in doubt. Richard was in the north when his brother died, making it impossible for him to influence, much less control, events at court. The Woodvilles, and their supporters, were keen to isolate Richard and deny him access to his nephew, Edward V.

Edward V was in the care of his uncle Anthony, Earl Rivers, at Ludlow and it was proposed to bring him to London at the head of an army. On arrival, Edward would be quickly crowned king so as to prevent any interference from Richard or anyone else who might oppose them. As King Edward V, the 12-year-old monarch could then exercise his authority, in consultation with the Woodville-dominated council, to appoint a protector of his choice to rule the kingdom while he grew to manhood. Unfortunately for the Woodvilles, they were unpopular and had few friends among the nobility. The first to turn against them was William, Lord Hastings, who had been one of Edward IV's most loyal friends and servants. He advised Richard to make his way to court as quickly as possible to support him in opposing the Woodville plan to seize control of the crown.

Edward IV's will has not survived, so it is impossible to say whether he intended his brother to rule on behalf of his son as protector. However, the fact remains that as the only living close male relative, Richard had a better claim to that role than anyone else. Richard wrote to the queen to reassure her that his intentions were honourable and that his sole objective was to see his nephew safely on the throne. Rivers appears to have believed Richard and the two men met at Northampton. All appeared well, but following a night's revelry, Richard, aided by Henry Stafford, Duke of Buckingham, had Rivers, Sir Thomas Vaughan, Sir Richard Grey and other key members of the young king's household arrested, after which he took Edward into custody.

Bewildered and confused, the Woodvilles in London, led by the queen's son, the Marquis of Dorset, tried to raise an army but failed. They fled into **sanctuary** at Westminster Abbey when they realised there was nothing they could do to stop Richard entering the capital. Richard's success and conduct thus far – he promised to have Edward V crowned on 22 June – had earned the respect if not the wholehearted support of the nobility. John, Lord Howard, Francis, Lord Lovel and Henry Percy, Earl of Northumberland, were among the few that openly threw in their lot with Richard.

The overthrow of Edward V

Historians remain sharply divided in their opinion of the nature and cause of the usurpation. Some argue that it was carefully planned and skilfully executed by Richard and his chief supporter, the Duke of Buckingham. Others view Richard's seizure of the throne as a haphazard sequence of ill-considered impulsive reactions. The most widely held view is that Richard acted on the spur of the moment to prevent the queen's family from robbing him of the position of protector. Richard feared that the Woodvilles might try to destroy his power by turning his nephew against him. He may even have feared assassination. Therefore, self-preservation rather than ambition is thought to be the most likely cause of the usurpation.

Events leading up to the usurpation

The events leading up to the usurpation began on 4 May 1483 when Richard, Buckingham and Edward V entered London in triumph. Within days the king's council had confirmed Richard's appointment as protector and had invested him with greater powers than those enjoyed by his father, Richard of York, during his protectorates in the 1450s. Almost immediately, Richard promoted Buckingham, Howard and Lovel to positions of power within the government. This would certainly have worried the Woodvilles, but it seems also to have caused Hastings some anxiety. Whether or not they combined to plot Richard's downfall is not known but, on 10 June, the protector requested the military assistance of his northerners to crush what he called a Woodville conspiracy to 'murder and utterly destroy' himself and Buckingham.

Three days later, on 13 June, Hastings was arrested and accused of treason; a week later he was executed. On the same day, 20 June, Edward IV's most loyal and trusted ecclesiastical servants, Thomas Rotherham, Archbishop of York, and John Morton, Bishop of Ely, were removed from the council. Thomas, Lord Stanley, was also arrested but later released by Richard. On 16 June a reluctant Thomas Bourchier, Archbishop of Canterbury, was pressured into forcing the queen to release her younger son, Richard, from sanctuary so that he could join his brother in the Tower. Following these events, Richard of Gloucester and Buckingham, according to the Crowland chronicler, 'did thereafter whatever they wanted'.

Written at the Benedictine Abbey of Crowland, in Lincolnshire, the **Crowland Chronicle** is an important source for events in late fifteenth-century England. The section that covers the years 1459–86 was written in April 1486 (after Henry Tudor ascended the throne as Henry VII) by someone who had access to information from the court of Richard III. Some historians believe the author was John Russell, Bishop of Lincoln, who was Richard's chancellor for most of his reign (until Richard dismissed him in July 1485) but others conclude the work was written by an unknown Crowland monk.

Key dates

Edward V's brother handed to Richard and Buckingham: 16 June 1483

Lord Hastings executed: 20 June 1483

Key term

Crowland Chronicle Also known as the *Croyland Chronicle*, this important chronicle was written by a well-informed monk from the Benedictine Abbey of Croyland in Lincolnshire. The most significant part of the chronicle, covering the years 1459–86, was written sometime in April 1486.

Usurpation

On the day appointed for Edward's coronation, sermons were preached at St Paul's calling into question Edward IV's legitimacy and that of his son. The carefully orchestrated event was clearly designed to declare publicly Edward IV a bastard while at the same time highlight Richard's legitimacy and claim to the throne. Four days later, on 26 June, in another choreographed or carefully staged event, a petition was submitted by parliament calling on Richard to take the crown. On 6 July 1483 Richard was crowned King of England. The overthrow had taken a little over eight weeks. The princes lodged in the Tower were never seen alive again and it is thought they had been disposed of some time between July and October 1483.

Key dates

Parliament petitioned Richard to take the throne: 26 June 1483

Richard III crowned king: 6 July 1483

A nineteenth-century painting of the 'Princes in the Tower'. Why did the artist, J.E. Millais, deliberately romanticise the fate of the princes?

Summary diagram: Richard, Duke of Gloucester, and the overthrow of Edward V

```
Edward IV ────────┐
                   ├──── Richard: protector
Edward V ──────────┤
                   └──── Overthrow
                              │
                         Richard III
```

Key question
Why did nobles such as Buckingham challenge Richard's rule?

2 | 'Uneasy Lies the Head that Wears the Crown': Challenges to Richard's Rule

All was not to run smoothly for Richard. He lost much support in the aftermath of his usurpation or overthrow of Edward V, and court and country became disunited again. Richard's ruthless disposal of his enemies, the leader of the Woodvilles, Earl Rivers, and former allies, William, Lord Hastings, deeply divided the nobility. Earl Rivers was accused of plotting to remove Richard as protector and make his sister, the queen, regent. Hastings shared Richard's fear and distrust of the Woodvilles, so he supported the execution of Earl Rivers. He also supported Richard's regency but he would not agree to the deposition of Edward V. Hastings' refusal to support the usurpation made him a threat to Richard, so he was eliminated.

Buckingham's rebellion

The Duke of Buckingham, who was ruthlessly ambitious, encouraged Richard to dispose of Earl Rivers and Hastings and to seize the throne for himself. Buckingham disliked the Woodvilles and was jealous of Hastings' power and influence. Edward IV had judged Buckingham to be dangerously untrustworthy and he was kept out of power. Buckingham struck up a friendship with Richard that saw them plot the usurpation together. Buckingham was lavishly rewarded and became the most powerful noble in the kingdom. However, within four months of Richard's coronation, this 'over-mighty' subject rebelled. He failed and was executed in November 1483.

Key date
Buckingham rebelled and was executed: 2 November 1483

The reasons for Buckingham's rebellion are a matter for debate. For example, there has been a great deal of speculation about the fate of the two young sons of Edward, the 'Princes in the Tower', neither of whom was seen alive again. Some historians have argued that their murder by Richard may have turned Buckingham against him. Others have accused Buckingham of murdering them himself. The real reason why Buckingham rebelled will probably never be known but the following may have been possible motives:

- dissatisfaction with the rewards and position of power given to him by Richard
- conversion to Henry Tudor's cause
- ambition to take the crown for himself.

Of course, Buckingham could simply have been swept along with the rising tide of opposition to Richard so that self-preservation was the primary motive for his rebellion. It is known that rising resentment among the gentry classes in the southern counties of England had begun to grow. In common with many of the southern-based nobility, the gentry of Kent, in particular, resented the power and influence of Richard's '**northern affinity**'. The result was a rebellion in which Henry Tudor, the exiled Lancastrian claimant to the crown, was invited to take the throne. He had been in exile in Brittany and France for over 12 years but had still been able to communicate with Buckingham, who now pledged his support.

In light of the events in Kent and Henry Tudor's preparations to land in England at the head of an army, Buckingham might have reasoned that Richard III's days were numbered and that he himself should be seen to support the winning side. In the event,

Northern affinity
Used to describe the noble and gentry supporters of Richard III who came from northern England.

Key term

Profile: Henry Stafford, Duke of Buckingham 1455–83

1455	– Birth of Henry Stafford. His parents were Humphrey Stafford, Earl of Buckingham and Lady Margaret Beaufort, daughter of Edmund Beaufort, Duke of Somerset (killed in battle on 22 May 1455)
1460	– Created Duke of Buckingham, aged 4, by Henry VI
c.1465	– Married aged 10 to Katherine Woodville, sister of Edward IV's queen
1471	– Edward IV appointed him to serve on royal commissions of the peace. His role was to help pacify resentful Lancastrians after the battles of Barnet and Tewkesbury
c.1472–3	– Appointed to serve on the king's council
1475	– Served as a captain of soldiers in Edward IV's campaign against the French
1476	– Dismissed from the council and kept out of office. No explanation offered other then a possible falling out with Edward IV
1478	– Served briefly as Lord High Steward of the Kingdom
1483	– On the death of Edward IV, allied himself to Richard, Duke of Gloucester. Was instrumental in putting Richard III on the throne
	– Rebelled against Richard III. Captured and executed

his judgement on Richard was misplaced, since Lord Howard crushed the rising in Kent, while the king dealt swiftly with the rebels. Henry Tudor's invasion did not take place for, on hearing the news of Buckingham's failure, the fleet, hampered by bad weather, turned back to France.

The role of powerful nobles in Richard's kingship

It has been said that only under-mighty kings have over-mighty subjects, but this does not apply to Richard III, who was anything but 'under-mighty'. Nevertheless, Richard's relationship with the Duke of Buckingham points to a dependency that reveals the weakness of his position. The success of Richard's kingship relied on maintaining the loyalty of a small group of powerful nobles:

- Henry Stafford, Duke of Buckingham
- John, Lord Howard
- Henry Percy, Earl of Northumberland
- Thomas, Lord Stanley
- John de la Pole, Earl of Lincoln
- William Herbert, Earl of Huntington.

As his reign wore on, Richard came increasingly to rely on the support of John, Lord Howard, who he created Duke of Norfolk, as reward for crushing the Kent rebellion. As for the others:

- Buckingham had rebelled and been executed.
- Henry Percy, Earl of Northumberland, gradually grew resentful at Richard's failure to confirm him as his successor in the north.
- Lord Stanley's loyalty had to be secured by Richard's taking of his eldest son, George, as a hostage.
- Lincoln and Huntington offered their support and were rewarded with positions on the council, but for much of the reign the latter remained lukewarm.

The bulk of Richard's core support came from northerners, men such as Sir William Catesby and Sir Richard Ratcliffe, which made him unpopular in the south. This southern resentment of northern interference in the affairs of state and the operation of patronage is expressed in William Collingbourne's famous rhyming couplet:

> The Cat [Catesby], the Rat [Ratcliffe] and
> Lovel [Francis Lord Lovel] our dog
> Rule all England under the **Hog**

Key term

Hog
Refers to Richard's emblem of the white boar.

'The Hog' (Richard) did his best to widen his support-base but he met with limited success. In return for his not ungenerous patronage, a few nobles, such as Walter Devereux, Lord Ferrers, John Brooke, Lord Cobham and Lord Henry Grey of Codnor, offered their service, but many were unwilling to commit to a usurper.

Summary diagram: 'Uneasy lies the head that wears the crown' – challenges to Richard's rule

Challenges to
Richard III's rule

Buckingham's rebellion

Disaffected nobles

3 | Politics and Government in the Reign of Richard III

Key question
How able a king was Richard?

The government of medieval England was in the hands of the king and whoever he chose to advise him and to sit on his council. It was an age of personal monarchy. This meant the country prospered or stagnated depending on the ability of the ruler. Richard proved to be a capable and energetic king. He was determined to stamp his authority on the kingdom by promising to outlaw corruption, restore peace and reform the legal system. He participated in government and moved around the kingdom to show himself to his subjects. He was also prepared to retain, and reward, talented councillors who had served his brother. Of the 54 councillors employed in Richard's government, 24 of them had once been in service to Edward IV. Richard was also prepared to innovate if the reason for doing so was sufficiently strong. In July 1484, he transformed his household council into a more formal Council of the North with full powers to govern the region on behalf of the king. Its first president was John de la Pole, the Earl of Lincoln. More significantly, the king founded a new body called the Council of Requests and Supplications, which was intended to help poor people in search of justice.

In 1471 Sir John Fortescue (see page 67), Chief Justice of the King's Bench under Henry VI, wrote *The Governance of England*, in which he offered Edward IV advice on how to restore the Crown's authority, political strength and stability. Fortescue identified two major problems and the means to deal with them:

- *The financial weakness of the Crown*. To solve this problem, Fortescue advocated **retrenchment** to halt the decline in royal revenue and **re-endowment** to increase the monarchy's income.
- *The increasing power of the nobility*. To combat the power of the nobility, especially the 'over-mighty' subject, he advocated a code of strict discipline mixed with reward and punishment.

When Richard became king he tried to follow this advice. He sought stability by continuing the financial policies of his brother Edward IV and raised much needed revenue from the forfeited estates of people attainted for treason. This enabled Richard to

Retrenchment
Cutting down on expenditure.

Re-endowment
Reinvestment, or finding other ways of raising money for the Crown.

Key terms

A contemporary illustration showing Richard III and his wife, Queen Anne, dressed in their coronation robes. Why has the illustrator shown Richard armed and wearing armour beneath his coronation robe?

grant away revenues worth around £12,000 (£6 million in today's money) a year as rewards for loyal service. He also tried to improve the efficiency of revenue collection in Crown lands. Although he did not rule long enough to solve the financial weakness of the Crown, Richard had introduced a measure of stability and efficiency in the collection of royal revenue.

Richard III and the nobility

Key question
How did Richard III deal with the nobility and parliament?

Richard hoped to stabilise the government by recruiting the nobility. He won many of them over by offering financial rewards, grants of land and important offices. Although this added to his financial problems, he thought that gaining noble support was worth the risk. He relied on the likes of the Duke of Norfolk, the Earl of Huntington and the Earl of Lincoln to advise him in council and provide stability in the provinces. The execution of Buckingham showed that he was not afraid to punish nobles who betrayed him. Although most of his support came from northern lords, it is a measure of his success that no English peers declared their support for Henry Tudor until after the battle of Bosworth.

Richard III's parliament

Richard's only parliament has been held up as an example of how great a king he might have been had he been given the time. Meeting in January 1484, parliament was required to fulfil three basic aims:

Parliament met: January 1484

Key date

- To ratify Richard's claim to the throne.
- To pass legislation leading to the attainder of 114 traitors and the confiscation of their lands.
- To enact reforming legislation to end the abuse of power by local officials, to improve the operation of justice in local courts, to tighten up the rules on those chosen for jury service and to end benevolences or forced loans.

Richard also offered individuals the opportunity to submit private bills to parliament, mainly in connection with disputed property rights. Although short lived, Richard's parliament hints at the direction in which the king wished his government to go: along the path of reform.

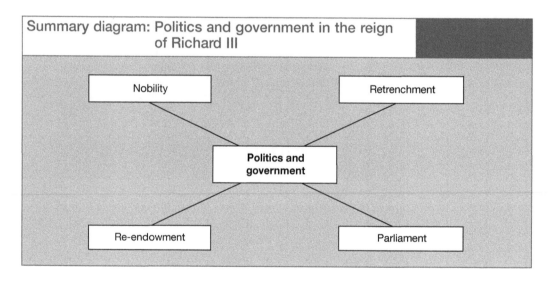

Summary diagram: Politics and government in the reign of Richard III

4 | Bosworth and the Overthrow of Richard III

Invasion and the march to Bosworth

Key question
Why did Bosworth lead to the overthrow of Richard III?

Henry Tudor, Earl of Richmond, had been in exile since 1471. Much of this time had been spent in Brittany, where he and his uncle, Jasper, Earl of Pembroke, found safe refuge. However, in 1484 this changed when Richard III negotiated a deal with Duke Francis II whereby he agreed to supply the duchy with a company of English archers to help defend it from possible invasion by France. Fearing for his safety, Henry crossed into France, where he was welcomed by the French king, Charles VIII. Angered by Richard's intervention and his support for the Bretons, Charles VIII decided to back Henry and his Lancastrian exiles by offering them financial and military assistance. The French king was willing to support and supply an invasion of England in the hope that it would prevent Richard from helping Brittany. Charles had long wished to annex the duchy and he was certain that Henry could provide him with the opportunity to achieve his ambition.

Henry set sail, in ships provided by the French, from Harfleur on 1 August 1485. He was accompanied by between 400 and 500 English and Welsh loyalists who had joined him in exile, and at least 1500 French and Flemish troops paid for by Charles VIII. Although half of Henry's troops lacked quality – Phillipe de Commines, a French chronicler, described them as 'the worst rabble one could find' – the remainder were tough mercenaries hired to provide the invading army with some military professionalism.

Henry sailed for Wales, his homeland, because he thought he might receive a warm welcome from his countrymen. Henry's force landed at Mill Bay near Dale in Pembrokeshire on 7 August and, over the next six days, it marched northwards through the second largest town in Wales, Haverfordwest, and up along the Cardiganshire coast. Henry attracted recruits from across mid-Wales and north Wales, and as his army grew in size he felt confident enough to turn inland and march through the Cambrian mountains and along the Severn to the border with England. By 12 August Henry had won over William ap Gruffudd and Rhys ap Thomas, two of the most influential landowners in north and south Wales, respectively. They were persuaded with promises of land and office should Richard be defeated. According to one eyewitness, Thomas brought with him 'a great band of soldiers' some 800 strong, while Gruffudd led a contingent of over 500 men.

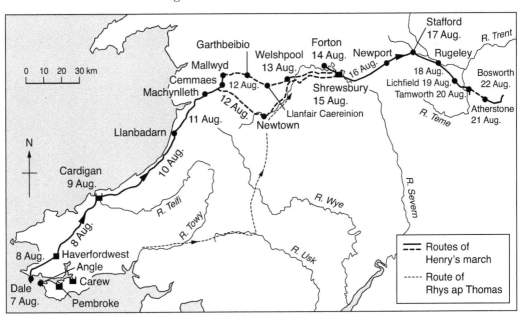

Figure 5.1: Map of Henry's march through Wales into England and the gathering of his supporters.

Henry reached Shrewsbury on 15 August with an army swollen to around 5000 men, mainly Welsh recruits, but could not hope to win a battle unless he obtained more support from the English nobility. Henry's main hope of success lay with two brothers – his stepfather, Thomas, Lord Stanley, and Sir William Stanley – whose lands included much of north Wales, Cheshire and the Borders. The brothers offered their support in secret because Richard held Lord Stanley's eldest son and heir, George, as a hostage to ensure his father's good behaviour. The Stanleys, particularly Sir William, had earned a reputation for changing allegiance during the Wars of the Roses and so could not entirely be trusted. However, Henry had no choice but to rely on their promises of support and so he pressed on and marched further into England. On the way to Bosworth, Henry was joined by Gilbert Talbot, the powerful uncle of the Earl of Shrewsbury, who brought with him nearly 500 men.

The battle of Bosworth and the death of Richard III

Richard was at Nottingham Castle with an army 10,000 strong when he learnt of the invasion. He had hoped that his rival would be defeated in Wales by either Rhys ap Thomas in the south or the Stanleys in the north. Within days he came to realise his mistake and in an effort to make up for time wasted, he moved his troops to Leicester, where they prepared for battle.

The two armies confronted each other just outside the small village of Market Bosworth in Leicestershire on 22 August. Tired and hungry after a three-week forced march covering over 240 km, Henry's army now numbered between 5000 and 6000 men. They were faced by a rested and well-prepared army almost twice their number led by an experienced soldier in Richard III. The records do not make clear whether or not this included the Stanleys' force of 3000, which remained on the sidelines for most of the battle. Neither Richard nor Henry knew for certain on whose side the notoriously unreliable Stanleys intended to intervene.

Henry's army

The majority of the recruits to Henry's army were not professional soldiers but they had probably seen some active service during the civil wars. For the most part they were tenant farmers recruited by their landlords to serve for a limited period. They were lightly armed and tended to fill the ranks as archers and spearmen. The more professional troops or retainers and mercenaries fought as men-at-arms, with sword, shield and pike. The landowners, the majority of whom were nobles, knights and squires, wore armour and fought on horseback. They were the cavalry that provided Henry's army with the necessary mobility on the battlefield. Henry relied on the military expertise of his uncle Jasper and John de Vere, Earl of Oxford, to guide him in battle.

Richard's army

Since England had no regular standing army, Richard's troops were probably similar in quality and background to those of his enemy. However, Richard's troops were better equipped and he had considerably more cavalry than Henry. They were fresher than Henry's troops, who had had a fortnight's hard marching, whereas Richard's army had come a much shorter distance. What artillery Henry had been able to bring with him consisted of light **field guns**, certainly inferior to the heavier **artillery** available to Richard's army. Richard had vastly more experience of warfare and military command than Henry and he had had ample time to prepare his defences. This enabled Richard to occupy the more favourable tactical position on the battlefield, the high ground on Ambion Hill with marshland protecting the flank.

The events of the battle

No eyewitness account of the battle exists but, by piecing together later accounts, we learn that fighting began early in the morning with Henry's forces charging across a marshy area towards the king's army. The battle lasted about three hours, but was bitterly

Key terms

Field guns
Small cannons mounted on wheels.

Artillery
Wheeled cannons of various sizes.

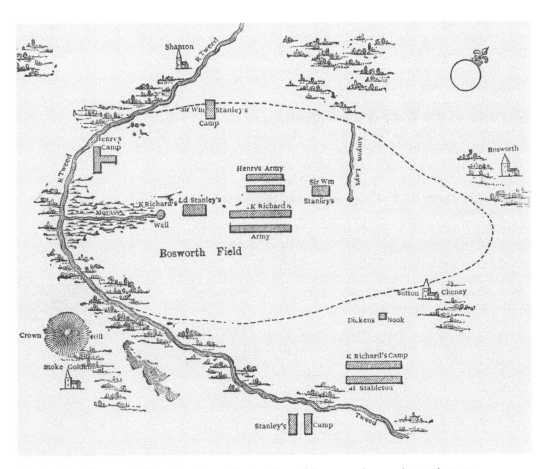

The battle of Bosworth. The plan shows the location of the opposing armies and, more importantly, the key positions occupied by the forces of the Stanley brothers. This plan was drawn some years later.

contested with heavy casualties on both sides. According to Polydore Vergil, Henry fought bravely and 'bore the brunt longer than his own soldiers … who were almost out of hope of victory'. The turning point came when Richard suddenly decided to strike at Henry himself. This apparently reckless action (Richard could have fled the field to fight another day) was caused in part by the Earl of Northumberland's refusal to move his reserve up in support. Having spotted Henry riding towards the Stanleys in the company of a relatively small band of men, Richard, accompanied by no more than 100 men, launched a furious assault on him. He almost succeeded, slaughtering Henry's standard-bearer before Henry's personal guard closed ranks.

At this crucial moment, Henry's step-uncle, Sir William Stanley, waiting in the wings to see the direction the battle would go, rushed to his rescue. Stanley's cavalry, perhaps some 500 strong, overwhelmed Richard, who refused to quit the battlefield. Richard's death concluded the battle and the leaderless Yorkists fled. The most prominent Yorkist, the Duke of Norfolk, was killed in the battle but the Earl of Northumberland survived. Northumberland's betrayal of Richard III did not earn the respect of the victor Henry Tudor, who had him arrested and imprisoned after the battle.

Key date

Battle of Bosworth. Richard killed: 22 August 1485

The crown was picked up by Lord Stanley from the field of battle and it was placed on Henry Tudor's head. Richard's naked body was tied to a mule and taken to Leicester to be buried. Henry's long years in exile were over.

The end of the Wars of the Roses

Bosworth was, arguably, the final act in the conflict known as the Wars of the Roses, which had dominated England's political, social and economic life throughout the second half of the fifteenth century. For this reason, 1485 is often seen as a turning point in the history of England. It is a date frequently used as a division between what historians call the medieval and the early modern periods. The reign of Henry VII ended the civil war and heralded the foundation of a new dynasty, the Tudors.

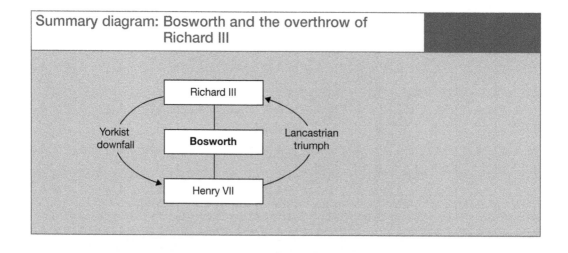

Summary diagram: Bosworth and the overthrow of Richard III

Study Guide: AS Questions

In the style of AQA

(a) Explain why Richard III's position as king was unstable in the years 1483–5.

(b) How far was Richard III responsible for his overthrow by Henry Tudor in 1485?

Exam tips

The cross-references are intended to take you straight to the material that will help you to answer the questions.

(a) In this question you have to demonstrate a confident understanding of a range of factors, make links and draw conclusions to show why Richard's position as king was unstable, for example:

- The splits caused in the Yorkist party by Richard's usurpation that led to Buckingham's rebellion (pages 95–6).
- The instability caused by former Yorkists fleeing to join Henry Tudor in exile (page 96).
- The unpopularity of Richard's policy of planting northerners in southern counties after the failure of Buckingham's rebellion (page 96).
- The rumours circulating about the fate of the 'Princes in the Tower', the death of Richard's wife and that of his son in 1484 (pages 94–5).

(b) In this question the key element is why Richard III was overthrown by Henry Tudor and whether or not he was to blame. You need to consider the arguments on both sides before making your essay plan. Points to consider might be:

- Was Richard's overthrow due to the divisions among the Yorkists caused by his usurpation (pages 94–5)?
- Did Henry exploit the rumour that Richard killed the 'Princes in the Tower' (pages 94–5)?
- How important is the fact that Richard had no heir?
- How unpopular was Richard and why did the southern nobility mistrust him (page 97)?

You should be able to come to a judgement on whether Henry's overthrow of Richard was due to his actions or to the actions of others (pages 102–4).

In the style of Edexcel

How accurate is it to say that Henry Tudor was able to seize the crown primarily because of Richard III's inability to secure the support of the great nobles of England?

Exam tips

The cross-references are intended to take you straight to the material that will help you to answer the question.

Do not be tempted to dismiss the statement in favour of stating the obvious – that Henry gained the crown on Richard's death – and concentrating your answer simply on the battle of Bosworth. The question requires a focus on what made Henry 'able to seize the crown' and that will include an exploration of what put him in a position to challenge Richard on the battlefield.

The answer requires exploration of two key elements:

- What enabled Henry VII to mount a successful invasion of England?
- What enabled Henry to win the battle of Bosworth and take the crown?

For the first element you should consider:

- Richard's weakened position – usurper, overly dependent on maintaining the loyalty of a small group of noble families whose support waned rapidly (page 97).
- Crucial support of Charles VIII of France (pages 100–1).
- Securing the support of Rhys ap Thomas in Wales (page 101).
- The decision of the Stanleys not to halt Henry's advance (pages 101–2).

For the second element you should consider:

- Richard's mishandling of the battle of Bosworth in spite of his military advantages (pages 102–3).
- Northumberland's reluctance to intervene and Stanley's decisive intervention (page 104).
- Death of Richard in battle (page 104).

In reaching a conclusion you should explore how many of these factors are connected with the issue of support for Richard from the great noble families of England. You can show that this was ultimately decisive in influencing the events and outcome of the battle of Bosworth, although Richard's own misjudgements and recklessness played their part. Additionally, mention that Henry's initial landing was prompted by the knowledge of Richard's weakness. However, you will need to take into account that Henry's expedition was made possible only by the support of the King of France, and that the support Henry gained in Wales was crucial to the invasion of England.

In the style of OCR

Assess the reasons why Richard III lost the battle of Bosworth.

Exam tips

The cross-references are intended to take you straight to the material that will help you to answer the question.

This question does not ask you to explain why Richard lost his throne, so do not analyse the long-term causal reasons behind problems in 1483–5. Equally, the question does not ask you to describe the battle of Bosworth. The question's focus is very specific: short-term reasons in the summer of 1485 for Richard's defeat at Bosworth, for example:

- the quality of generalship (pages 102–4)
- the quality and motivation of troops (page 101)
- the behaviour of the Stanleys (pages 102–4).

Weigh reasons against each other, putting them in a clear rank order of importance. When you do that, do not forget to justify your decisions, explaining why one factor was more or less important than another. As you consider some reasons, examine how they affected each side in the battle.

Some reasons will require a specific focus on one side, for example, for the Yorkists:

- the failure of parts of Richard's army to join in the battle (page 104)
- Northumberland's lack of support for Richard (page 104).

It is possible to argue that Richard, although an experienced and previously successful soldier, was reckless in his tactics. Good answers might discuss whether Richard was damaged by rumours of the death of the 'Princes in the Tower'. Henry Tudor proved to be an adept opponent, careful to engage Richard on the battlefield only when he had maximised his support, foreign and domestic (including his promise to marry Elizabeth of York, pages 100–1). Strong answers might push a little way back to assess very briefly the situation in 1484–5, noting that Richard's position was already weakened by the unpopularity of forced loans, that his patronage of northerners' causes harmed his reputation and that the death of his son was a serious blow. Nonetheless, the focus of your answer must be kept on 1485 and the battle itself. In that context, you might also consider the significance of luck as a factor on the battlefield. After all, Richard came close to killing Henry Tudor (page 104).

6 Henry VII: Establishing the Dynasty

POINTS TO CONSIDER

Winning the battle of Bosworth secured Henry the throne but it did not give him security. His claim to the throne was considered by some to be weak and so Henry faced a number of challenges to his rule. The most dangerous threats to his power centred around the pretenders – Lambert Simnel and Perkin Warbeck – and their Yorkist supporters. The threats to the Tudor dynasty and the means by which Henry VII secured his throne by taming the nobility and befriending the Church are examined as four themes:

- Henry Tudor's claim to the throne
- The aims and character of the new king
- Securing the throne: pretenders, protests and threats
- Taming the nobility and befriending the Church

Key dates

1485		Henry crowned as King Henry VII
1486	January	Marriage of Henry and Elizabeth of York
	September	Birth of Arthur, a son and heir to Henry
	November	Elizabeth of York crowned Queen of England
1487		First law passed against illegal retaining
	June	Battle of Stoke
1489		Release from the Tower and restoration of the lands and title of Thomas Howard, Earl of Surrey
		Rebellion in Yorkshire. Earl of Northumberland killed by rebels
1497		Rebellion in Cornwall
1499		Warbeck and the Earl of Warwick executed
1504		Second law passed against illegal retaining

Key question
How strong was Henry Tudor's claim to the throne?

1 | Henry Tudor's Claim to the Throne

To the majority of Englishmen the battle of Bosworth on 22 August 1485 was just one more battle in the long struggle for the crown that dominated the second half of the fifteenth century. On this occasion the victor happened to be the relatively unknown Lancastrian claimant, the 28-year-old Henry Tudor, Earl of Richmond. Henry was well aware that his claim to the throne by inheritance was weak and that it was only victory in battle that had brought him to power.

Henry's claim lay through his mother, Margaret Beaufort, who was a direct descendant of Edward III by the marriage of his third son, John of Gaunt, Duke of Lancaster, to Katherine Swynford (see the family tree on page 15). Their children had been born when Katherine was Gaunt's mistress and, although an act of parliament in Richard II's reign had legitimised them, a further act in Henry IV's time had excluded them from the line of succession.

A portrait of Henry VII. How does the portrayal of Henry VII in this painting differ from that of Richard III?

Henry VII also inherited royal blood, although not a claim to the throne, from his father Edmund Tudor. This was because Edmund's mother, Catherine, was a French princess who had been married to Henry V of England before she became the wife of Edmund's Welsh father, Owen Tudor, a squire from Anglesey. After the death of her husband, Henry V, Queen Catherine had no claim to the throne. By virtue of this marriage, Edmund and his brother Jasper were the half-brothers of the king, Henry VI. In 1452 Henry VI raised his half-brothers to the peerage by creating Edmund Earl of Richmond and Jasper Earl of Pembroke. Therefore, Henry VII was the half-nephew of the King of England and a member of the extended royal family.

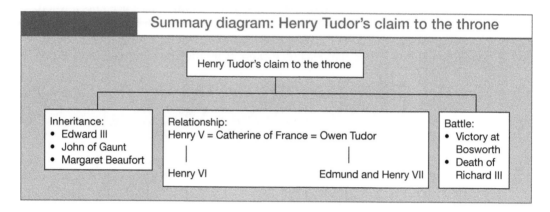

Summary diagram: Henry Tudor's claim to the throne

2 | The Aims and Character of the New King

Aims

Key question
What kind of man was Henry VII and what were his aims and ambitions?

Henry VII had one essential aim: to remain king and establish his dynasty by handing on an unchallenged succession to his descendants. His policies at home and abroad were shaped and dictated by this aim. Therefore, his goals were simple: to secure and strengthen his dynasty. He knew that if he was to prove himself a strong king and retain full control of his realm he would have to establish effective government, maintain law and order, control the nobility and secure the Crown's finances. He would also need good advice, friends abroad and a considerable amount of luck.

Character and personality

The character and personality of Henry VII remain as shadowy and elusive today as they did to his own subjects in 1485. The evidence is such that we know far less about him than any other of the Tudors. This uncertainty about the character and personality of the first Tudor monarch is a good example of how limited evidence can lead to widely differing opinions. Historians tend to disagree about Henry's character, mainly because kings rarely recorded their own thoughts, with the result that historians have had no choice but to draw their own conclusions from his actions and policies.

However, some of the views of his contemporaries have survived. Among the more interesting, if not necessarily the most useful, is the portrait of Henry VII by Sittow, a talented Renaissance artist working in Flanders. It was painted from life 20 years after the battle of Bosworth, in 1505. The following brief description is by Polydore Vergil, a brilliant Italian scholar and papal tax collector who arrived at the English court in 1501. Henry was so impressed by his understanding of history that he encouraged him to write a history of England. Henry VII is described by Vergil in his book *Anglica Historia*:

> His appearance was remarkably attractive and his face was cheerful, especially when speaking; his eyes were small and blue, his teeth few, poor and blackish; his hair was thin and white; his complexion sallow.

It is worthwhile comparing Vergil's description with the impression that we gain from studying Sittow's portrait. Vergil is probably more truthful and reliable because he wrote a few years after Henry's death, and was, therefore, not concerned about the king's reaction.

Francis Bacon's *History of the Reign of King Henry VII*, published in 1622, remained the major work on the reign for over 300 years. Indeed, Bacon's conclusions were not challenged by historians until the middle of the twentieth century. His description of Henry as 'one of the best sort of wonders: a wonder for wise men' has the ring of truth and implies that Henry was admired for his intellectual ability. But the fact that Bacon goes on to say that 'for his pleasures, there is no news of them' suggests that his lifestyle was rather dull. Bacon wanted his contemporaries and future generations to learn from his *History*, which is why he was prepared to pass judgement on those who came under his scrutiny.

Henry VII devoted so much of his time to replenishing the Crown's empty coffers that historians have accused him of being a miser. In fact, his account books make fascinating reading, for we catch a glimpse of Henry the man, as well as Henry the king.

A coin depicting Henry VII and Queen Elizabeth. Why was the minting of a coin such a significant event?

Profile: Jasper Tudor c.1431–95

c.1431	– Second son born to Owen Tudor, a Welsh squire in the service of the royal household, and Queen Catherine of France, the widow of King Henry V
1452	– Created Earl of Pembroke by his half-brother King Henry VI
1457–61	– Ruled south Wales on behalf of King Henry VI
1461	– Fled into exile after defeat in the battle of Mortimer's Cross
1462	– Deprived of his earldom and title
1470–1	– Restored to power during Henry VI's brief second reign
1471	– Fled for a third time into exile after the Lancastrian defeat at the battle of Tewkesbury, taking his nephew, Henry, with him
1471–85	– Spent 14 years in France bringing up and protecting his nephew from various Yorkist plots intended to murder him
1485	– After victory in the battle of Bosworth he was restored to his Earldom of Pembroke and created Duke of Bedford
1495	– After 10 years' loyal service on the king's council Jasper died childless

Jasper Tudor did much to influence the way in which Henry VII ruled the kingdom. He was the first one to whom the young and inexperienced king turned to for advice. He was a permanent member of the king's council and his appointment to positions of power in Wales and Ireland kept these distant parts of the realm under firm royal control.

From them we discover his weakness for dicing and playing cards, and the way he indulged his own and his younger daughter's love of music. This 'miserly' king was rash enough on occasions to pay £30 'for a little maiden that danceth' and around £13 on a leopard for the Tower menagerie!

A European visitor commented on Henry's sumptuous table for 600 guests and the fact that he celebrated St David's day in which he offered an annual prize of £2 for the winner of an **Eisteddfod**-style musical competition. The king was a keen sportsman, playing tennis and chess regularly, but his great passion was the hunt and he kept an impressive stable of horses and pack of hounds. Henry is portrayed as rather a cold man but his caring, more human side was revealed on the death of his eldest son, Prince Arthur, when, though grief-stricken, he rushed to comfort his wife. When Elizabeth herself died only a year later an inconsolable Henry 'privily departed to a solitary place and would no man should resort unto him'.

Eisteddfod
An annual Welsh cultural festival in which prizes are offered to competitors in poetry and music.

Key term

Summary diagram: The aims and character of the new king

Henry VII

Aims:
• To remain king
• To establish a dynasty

Character and personality:
• Quiet and reserved
• Strong and thoughtful
• Passion for hunting and music
• Strong family man

Key question
How was Henry able to secure the throne in the face of such serious threats and opposition?

Key dates

Henry crowned as King Henry VII: 1485

Marriage of Henry and Elizabeth of York: January 1486

3 | Securing the Throne: Pretenders, Protests and Threats

First steps to securing the throne

Henry's first steps to securing the crown revealed his concern to stress the legitimacy of his position. He was anxious to show that his claim to the throne did not simply depend on his defeat of Richard and his marriage to Elizabeth of York. For example:

• He dated the beginning of his reign from the day before Bosworth, which enabled Richard and his supporters to be declared traitors. This was a shrewd decision because it meant that he could use acts of attainder to confiscate their estates which thus became the property of the Crown.
• He deliberately chose 30 October to be the date of his coronation because it fell a week before the first meeting of parliament on 7 November. Thus it could never be claimed that parliament made Henry VII king.
• He applied for a papal dispensation to marry Elizabeth of York. This was necessary because they were distant cousins but it was also desirable since it meant he obtained the support, and blessing, of the Pope. Henry and Elizabeth were married on 18 January 1486, finally uniting the Houses of Lancaster and York.

After victory at Bosworth, Henry's most immediate problem was ensuring that he kept the crown. He was fortunate in that many potential candidates had been eliminated from the succession during the Wars of the Roses, but it was not until 1506, only three years before the end of his long reign, that Henry could feel secure on his throne. By that time the most dangerous claimants to the crown were either dead or safely imprisoned.

Rival claims to the throne

In 1485 there were a number of important Yorkists alive with rival claims to the throne. The strongest claim belonged to Richard III's 14-year-old nephew, Edward, Earl of Warwick (son of his brother Clarence). Henry successfully disposed of him, at least in the short term, by sending him to the Tower. Although it was a royal stronghold and prison, the Tower was also a royal residence, so Warwick lived in relative comfort although he was denied the freedom to come and go as he wished. When his own son died in infancy, Richard had named another nephew, John de la Pole, the Earl of Lincoln, as his heir. The threat posed by Lincoln was reduced when he, and his father, the Duke of Suffolk, publicly declared their loyalty to Henry. If Henry remained suspicious about Lincoln's loyalty he did not show it; on the contrary, he not only accepted the earl's submission but invited him to join the king's council.

The surviving Yorkist nobility

Richard's supporters at Bosworth were naturally treated with suspicion, but Henry was prepared to give them a second chance as long as he could be convinced of their loyalty to him. Henry's treatment of two of the most prominent Yorkists is quite interesting. For example:

- Thomas Howard, Earl of Surrey, who had fought on the Yorkist side with his father, John, Duke of Norfolk, who had died at Bosworth, was kept in prison until 1489. Only when Henry was persuaded to trust Surrey's professions of loyalty did he release him.
- Henry Percy, Earl of Northumberland, was released after a mere four months in prison, at the end of 1485, when he begged the king to be given the opportunity to prove his loyalty. Henry accepted his promise of support in return for resuming his old position as governor of the north of England.

Key date
Release from the Tower and restoration of the lands and title of Thomas Howard, Earl of Surrey: 1489

Henry was well aware that those who pledged loyalty to the new regime might simply be playing for time perhaps in expectation of its collapse. Nevertheless, it is clear that in spite of his suspicions, and misgivings, Henry was determined that ex-Yorkists would not automatically be excluded from the Tudor court: loyalty was the new king's only requirement for them to regain royal favour.

Minor risings and protests 1485–6: Lovel, Stafford and Vaughan

Key question
What caused the risings and protests of 1485–6?

When Henry came to power he was a largely unknown and untried nobleman. His knowledge of Wales, Brittany and France was better than that of England. Few of his subjects believed that the civil wars were over or that he would remain king for more than a few months. The uncertainty of his rule, the continuing political instability and the economic dislocation caused by war affected nobleman and commoner alike. Therefore, Henry had to deal with the disgruntled – protestors against such things as high taxes – alongside the dangerous – pretenders or rival claimants to the throne. Henry could not afford to ignore or treat lightly any protest or rebellion but it was clear that the main threat to his position came from the pretenders Lambert Simnel and Perkin Warbeck (see pages 118–25).

Lovel and the Stafford brothers

Ironically when rebellion struck it came not from Simnel or Warbeck but from a group of minor Yorkist nobility and gentry, namely, Francis, Lord Lovel and the Stafford brothers, Thomas and Humphrey. Trouble broke out while the king was on royal progress in the north of England. This was a public relations exercise in an unruly and pro-Yorkist area, in which the king travelled to York to show himself to his people in an attempt to secure their support. Since their defeat at Bosworth, Lovel and the Stafford brothers, faithful adherents of Richard, had been in sanctuary at Colchester. Protected from arrest and imprisonment by the Church, the conspirators repaid their clerical hosts by plotting to overthrow the new king. Unaware of their plotting, Henry reluctantly agreed to respect the right of the Church authorities to shelter his enemies. Perhaps Henry hoped that the conspirators might contemplate the futility of their position and give themselves up to his mercy: he was wrong.

As Henry travelled to Yorkshire in April 1486, the conspirators broke sanctuary. Lovel headed north and planned to ambush the king, while the Staffords travelled to Worcester to stir up rebellion in the west. News of the uprisings was brought to the king while he was at Lincoln. Undaunted, he continued with his progress, but sent an armed force to offer the rebels the choice of pardon and reconciliation or, if they fought and lost, excommunication and death. The rebels dispersed, but Lovel evaded capture and fled to Flanders. Bereft of support, the Staffords sought sanctuary once again. A reluctant Church offered them protection but did nothing to prevent their arrest when the king ordered his troops to remove them. The king and his judges felt that it was unreasonable for declared traitors to be allowed sanctuary a second time, and so the Staffords were sent to the Tower. Humphrey was executed but the younger brother, Thomas, was pardoned and remained loyal thereafter.

Vaughan

At about the same time there was trouble in Wales from a group of dissatisfied Yorkists drawn from among the Vaughans and Herberts. Led by Sir Thomas Vaughan of Tretower, they conspired to kill Henry and seize Brecon Castle. The rebellion was crushed by Henry's old ally Rhys ap Thomas, who the king had knighted at Bosworth.

Henry's reaction to the minor risings and protests

Henry's policy of severity towards the ringleaders and clemency to the rank and file proved successful. Not only did Henry gain the respect of his people, he was seen as the upholder of justice and order. The royal progress to the disaffected areas of the north and west provoked the required reaction of loyalty, submission and obedience. Less than six months after the quelling of these uprisings Henry's wife, Queen Elizabeth, gave birth to a healthy son at Winchester, England's ancient capital. Amidst the celebrations Henry sought to establish the ancient roots of his

Key date

Birth of Arthur, a son and heir to Henry: September 1486

dynasty by having the baby christened Arthur. In a carefully orchestrated campaign of propaganda, Henry hoped to stir the nation by evoking memories of the country's great past. The king had not yet reached 30 and was still young enough to have more children and to see his heir reach maturity. These events helped towards securing the dynasty by giving it an air of continuity.

Rebellions in Yorkshire (1489) and Cornwall (1497)

These rebellions stemmed not from dynastic causes but from the king's demands for money through taxation. However, they did influence the way in which Henry responded to dynastic challenges and showed how thin the line was between public order and lawlessness.

Yorkshire

In an effort to deter a French attack on Brittany Henry declared his intention to offer aid to the duchy. For this he required a substantial sum of money, much of which he expected the parliament of 1489 to provide. Pressure was brought to bear and parliament agreed to grant the king a subsidy of £100,000. The size of the subsidy caused widespread resentment because to pay for it a new system of taxation was introduced that resulted in a form of income tax. In spite of the king's demands it seems only £27,000 of the total was raised. The subsidy was particularly badly received in the economically poor and pro-Yorkist county of Yorkshire which was suffering the after-effects of a bad harvest the previous summer. The people also resented the fact that the counties to the north of them – Northumberland, Cumberland Westmorland and Durham – were exempted from the subsidy because they were expected to contribute to the defence of England from the Scots. Henry Percy, Earl of Northumberland, put the case for Yorkshire to the king, but Henry refused to negotiate. When the earl returned north with the news, he was murdered by an angry gang in York. What had begun as localised mob violence soon turned into a serious and widespread rebellion led by Sir John Egremont, an illegitimate member of the Percy family. By taking advantage of Northumberland's declining popularity in the area, because he had supported the subsidy, Egremont was able to stir the people into action.

The Earl of Surrey was sent north with an army and he defeated the rebels outside York. However, Surrey failed to capture Egremont, who escaped to Flanders. The king travelled north to issue a pardon to most of the prisoners as a gesture of conciliation, but he failed to collect any more of this subsidy. He faced no more trouble in the north because the new Earl of Northumberland was only a minor and a ward of the Crown. Henry therefore appointed the Earl of Surrey as his Lieutenant in the north. Surrey, who had no vested interest in the region, seized the opportunity to demonstrate his loyalty to the new regime in the full knowledge that the restoration of his own estates rested on his success there.

Key dates

Rebellion in Yorkshire.
Earl of
Northumberland killed
by rebels: 1489

Rebellion in Cornwall:
1497

Cornwall

Taxation and the heavy financial demands of the king lay at the root of the rebellion in Cornwall. In January 1497 parliament was encouraged to provide Henry with the means to finance an armed expedition north to resist an expected invasion of England by the Scottish king, James IV, and the pretender Perkin Warbeck (see pages 124–5). The Cornish refused to contribute to the defence of the northern part of the kingdom because it offered little threat to them. In May the rebels set out from Bodmin and marched through western England towards the capital, London, acquiring their only leader of any significance, the impoverished and disaffected Lord Audley, at Wells in Somerset. On 16 June, the rebel army, now some 15,000 strong, reached the outskirts of London and encamped on Blackheath. The Cornishmen were confronted by a royal army under the command of the Earl of Oxford, Lord Daubeney and Sir Rhys ap Thomas.

Historians estimate that between 500 and 800 rebels were killed in the battle and that the rest swiftly fled. Following his policy of severity towards the ringleaders and clemency to the rank and file, only Audley and around half a dozen of the original local leaders were executed. Despite the fact that the rising had been defeated, it must have concerned the king that the rebels had been able to march as far as they did before facing any opposition. Distracted by events in Scotland and by the Warbeck conspiracy (see pages 124–5), Henry had not responded to the Cornish rising until it was nearly too late. The rebellion may not have endangered his throne, but he did not know this at the time. To Henry and his contemporaries the rebellion looked threatening and it had shown that he could not afford to involve himself in a military campaign against Scotland. Henry opted for diplomacy and attempted to come to terms with James.

The impact of the rebellions

The uprisings in Cornwall and Yorkshire had little to do with any Yorkist conspiracy but their impact on Henry must not be underestimated. They showed that there was a groundswell of opinion opposed to heavy and regular taxation, and that the country at large was unwilling to finance a major war in defence of the Tudor regime.

Henry was fortunate because:

- The rebellions were essentially regionalised and did not spread throughout the kingdom. The Cornish rebels found that when they left the West Country on their march to London, people were reluctant to join them.
- Many of Henry's subjects were apathetic and not inclined to take up arms. The majority of people wished to lead a simple, peaceful life and they had no desire to see a resumption in civil war.
- The stability that he was working towards led many to be content with his leadership and style of government.

A near contemporary print showing the hanging of Cornish rebels at Canterbury in 1497. Why did Henry VII insist on having public executions for the rebels?

Henry seems to have preferred negotiation to fighting and he only took up arms when absolutely necessary. Financially and militarily this was less burdensome and, therefore, preferable to both the king and his subjects. This naturally affected the way in which Henry dealt with the pretenders – Simnel and Warbeck. Rather than confront them in battle, unless he had no choice as happened at Stoke (see pages 120–1), Henry turned to diplomacy in an effort either to make peace or to persuade foreign rulers not to support his enemies.

The pretenders: Lambert Simnel and Perkin Warbeck

Henry was king because he had been victorious in battle. The manner of his victory was such that a rising from Richard's surviving Yorkist followers was almost inevitable. The uprisings led by Lovel, the Stafford brothers and Vaughan demonstrated how vulnerable Henry was and how alert he must be if he was to remain on the throne. He developed an intelligence system that

Key question
How serious a challenge to Henry's rule was Lambert Simnel's rebellion?

employed agents to gather information that could be used to warn him in advance of any plot or conspiracy.

This intelligence system was in its infancy when the Simnel plot emerged, but it repaid Henry's faith in it when it uncovered the Warbeck conspiracy. The Yorkist-inspired Simnel and Warbeck conspiracies were the two most dangerous challenges to confront Henry in the 14 years after Bosworth. This was because:

- Henry was forced into fighting a battle.
- They caused entanglement with other European states, particularly Burgundy.
- They lingered on for such a long time, from 1486 to 1499.
- They encouraged some of his subjects to contemplate committing treason.

In hindsight, it may seem incredible that the two pretenders to the throne – the 10-year-old Lambert Simnel and the 17-year-old Perkin Warbeck – were taken seriously at the time, but the fact that they were meant that Henry could not afford to ignore them for fear of appearing weak and indecisive.

Lambert Simnel 1486–7

The conspiracy involving the first of the two best-known rebels against Henry VII emerged in the winter of 1486 when conflicting rumours began to circulate about the fate of the Earl of Warwick (Edward, son of George, Duke of Clarence, see page 15). Many thought that, following his arrest and detention by Henry, Warwick must have died in captivity, as he had not been seen for some time. In this unsettled climate, a priest from Oxford, Richard Symonds, seized his opportunity. Although Symonds had never seen the young sons of Edward IV, he claimed that one of his pupils, the 10-year-old Lambert Simnel, the son of an organ maker, bore a striking resemblance to the missing, presumably murdered, princes.

Relying on his clerical background to sway the opinion of the common people, who had themselves never seen the missing princes, Symonds decided to pass Simnel off as the younger prince, Richard of York. When this met with a lukewarm response he changed his mind and, responding to rumours suggesting Warwick had died in imprisonment, Symonds decided that Simnel would now impersonate the teenage earl. The whole enterprise seemed doomed from the start and had it not been for the interest shown in the conspiracy by some Yorkist nobility, chief among them John de la Pole, Earl of Lincoln, it might have withered and died.

Funded by sympathetic Yorkists, Symonds took Simnel to Ireland hoping for a better reception there. Ireland was chosen because it had been a centre of Yorkist support since Richard, Duke of York, had been Lord Lieutenant there in the 1450s. Symonds hoped that passing Simnel off as Warwick might gain support because he was the grandson of Richard of York. Although the current Lord Deputy, the Earl of Kildare, probably did not believe that Simnel was who he claimed to be, the earl and some other prominent Irish leaders, Walter FitzSimons, the Archbishop of Dublin, prominent among them, decided to take advantage of the opportunity to discomfort the new king. Kildare and his Irish allies were motivated by a combination of anger, ambition and greed:

* Anger at Henry's failure either to confirm Kildare's position as Lord Deputy of Ireland or to acknowledge Walter FitzSimons's position as Irish Archbishop.
* Ambition for greater power and the opportunity to govern Ireland with a free hand.
* Greed in the hope of winning substantial concessions in land.

Accordingly, Kildare and his adherents proclaimed Simnel king in Dublin. On hearing the news from Ireland, Edward IV's sister, Margaret, Dowager Duchess of Burgundy, offered her support to the pretender. Margaret was a determined enemy of Henry VII and was intent on seeking revenge for the death of her brother, Richard III, at Bosworth. Seizing the opportunity to strike at Henry she sent money and a force of 2000 German mercenaries to Ireland, commanded by the experienced and capable Martin Schwarz. The international nature of this support encouraged the Irish to go as far as to crown Simnel as king Edward VI in a ceremony held in Dublin in May 1487. Unfortunately, they realised they had no crown and so had to improvise one by borrowing a coronet from a nearby statue of the Virgin Mary.

Although the conspiracy had begun late in 1486, Henry himself does not appear to have been aware of it until January 1487. Henry moved quickly and decisively. Edward IV's queen, Elizabeth Woodville, and her son by her former marriage, the Marquis of Dorset, were put under house arrest and deprived of their lands. This was followed by the arrest of some minor nobles with Yorkist connections who were declared traitors. What exactly any of them were thought to have done remains obscure, but this suited Henry's purpose in seeking to strike fear into the minds of his enemies.

The real Earl of Warwick was exhibited in London to expose the imposter but the damage had already been done and the conspiracy soon developed a momentum of its own. The sudden flight of Lincoln to join Lord Lovel in Flanders at the court of his aunt, Margaret of Burgundy, made clear the gravity of the situation. By May, Lincoln, Lovel and Schwarz had arrived in Ireland, where they joined Kildare. Lincoln clearly knew that Simnel was an imposter but this did not deter him from offering his support or from taking over the leadership of the rebellion. It is likely that on toppling Henry VII, Lincoln planned to put forward his own claim to the throne when he judged the time to be right.

The battle of Stoke 1487

On 4 June 1487, Lincoln and his multinational army landed in Lancashire, marched across the Pennines and then turned south. Lincoln had expected a flood of recruits but he was to be

Battle of Stoke: June 1487

Key date

disappointed. A population weary of war was further dissuaded from joining the rebels because they feared the Irish troops, who had a reputation for plunder and carnage. The king was fully prepared to meet the insurgents and the two sides clashed just outside Newark at East Stoke on 16 June 1487. Although the royal army outnumbered the rebels – Henry had 12,000 to Lincoln's 8000 – the outcome of the battle was by no means a foregone conclusion.

After three hours of fierce combat, the Yorkist forces were defeated. Lincoln, Lovel, Schwarz, and Kildare's brother, Thomas Fitzgerald, the chancellor of Ireland, all perished, along with nearly half their army. Lambert Simnel and Richard Symonds were both captured. The cleric Symonds was sentenced to life imprisonment in a bishop's prison. The king, recognising that Simnel was no more than a child manipulated by ambitious men, made him a turnspit in the royal kitchen. He was later promoted to be the king's falconer as a reward for his good service.

Henry's calculated mercy found expression in his treatment of the defeated rebels. He could afford to be reasonably generous to Simnel because Symonds was now in prison and the ringleaders, Lincoln and Lovel, were dead. As a deterrent to others in the future, those nobles who had fought at Stoke and survived were dealt with swiftly in Henry's second parliament, which met from November to December 1487. Twenty-eight of them were attainted and their lands were confiscated.

Some historians regard Stoke as being the last battle of the Wars of the Roses. Certainly, Henry never again faced an army composed of his own subjects on English soil. Indeed, Stoke could have been a second Bosworth, with Henry this time in the role of Richard III. However, the fact that such a ridiculous scheme almost succeeded indicates that the country was still very unsettled and shows how fragile Henry's grasp on the crown was. It was no coincidence that, on 25 November, his wife, Elizabeth, and mother of his heir, was finally crowned queen. This was designed to:

- provide a 'feel-good' factor by means of a public spectacle and celebration
- unite the nation by securing the goodwill of the people
- satisfy disaffected Yorkists.

Key date

Elizabeth of York crowned Queen of England: November 1486

Perkin Warbeck 1491–9

Henry's crushing victory at Stoke did not end the challenges to his rule, nor did it dissuade others from plotting his overthrow. Ironically, his military success may have had the opposite effect to that intended because instead of eliminating any threat or challenge it bred resentment and thoughts of revenge. Indeed, in the opinion of the distinguished Welsh historian Sir Glanmor Williams: 'Mention of Perkin Warbeck reminds us that it took time for many dissidents to give up the thought of re-opening the civil wars.' So desperate had some dissident Yorkists become that they were willing to support virtually any pretender to the throne no matter how incredible the claim or ridiculous the plan. Perkin Warbeck may fairly be said to fall into both those categories because:

- his claim to be Richard, Duke of York, one of the missing 'Princes in the Tower', was incredible
- his plan to seize the throne from Henry VII and make himself king was plainly ridiculous.

So who was Perkin Warbeck and why did so many contemporaries take him seriously? The fact is we know very little about him other than he was a 17-year-old youth from Tournai in France who was apprenticed to a Breton merchant. He first emerged in November 1491 when he arrived in Cork, Ireland, aboard his master's ship with the sole intention of selling silk merchandise. The way in which this French-speaking merchant's apprentice of humble origin was plucked from obscurity to play a leading role in one of the most serious conspiracies in Henry VII's reign is not known.

The majority of historians are content to simply repeat the story that his 'noble' bearing and silk-wearing exploits so impressed the townsfolk that they assumed he was the Earl of Warwick. Why they would make this assumption and why, when told of the people's reaction, Warbeck is reported to have denied it, claiming instead to be the younger son of Edward IV, is unknown. There are no clear-cut answers to these questions but it is thought that the plot had probably been hatched before Warbeck set foot in Ireland. The plot gained credibility from the fact that the fate of Edward IV's children was not known: had they been murdered or were they still imprisoned, or, as Warbeck claimed, was he the living proof that at least one of them had escaped?

In the opinion of Henry VII's modern biographer, the historian Professor Stanley Chrimes, Warbeck's appearance in Ireland was 'no accident but was the first overt action in the unfolding of a definite plan'. Part of that 'plan' involved a man called Edward Brampton, a Portuguese Jew recently converted to Christianity, who is said to have 'trained' Warbeck for his role as a Plantagenet prince. Although it cannot be proved at such an early stage, the key players in the whole conspiracy are thought to be Charles VIII of France and Margaret of Burgundy. Both had a vested interest in wishing either to unsettle or to unseat Henry VII. For example:

- Charles wanted to use Warbeck as a diplomatic counter in order to dissuade Henry from interfering in France's attempted takeover of Brittany (see pages 164–5).
- Margaret's intended use of Warbeck was altogether more sinister. She wanted nothing less than Henry's overthrow even if it meant supporting the accession to the English throne of someone who she did not believe was her nephew.

Charles VIII of France

If Warbeck's own confession, which he made shortly before his execution, is to be believed, the plot was the brainchild of Charles VIII:

> The French king sent an ambassador into Ireland ... to advise me to come into France. And I went to France and from there into Flanders, and from Flanders into Ireland, and from Ireland into Scotland, and so into England.

The conspiracy achieved international recognition when Warbeck, frustrated at the lack of support in Ireland, accepted the invitation of the French king to meet him in Paris. In March 1492, Charles VIII welcomed the pretender to the French court, where he was treated as an honoured guest. The French king's acceptance of Warbeck as Richard of York provided the conspiracy with the stamp of authority it had hitherto lacked and the kind of publicity guaranteed to attract followers. By the middle of that summer, less than six months after Warbeck had set foot in France, over 100 English Yorkists had joined him in Paris.

Unfortunately for Warbeck the hospitality of the French king was suddenly cut short when, in November 1492, Charles VIII and Henry VII negotiated and signed the Treaty of Étaples (see pages 165–6). In among a number of clauses dealing with war, finance, trade and territory was one in which the French king agreed not to support any of Henry VII's enemies. This meant that Warbeck had to flee and he did so to Flanders, where Margaret of Burgundy offered him shelter and support.

Margaret of Burgundy and the Emperor Maximilian

In publicly acknowledging Warbeck to be her nephew, Margaret hoped to:

- attract dissident Yorkists, both at home and in exile, to her court
- stir up trouble in England by encouraging Yorkists there to rise in rebellion.

Margaret's support of Warbeck worried Henry to the extent that in 1493 he temporarily broke off all trade with Flanders, even though this jeopardised the cloth trade that was a vital and lucrative part of the English economy.

Soon anyone with a grudge against Henry was prepared to support the growing conspiracy. With the active encouragement of Margaret, Maximilian, the newly elected Holy Roman Emperor, pledged his support for Warbeck, who he recognised as Richard IV in 1494. However, to Warbeck's obvious frustration it would take more than a year before Margaret and Maximilian had the resources available to finance an invasion of England.

Conspiracy at home: Stanley, Radcliffe and Fitzwalter

In the meantime, Henry's intelligence network had identified and drawn up a list of those implicated in plotting treason, both at home and abroad. Armed with this information Henry moved quickly and in the parliament of 1495 a number of acts of attainder were passed against dissidents such as Lord Fitzwalter, and the king's own steward, John Radcliffe.

The most significant victim was Sir William Stanley, Henry's step-uncle and Chamberlain of his Household. Henry was shaken by the revelation that a man in whom he had placed a great deal of trust had betrayed him. According to Polydore Vergil, Stanley was only peripherally implicated in Warbeck's schemes and that his crime had been to admit, in conversation with Sir Robert Clifford, that 'if he were sure that the man [Warbeck] was Edward's son, he would never take up arms against him'. This was hardly treason but neither was it the ringing endorsement of his royal credentials that Henry demanded of his subjects, let alone his friends and family.

Henry was determined to send out a clear message that he would spare no traitor, no matter how eminent, and so Stanley followed Fitzwalter and Radcliffe to the executioner's block. It was unfortunate for Stanley that the man in whom he confided his thoughts, Sir Robert Clifford, a supposed adherent of the plot, was likely to have been one of Henry's agents, since he alone received a pardon and reward for breaking the conspiracy.

Failure at Deal and refuge in Scotland

With the financial backing of Margaret and Maximilian, Warbeck launched his invasion of England. However, his attempted landing at Deal in Kent in July 1495 was a fiasco. He failed to gather sufficient local support and so he set sail for Ireland, ruthlessly abandoning those of his men, most of whom were hired mercenaries, who had already gone ashore. In Ireland, he laid siege to the town of Waterford for 11 days without success.

Warbeck then departed for Scotland, where he was welcomed at Edinburgh by James IV, who gave him refuge and support. In spite of his doubts about Warbeck's identity, James thought he would prove useful as a weapon against Henry VII, who he distrusted. James went so far as to give Warbeck his cousin, Lady Catherine Gordon, in marriage together with an annual pension of £1200 (£500,000 in today's money). He even promised Warbeck to invade England should a suitable opportunity present itself.

Henry considered these events to be serious because they threatened:

- his security
- his legitimacy and position on the throne
- his marriage alliance with Spain.

Henry's greatest fear was that King Ferdinand and Queen Isabella of Spain would fail to honour their promise, made in the Treaty of Medina del Campo in 1489 (see pages 166–7), to send their daughter, Catherine of Aragon, to England to marry his eldest son and heir Arthur, Prince of Wales.

Fortunately for Henry, the Scottish invasion of England was a disaster. This was due as much to the efficient work of Henry's agents informing him of the attack as to Warbeck's poor leadership. The pretender received no support south of the border mainly because his Scottish troops preferred raiding and pillaging to fighting. Warbeck had no choice but to retreat.

Disillusioned with Warbeck, James, like the French king before him, thought that Henry's conciliatory offer of a treaty was more to Scotland's long-term advantage. In September 1497 a seven-year truce was agreed at Ayton which was ratified in 1502 – the first full peace treaty with Scotland since 1328. To make the terms of the treaty more concrete Henry agreed to give his eldest daughter, Margaret, in marriage to James.

Warbeck's conspiracy ends in failure

To avoid possible detention, Warbeck fled Scotland for Ireland in July 1497, hoping to find support there. He was to be disappointed. Kildare and the other Irish leaders did not want to risk a confrontation with Henry. Warbeck was encouraged to leave Ireland and on hearing of the Cornish rebellion, he set sail for the south-west of England hoping, as a last resort, to enlist the support of the rebels.

Again, Warbeck was to be bitterly disappointed for, having landed in Devon, he found the rebellion had ended in failure: he was too late. In an effort to reignite the flames of revolt, Warbeck appealed to the West Countrymen for support. To the king's horror a few thousand men rallied to the impostor and they marched on Exeter, besieged it but failed to take the city. This was the high point of Warbeck's 'English enterprise' for as soon as the rebel army reached Taunton it broke and fled when confronted by the royal army. Within a fortnight it was all over, Warbeck once again abandoned his followers and he sought the sanctuary of Beaulieu Abbey in Hampshire. In August 1497 he was persuaded to give himself up and to make a full confession.

Since Warbeck was a foreigner, English law did not apply and so Henry could not accuse him of treason. In a conciliatory gesture, Henry allowed Warbeck to remain at court with his young Scottish bride, but he spurned the opportunity to win the king's trust by trying to escape in 1498. He was recaptured, publicly humiliated by being forced to sit in the stocks, and was then imprisoned in the Tower. As for his wife, she remained at court and, with the approval of King James, she became a lady-in-waiting to Henry's queen.

Key date
Warbeck and the Earl of Warwick executed: 1499

The execution of Warbeck and Warwick

Historians have long argued over whether Warbeck and Warwick entered into a plot to escape from the Tower and murder the king. Some suggest that the prisoners were the victims of a cynical attempt by the king's agents to manipulate them into conceiving a plot. Others believe that Warwick, weary of

Key question
Why were Warbeck and Warwick executed?

imprisonment, was persuaded by Warbeck to enter into a conspiracy. The truth will probably never be known and all that can be said with certainty is that Henry's patience with Warbeck had been exhausted. The pretender, and his powerful foreign backers, had succeeded in causing Henry eight years of considerable anxiety and expense. Consequently, in November 1499, Warbeck was convicted of trying to escape yet again and this time he was hung, drawn and quartered.

The Earl of Warwick was found guilty of treason and was beheaded two weeks later. Although Warwick himself might not have been dangerous, he was there for others to manipulate and weave plots around. It is possible that pressure from Spain induced Henry to act as ruthlessly as he did. Ferdinand and Isabella wanted to ensure that their daughter would become the wife of the next king of England. In short, they were seeking a secure inheritance for their child and not a contested crown.

De la Pole and the end of Yorkist threats 1499–1506

Following Warwick's execution, the only remaining Yorkist with a reasonable claim to the throne was Edmund de la Pole, Earl of Suffolk. As the brother of the rebellious Earl of Lincoln, killed at Stoke, he was treated with suspicion by Henry VII. This may be the reason why the relationship between the two men was tense, a tension made worse by the king's refusal to grant Suffolk the dukedom enjoyed by his father.

What prompted Suffolk suddenly to flee the kingdom for France in July 1499 is not certain. That Henry was caught by surprise suggests that neither he nor his usually reliable agents knew anything about the earl's intentions. Henry persuaded Suffolk to return but within two years, in 1501, he fled again. This time he took his brother, Richard, with him. Suffolk's decision to flee may have been influenced by the Emperor Maximilian, who offered them safe conduct to his court in Flanders.

The remainder of the dwindling band of Yorkist exiles gathered in Flanders to offer their allegiance to Suffolk. Fearing another foreign-backed invasion by a rival claimant to his throne, Henry acted more ruthlessly than before:

- Suffolk's relations in England were imprisoned.
- In the parliament of January 1504, 51 noble and gentry landowners with links to Suffolk were attainted.

The most notable victim of Henry's purge of suspected Yorkists was Sir James Tyrell, once Constable of the Tower, and latterly Governor of Guisnes, where Suffolk had temporarily sought refuge. Before his execution, Tyrell confessed to murdering the two young princes, the sons of Edward IV, thus discouraging any further imposters. Of course, the reliability of this confession, obtained under torture, is debatable.

Henry was determined to destroy Suffolk but, so long as the latter remained on the continent protected by foreign princes, there was little he could do. However, Henry's luck seemed to change in 1506 when Maximilian's son, Philip, was persuaded to negotiate an alliance. Among the many terms of the Treaty of Windsor was a clause in which Philip agreed to surrender Suffolk but only on condition that the earl's life would be spared. Henry kept his promise; Suffolk remained in the Tower until his execution by Henry VIII in 1513. Suffolk's brother, Richard de la Pole, escaped and remained at large in Europe trying in vain to muster support for his claim to the English throne.

It was not until 1506 that the persistent threat of Yorkist claimants was, for the most part, eliminated. Thereafter, the security of the dynasty rested on the heartbeat of his only son, Prince Henry. Arthur had died in April 1502, followed by the death of Queen Elizabeth in February 1503. Henry's fear for the future of his dynasty is seen in the way he searched the courts of Europe for a second wife. Nevertheless, it is a credit to Henry's clear, decisive judgement and diplomatic skill that he managed, unlike the three previous English kings, to hand on his throne intact to his son.

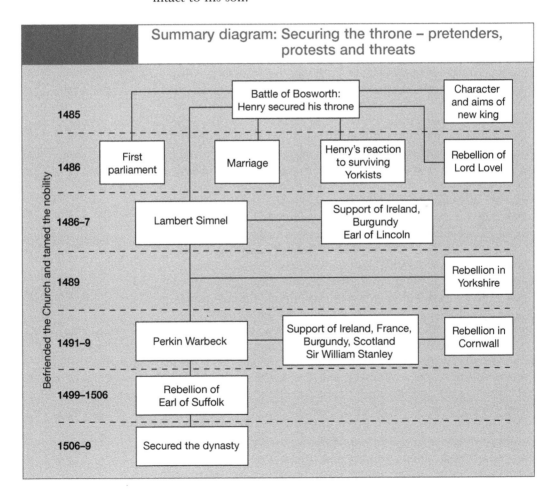

Summary diagram: Securing the throne – pretenders, protests and threats

4 | Taming the Nobility and Befriending the Church

Key question
How did Henry tame the nobility and befriend the Church?

A wise king recognised the importance of keeping control of the nobility and befriending the Church. Both had the wealth and power to challenge the monarchy. In order to safeguard the throne, Henry employed a number of strategies to combat and master the disaffected nobleman and the disgruntled priest.

The 'problem' of the nobility

Key question
Why do some historians consider the nobility to be a 'problem'?

The stability and security of the realm rested on the relationship between the king and his nobility, and their willingness to co-operate. According to the teachings of the Church, the nobility had a duty to serve their anointed king, who was held to be God's deputy on earth. By the same token, the king was obliged in return to protect them, to reward them for their loyalty and service and, above all, to rule wisely and fairly. This theory of obligation, known as the Great Chain of Being (see page 8), was the natural order of society. However, this theory did not always work well in practice.

The Wars of the Roses had temporarily upset this natural order of society with the crown being fought over by rival factions. This damaged and reduced the status of the monarchy. The nobility had profited most from this, seizing the opportunity to take the law into their own hands and govern as **semi-regal princes** in their own localities. Although they had always tried to have the last word in their own area, they now took this a step further, using their servants and retainers as private armies to settle their petty quarrels and to make or unmake kings on the battlefields of the recent civil wars. This was the norm in Wales, where each Marcher lordship was virtually an independent territory in whose affairs the Crown could not legally interfere. A fair proportion of the English nobility, including the dukes of York, Lancaster, Norfolk and Buckingham, were also Marcher lords and it is the freedom they enjoyed in Wales that may have inspired them to take greater control of their landholdings in England.

In 1485 it was this class over whom Henry had to assert his authority if he was to restore the dignity and authority of the monarchy. His problem, according to one modern historian, S.T. Bindoff, was 'how to suppress the magnates' abuse of their power while preserving the power itself'. The nobility had the power to provoke disorder and even revolt, but they could also quell rebellion and act as a mediator between the king and his subjects. Henry hoped that by ruthlessly imposing his will, the nobles might learn to accept that their position was one of obedience, loyalty and service to the Crown. If this was achieved the rest of his subjects would follow suit because the nobility were the natural leaders of society. In this context it can be argued that Henry's reign marks the end of an independent **feudal** nobility and the beginning of a **service nobility**.

Key terms

Semi-regal princes
Nobles exercising the powers of a monarch in a particular lordship or locality.

Feudal
The medieval social and political system by which lords were given land in return for serving the king in time of war.

Service nobility
Nobles whose power and promotion rested on serving the king in government office.

Size of the nobility

It is a common misconception that most nobles were killed during the Wars of the Roses, and that Henry only had a small upper class to control. In fact, the evidence from **inquisitions post mortem** suggest that there had always been a high extinction rate, with the result that peers too often failed to leave sons to succeed them. On average in the later Middle Ages in every 25-year period a quarter of noble lines died out and were replaced by newly ennobled families. In order to make his task of bringing the nobility to heel easier, Henry deliberately kept the peerage small by limiting the number of titles he either bestowed or created. This was unusual and in direct contrast to the policies of Edward IV and Henry VIII, in whose reigns the nobility grew significantly in size.

Henry VII deliberately refrained from making new creations for three reasons:

- A limited noble class was easier to control.
- He so rarely elevated anyone to the peerage that it was regarded as a distinctive honour when it did happen.
- The bestowal of a title might bring with it vast estates, the majority of which were granted from Crown lands. If titles and estates were handed out on a large scale, it could result in a considerable drop in income for the Crown.

Key term

Inquisitions post mortem

Local enquiries into the lands held by people of some status and wealth, in order to discover whatever income and rights were due to the Crown. Such inquisitions were only held when people were thought or known to have held lands of the Crown.

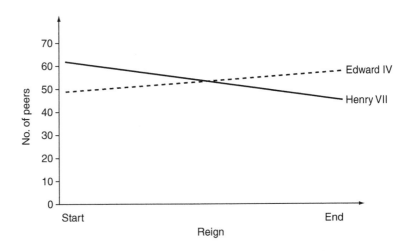

	Number of peers		Number of major peers*	
	Start of reign	End of reign	Start of reign	End of reign
Edward IV	49	58	7	12
Henry VII	62	45	16	10

*Dukes, marquises and earls

Figure 6.1: The number of peers between 1487 and 1509.

Whereas Edward IV had created nine new earls, Henry created only three:

- His stepfather, Thomas, Lord Stanley, who became Earl of Derby.
- Philibert de Chandée who, in recognition of his military skill as captain of his mercenary troops at Bosworth, became Earl of Bath.
- Sir Edward Courtenay, who was invested with the title Earl of Devon, left vacant by the death of his cousin John at the battle of Tewkesbury in 1471.

As a consequence of Henry's policy, the peerage shrank from around 60 in 1485 to about 40 in 1509 as new creations failed to keep pace with the number of noble families that died out mainly through natural extinction. According to one modern historian, T.B. Pugh, 'Royal intervention was far more effective than the failure of male heirs in diminishing the group of great magnate families.' He cites the case of Sir Walter Herbert, whose claim to his late elder brother's earldom of Huntington was ignored by Henry, who thereby allowed the title to lapse. It counted for little that Walter was well known to, and well liked by the king, having been brought up with him at Raglan in Wales when the young Henry was put in the care of Herbert's father, the Yorkist Earl of Pembroke.

Henry found other ways to reward his loyal subjects that need not involve the granting of peerages. He revived and gave added prestige to the **Order of the Garter**, an award dating back to the reign of Edward III (1327–77). This old-established honour was in the gift of the Crown but involved it in no financial obligations. Some 37 of Henry's closest followers (including peers) received this privilege during his reign. Among those honoured were Sir William Stanley and Sir Rhys ap Thomas but, whereas the latter embraced the award with enthusiasm, Stanley considered it scant reward for his good service. For his sterling service at Bosworth, Stanley expected nothing less than a peerage: he was to be disappointed.

> **Order of the Garter** Founded in 1348, this honour was bestowed on the most important knights, who then became the senior rank of knighthood.
>
> *Key term*

Over-mighty subjects

Unlike Henry VI, Edward IV and Richard III, Henry VII did not have to confront over-mighty subjects. The reasons for this are many and varied, for example:

- Henry lacked close male relatives so he did not have to worry about family rivalries. Whereas Edward had had two powerful brothers with whom he had to contend, the Dukes of Clarence and Gloucester, Henry had none.
- Henry was cautious and refrained from over-rewarding his followers. The lands that came to the Crown from extinct peerage families were not given away but were retained. For example, the great estates acquired from the defunct Yorkist families of Warwick, Clarence and Gloucester were managed and exploited by the king's agents.

- Henry controlled the marriages of his nobles, thereby ensuring that they did not link themselves to great heiresses in order to create new and dangerous factions. For example, when Katherine Woodville, the widow of Jasper Tudor, married her third husband, Sir Richard Wingfield, without royal licence, Henry imposed a heavy fine of £2000 (nearly £1 million in today's money).
- Henry kept the families of great magnates such as the Percy earls of Northumberland, the Howard earls of Surrey and the Stafford dukes of Buckingham under close surveillance.
- Henry maintained a watchful eye over and kept firmly in check closely related families with the potential to become over-mighty, like the Stanley earls of Derby, to whom the king owed as much as Edward IV had owed to the Nevilles for his throne. For example, in 1506 Henry took the opportunity to fine Bishop Stanley, his stepbrother, the huge sum of £245,680 (£119 million in today's money) for illegal retaining.

In conclusion, it can be seen that partly through good fortune and partly through a carefully thought-out policy, the greater magnates posed less of a threat to Henry than they had in previous reigns.

The power of the nobility

Key question
Was Henry VII right to treat the nobility with suspicion?

There is no doubt that Henry was suspicious of the nobility. He feared their power and their potential for rebellion. He did not know the majority of them as he had been brought up in Wales and France but, as a usurper, he was naturally inclined to be cautious and distrustful. Henry's suspicion of and caution in his treatment of the nobility caused some historians to suggest that he was pursuing a consciously anti-noble policy. Indeed, it has been suggested that he deliberately set out to quell the nobility and thrust them from their traditional advisory role on the council, replacing them with professional lawyers and administrators. According to one of his most notorious agents, Edmund Dudley (see pages 135 and 144–5), Henry 'was much set to have the persons in his danger at his pleasure'; meaning that the king kept some nobles close to him at court so that he could keep an eye on them.

The fact is Henry's relationship with the nobility was far more complex and much less tense than was once thought. He enjoyed a good relationship with some of them, particularly the Earls of Oxford and Shrewsbury, who were among his closest companions, while others, such as the Dukes of Bedford and Buckingham, the Earl of Derby and Viscount Welles, were related to him. Of course there were some with whom he had a strained relationship like Thomas Grey, second Marquis of Dorset, suspicion of whom had been 'stirred in Henry' by others, and George Neville, Baron Bergavenny, who was the only nobleman to suffer the public disgrace of being tried, fined and imprisoned for illegal retaining (see pages 132–4).

Nevertheless, it is clear that Henry recognised the nobles' importance to him in controlling the provinces in the absence of a standing army and effective police force. He never attempted to interfere with their authority in the localities and they continued to dominate local government. Moreover, Henry continued the medieval practice of granting the overlordship of the outlying, and therefore more disturbed, areas of his kingdom to the greater magnates as a gesture of goodwill. So, despite his dubious support at Bosworth, Henry Percy, Earl of Northumberland, was released from captivity after only a few weeks and was regranted the wardenship of the north of England. In the opinion of historian Christine Carpenter, Henry was guilty not so much of a 'lack of trust' in his 'natural partners, the nobility' but more of a 'lack of judgement over how to delegate and to whom'.

Henry's attitude towards patronage and retaining

Patronage

Henry did not try to buy the loyalty of the nobility; rewards had to be earned. He was as careful in this as he was over the granting of titles. The beneficiaries of Henry's generosity were quite simply valuable servants of the Tudor government. Some were peers, such as Jasper Tudor, the Duke of Bedford; the Earl of Oxford in return for his military support; and George Talbot, Earl of Shrewsbury, a notable administrator; but many were not. Sir Richard Empson and Edmund Dudley, who rose to become two of Henry's most trusted advisers, were not made peers, but it is said they used their titles and positions of king's councillors 'as proudly as any peerage'. Loyalty and ability were Henry's sole requirements in his most important servants; **patronage** was not an automatic privilege of the upper class.

Patronage
The award and distribution of royal favours.

Key term

Retaining

Henry publicly condemned retaining at the beginning of his reign when he forced the members of both Houses of Parliament to swear that they would not retain illegally; that is without the king's licence. He followed this up by pushing through parliament two acts, in 1487 and 1504, to curb the practice. Henry knew that to allow retaining to continue unchecked was to invite trouble because the nobility would simply employ as many retainers as they could afford. The greater and wealthier the magnate the larger the number of retainers he could command. Retaining, or employing men purely on the basis of training them and arming them to fight, had contributed to the Wars of the Roses. Henry was seeking to establish peace and stability but he faced a dilemma because:

First law passed against illegal retaining: 1487

Key date

- He could not allow retaining to continue in its present form because it might threaten his position. To ignore it might make him look weak and indecisive.
- He dare not eliminate retaining because it would be difficult to enforce and might invite opposition. To ban it would be counter-productive because, ironically, the king needed the

retainers of his own supporters to maintain law and order and to form the core of a royal army in the event of war.

The only example Henry had to follow was that set by Edward IV in 1468 when he passed a law intended to restrain rather than eliminate retaining. Consequently, the act of 1487 did little more than repeat Edward's earlier statute. Thus, 'lawful' retaining was allowed to continue, if it was accompanied by a recognisance (see page 134) to ensure the retinue was not misused. In 1504 Henry went further when he introduced a novel system of licensing whereby nobles could employ retainers for the king's service alone. To do this, a lord had to have a special licence endorsed with the king's own seal, and the entire retinue had to be listed for royal approval. It was only valid during the king's lifetime.

The key difference between Henry VII and Edward IV over retaining is in their attitude to their friends. Whereas Edward turned a blind eye towards the misdemeanours of those close to him, Henry treated everyone alike. The list of those **indicted** for illegal retaining in 1504 included:

- the Duke of Buckingham
- the Earl of Derby
- the Earl of Essex
- the Earl of Northumberland
- the Earl of Oxford
- the Earl of Shrewsbury.

Even the king's own mother, the Lady Margaret, Countess of Richmond and Derby, was punished by fine for illegal retaining. One of the most celebrated victims of the king's displeasure over retaining was the Earl of Oxford, a friend and highly valued adviser. According to the seventeenth-century historian Francis Bacon, the king complimented the earl for putting on such an impressive show in honour of his visit and promptly fined him £10,000.

Although Henry's reign witnessed a reduction in the number of retainers that magnates maintained, the practice continued well into the reign of Elizabeth I. Nevertheless, Henry had succeeded in controlling it to a far greater extent than his predecessors and he did prevent it from becoming a significant problem.

Taming the nobility

Before Henry could control the nobility he first had to tame it by curbing its power. In addition to patronage and reward Henry used the power of the law to enforce his will over the nobility. The most favoured methods at his disposal were acts of attainder and bonds and recognisances:

- *Acts of attainder*. Henry frequently used acts of attainder as a way to punish disobedient magnates. After a period of time, he would often arrange for parliament to revoke them, but he would only gradually restore the confiscated lands as rewards for actions of particular loyalty and support. Lesser nobles were sometimes forced to pay large sums of money for such reversals

Key term

Indicted
Charged with a crime.

Key date

Second law passed against illegal retaining: 1504

Key question
What impact did the Crown's financial threats have on the nobility?

because they did not have as much to offer the king in terms of service or influence in their particular localities.

- *Bonds and recognisances.* These were written agreements in which a person who offended the king was forced either to pay up front, or promised to pay, a certain sum of money as security for their future good behaviour. This technique, sometimes with conditions attached, such as the carrying out of a certain duty, was used as a method of ensuring loyalty and faithful, if sometimes grudging service.

Henry used the system not only as a financial threat against potentially disloyal magnates, but also to raise much needed revenue for the Crown. The sums stipulated in these agreements ranged from £400 for a member of the gentry to £10,000 for a peer (£4.8 million in today's money). As with his policy over acts of attainder, the greater the magnate, the more likely Henry was to bring him under this type of financial pressure. The most important noble to suffer in this way was Edward IV's stepson, the Marquis of Dorset. Henry had believed him to be implicated in the Simnel plot and, after further reports of treachery in 1491, his friends signed bonds totalling £10,000 as a promise of his good behaviour. When Henry was planning the invasion of France in 1492, he even went so far as to take the Marquis's son as hostage in case he seized this opportunity to rebel again.

Even the Lords spiritual of the Church were not spared the king's ruthless treatment. For example, the Bishop of Worcester had to promise to be loyal and not to leave the country without the king's permission. As a further incentive the bishop was also forced to pay £2000 as a pledge of his good behaviour.

This policy of Henry's has been much commented upon, not so much because of its novelty but because of the extent to which he used it as a way of curbing the political power of the nobility. Use of such recognisances can be found throughout the fifteenth century, but other kings such as Edward IV employed them more haphazardly and infrequently. However, for Henry they were an integral part of his policy for controlling the nobility by threatening financial ruin on any family which dared to offend or oppose him.

The efficiency with which these bonds and recognisances were enforced and the money was collected was due to the skill and administrative ability of Empson and Dudley (see page 160). They were responsible for operating the system through the **Council Learned**. Henry expected nothing less than loyalty from all his subjects, rich and poor alike. The nobility suffered most during his reign because they posed the greatest threat to the authority and security of his dynasty.

Key term

Council Learned
Council staffed by legally trained officials entrusted with the task of defending the king's rights and imposing financial penalties on law-breakers.

Key figures

Sir Richard Empson and **Edmund Dudley**

The lawyers Sir Richard Empson (c.1450–1510) and Edmund Dudley (c.1462–1510) were two of Henry VII's most loyal servants.

Empson first came to prominence in the reign of Edward IV when he was appointed the chief law officer in the Duchy of Lancaster in 1477. He lost his office during the reign of Richard III but regained it for life on the accession of Henry VII. He was elected a member of parliament and served as the speaker of the House of Commons. He was knighted in 1504 and appointed Chancellor of the Duchy of Lancaster, and president of the Council Learned in the Law.

Dudley served as a member of parliament and as speaker of the Commons. He was appointed to the king's council in 1504 and became its president in 1506. He worked very closely with Empson in the Council Learned and their efficient running of that institution earned them the hatred of the gentry and nobility, who were subjected to the financial exactions known as bonds and recognisances.

Key question
Why did Henry VII consider befriending the Church to be so important?

Key terms

Orthodox
Accepting without question the doctrine of the Church.

Excommunicating
Expelling from the Church.

Befriending the Church

Henry VII was a loyal son of the Church. He was pious and entirely **orthodox** in his religious belief and attitudes. Although Henry was aware of the weaknesses within the Church he did not question its authority or try to reform it. He was keen to maintain good relations with the Church because it could prove to be a powerful ally in his claim to legitimacy and in his search for security. For example, Pope Innocent VIII was among the first foreign rulers to recognise Henry's claim to the throne. The Pope also supported Henry by **excommunicating** all those who rebelled against him. Henry responded by being the first English monarch to send an ambassador to Rome.

Henry's relationship with his bishops was equally good. He employed the most talented of them to serve him in government. The most senior churchmen – John Morton, Archbishop of Canterbury, Christopher Bainbridge, Archbishop of York, William Warham, Bishop of London, and Richard Fox, Bishop of Winchester – became the king's closest and most loyal advisers. Through their support for him, Henry was able to control and exploit the Church. The Church helped to add to the king's coffers with substantial amounts of money raised through clerical taxation, loans and fines. The bishops also ensured that the parish clergy reminded the people of the importance of obedience to authority and of the penalties for sinfulness and disorder.

Popular religion and the challenge of heresy

The parish church was the focal point of village life and its priest the most respected member of the community. The majority of English people were devout followers of the traditional practices and beliefs of the Church. They attended regularly and, as part of their routine of life, they followed the Church calendar, which marked the religious feasts, festivals and holy days. While the priest's main preoccupation was the teaching and preaching on matters of death and judgement, heaven and hell, the layperson was more concerned with baptism, marriage and burial. The religious fervour of the **laity** was frequently expressed in a materialistic way but with a spiritual motive, and in the fifteenth century many of England's 9000 parish churches were either built or improved by individuals hoping that their generosity would help reserve a place for them in heaven.

The only **heretical** idea to have acquired a significant following in England in the later Middle Ages was **Lollardy**. This laid stress on the reading of the Bible and urged the clergy to confine themselves to their pastoral duties. However, systematic persecution in the early fifteenth century had forced the Lollards underground, and there was no resurgence under Henry VII. About 73 Lollards are known to have been put on trial for heresy; of these, only three were actually burnt at the stake, the remainder confessing their sins and repenting.

Key terms

Laity
Laypeople; those who are not members of the clergy.

Heretic
A Christian who denies the authority of the Church and accepts or rejects some of its teachings.

Lollardy
A heretical movement that supported the translation of the Bible into English.

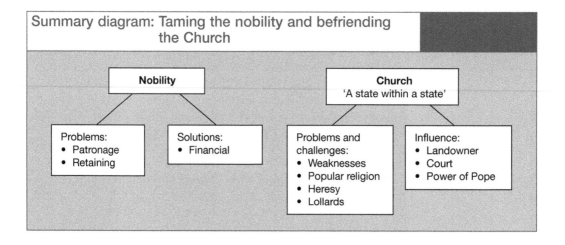

Summary diagram: Taming the nobility and befriending the Church

Study Guide: AS Questions

In the style of AQA

(a) Explain why Henry VII's position as King of England was insecure in 1487.

(b) How far was the rebellion of Perkin Warbeck a serious threat to Henry VII?

Exam tips

The cross-references are intended to take you straight to the material that will help you to answer the questions.

(a) You should re-read the sections on the minor rebellions of Henry's early years (pages 114–16) and on the Lambert Simnel rebellion (pages 118–21) before answering this question. When you have done so, make a list of reasons why Henry VII's position was insecure, referring both to the specific incidences of rebellion and concerns such as Lincoln's betrayal, and to more general factors, such as the position of the Yorkists and the fact that Henry himself had usurped the throne through battle.

You will need to show the links between these factors and should stress those which you feel to have been the most important. Try to develop your answer to lead to an overall conclusion.

(b) You need to re-read the material on pages 121–6 in the light of this question. Clearly you need to decide what would be understood as a serious threat and it might be helpful to define this in the first paragraph of your answer. You will need to assess Warbeck's personal threat and that posed by those who gave aid to this conspiracy, including Margaret of Burgundy, James IV of Scotland and the Emperor Maximilian. This might lead you to consider whether the rebellion was more of a threat to foreign relations than to internal ones.

To answer the question you will need to balance Warbeck's 'threat' against Henry's position as king. Would Henry have felt less threatened had his own position been more secure? The final essay should be argued throughout and lead the reader to a supported conclusion.

In the style of Edexcel

1. How accurate is it to say that Henry VII faced a much greater challenge from Lambert Simnel than he did from Perkin Warbeck?

2. How far do you agree that the Yorkists remained a serious threat to Henry VII's throne throughout this reign?

Exam tips

The cross-references are intended to take you straight to the material that will help you to answer the questions.

1. Questions which begin 'How accurate is it ...' can be followed by a range of statements. They can deal with causes, consequences, changes and so on. The question at the end of Chapter 5 began in the same way, but asked you for the causes of Henry's success. This one asks you to analyse some key features of the reign of Henry VII, compare them and reach a judgement. The question requires from you an assessment of the threat both pretenders posed. It does not require a narrative. For ease of comparison, you could organise your material to examine the following four elements:

   • strength of foreign backing
   • strength of support from within England
   • extent of the actual military threat
   • duration of the challenge.

   This will enable you to compare and contrast the two sets of challenges: Simnel's challenge led to the battle of Stoke, which could well have been 'another Bosworth' had the events on the field been handled differently (pages 120–1). In comparison, Warbeck's challenge enlisted foreign recognition and support, had an impact on England's trade, threatened the Spanish marriage alliance, but ultimately mounted no serious challenge in the field (pages 121–3).

   The question requires you to make a judgement. Do not be tempted to sit on the fence, but do make sure that your conclusion is in line with the argument you have developed in the body of your essay.

2. The key words to think about in planning your answer to this question are 'serious threat' and 'throughout'. You will need to be clear about the nature and extent of the threat and about whether the level of threat remained high until the end of the reign (pages 126–7).

   Select your material for relevance to the question. Not all rebellion and challenge to Henry was Yorkist (pages 116–18), but brief reference to non-dynastic challenges may help your assessment of Henry's overall position and his ability to deal with a Yorkist threat (pages 118–21 and 126–7).

   In dealing with the Yorkists' challenges to Henry (pages 113–14), there is no need to narrate the events. Provide a statement about the level of threat from the pretenders and from the Earl of Suffolk and support that with evidence. You could include the following: the weakness of Henry's claim to the throne (pages 109–10); the strength of support for the pretenders from the nobility and from abroad (pages 113–14); Henry's ability to deal with the threats (pages 121–7).

In assessing the seriousness of the threat, show how ineffective the Yorkists ultimately proved to be and how Henry's policies – in foreign affairs and in dealing with the nobility – contributed to his ability to reduce the level of the Yorkist threat (pages 114–16, 118–21 and 126–7).

Be sure to focus on the key words 'serious' and 'throughout' so as to come to a balanced conclusion. You should round off your answer by offering your judgement – do you agree or disagree with the statement in the question? One possible conclusion could agree that the Yorkists did represent some level of threat throughout Henry's reign, but that threat was only serious at the key points you have established in the main body of your answer.

In the style of OCR

1. To what extent was Henry VII threatened by pretenders?
2. How successful was Henry VII in establishing the Tudor dynasty?
3. 'Henry VII was fortunate still to be on the throne in 1499.' How far do you agree?

Exam tips

The cross-references are intended to take you straight to the material that will help you to answer the questions.

1. In this question you should examine and evaluate the extent to which Henry was threatened by rival claimants to the throne.

   Your evaluation should be balanced. You should also be able to come to a substantiated conclusion where an overall judgement can be offered. For example:

   - The weakness of Henry's claim to the throne and the way in which he became king might encourage others to try what he did at Bosworth (pages 102–4).
   - Owing to the frequent changes of kingship few expected Henry VII to last long on the throne (page 2).
   - The nature and extent of the support for the pretenders – from some of the nobility and from abroad – suggested they posed a very real threat to Henry.
   - On the other hand, Henry was well prepared to meet the expected threats from rivals and disaffected Yorkists.
   - The pretenders did not have the depth of support necessary to topple a regime – the majority of the nobility remained loyal and he could count on the support of Spain abroad.

2. In this question you should examine and consider the extent of Henry's success in establishing (securing) the dynasty.

   Your evaluation should be balanced. You should also be able to come to a substantiated conclusion where an overall judgement can be offered. For example:

   - The reign had survived for 14 years, longer than any of his Yorkist predecessors. (Note: Edward IV's two reigns – pages 48–62 and 65–86.)
   - Henry had two healthy sons so the future of the dynasty seemed assured (see page 15).
   - Henry had successfully defeated a number of rebellions and attempts to dethrone him (see pages 113–27).
   - On the other hand, there were still Yorkists roaming free on the continent, for example Edmund and Richard de la Pole (pages 126–7).
   - Henry's foreign relations remained fragile and needed constant repair (pages 162–71).
   - Henry had not won the wholehearted trust of all his nobles, for example Stanley's rebellion 1495 and the large number of attainders issued (page 124).

3. In a question like this, you must engage directly with the given quotation, decide how far you do or do not agree, and explain very clearly why. Note the question runs through to 1499 so make sure you cover that full period.

On the one side, Henry had been fortunate to win at Bosworth. He faced serious threats from ongoing Yorkist and other opposition across this period:

- from Margaret of Burgundy (pages 123–4)
- from the Pole family (pages 126–7)
- Lovel's revolt in 1486 (pages 114–15)
- conspiracies surrounding Lambert Simnel and Perkin Warbeck (page 11)
- rebellion in Yorkshire 1489 (pages 116–17)
- the Cornish rising 1497 (pages 117–18)
- disturbances in Ireland (page 120)
- foreign support for pretenders from Scotland and the Empire (pages 123–5).

The first 14 years of Henry's reign were filled with challenges that, singly or when combined, might have pulled him down.

Against that, the fact remains that he had survived those many troubles. Various Yorkist attempts had been defeated through vigorous action on Henry's part. The north, so crucial to the successful government of England, had been held for Henry and kept stable by his loyal ally, the Earl of Northumberland. He had been able to control the nobility to some degree, for example:

- action against retaining (pages 132–3)
- the use of bonds and recognisances (page 134)
- the use of attainders (pages 133–4)
- the king's council (pages 143–4)

and took swift action against them if needed (for example, the execution of William Stanley in 1495, page 124). He had built powerful international alliances, using them in part to legitimise his dynasty and undermine his Yorkist challengers (pages 113–14).

Strong answers will not just evaluate the threats to Henry's position, but assess how far those threats changed over time as he grew stronger. Was he safer after 1487 than before? With hindsight, we might think so, but Henry was still obsessed with the problem of security until at least 1504, and even to 1509.

In conclusion, you might also consider how far Henry was lucky to benefit from the mood in the country which, by 1485, stood strongly against further trouble. Henry may not have been too popular, but a renewal of civil war was far worse. For many, was Henry Tudor the least of the evils? However you decide, you have been given a chance to judge – so judge it, and judge it clearly one way or the other.

7 Henry VII: Governing the Kingdom

POINTS TO CONSIDER

Henry VII was determined to re-establish law, order and 'good governance' after the Wars of the Roses. To help him achieve this he sought to make the Crown solvent in the hope that financial security would contribute to consolidating the dynasty. Henry pursued an energetic foreign policy but he spurned confrontation and war unless it could not be avoided. His key aims were to be recognised by his fellow monarchs, and to secure trade and his throne. The way in which Henry governed the kingdom, restored the finances and established a vibrant foreign policy is examined as four themes:

- Government, law and the maintenance of order
- Seeking solvency: Henry's financial policy
- Diplomacy and alliance: Henry's foreign policy
- The dynasty secured

Key dates

1485	Henry's first parliament met
1486	Act of resumption
1489	Treaty of Redon
	Treaty of Medina del Campo
1492	Treaty of Étaples
1493	Council of Wales and the Marches re-established
1494	Sir Edward Poynings appointed Lord Deputy of Ireland
	Poynings' laws passed
c.1495	Council Learned in the Law established
1496	Trade agreement, known as the *Magnus Intercursus*, signed
1497	Truce of Ayton
1501	Marriage of Catherine of Aragon and Arthur, Prince of Wales
1502	Treaty of Ayton
	Death of Prince Arthur
1503	Office of Master of the King's Wards established
	Death of Queen Elizabeth
1504	Sir Richard Empson appointed head of the Council Learned

1506   Treaty of Windsor
1508   League of Cambrai

Key questions
How effective was Henry VII's government in maintaining law and order?

Why was it once thought that Henry VII had established a 'new monarchy'?

1 | Government, Law and the Maintenance of Order

'New monarchy'?

It was once thought that Henry VII governed in a way that was very different from that of his predecessors. Indeed, some historians went further and claimed that he introduced changes so revolutionary that he created a 'new monarchy'. The 'new monarchy' theory seemed to fit into what some historians of early modern Europe have described as the development of the 'nation state'. A state within which people sharing a common history, culture and language developed a sense of national identity, the bonds of which were cemented by the emergence of modern bureaucratic forms of government.

However, this idea that Henry VII was a 'new monarch' responsible for establishing a nation or sovereign state is no longer accepted. The reasons why historians thought Henry VII was so different is that he took a personal interest in the business of government. Unlike Edward IV, Henry enjoyed the paperwork that went with administering the kingdom and so he was able to stamp his unique authority on government. Henry made less use of the nobility but relied on a group of trusted advisers who came from the rising class of gentry. All of this gave the appearance of being new and different to what had been before.

Central government

Most historians now agree that there was little real change in the machinery of government between the accession of Henry VI (1422) and that of Henry VII (1485). Henry inherited a system that had been made more efficient by the Yorkists but there were no major changes in the institutions of central government during his reign.

The king's council

Key question
Why did Henry VII rely on such a small group of councillors?

The first serious test of Henry's kingship came within days of his accession: who would he choose to sit on his council? The king may have been at the heart of government but he could not rule effectively without the advice and assistance of his council. From the beginning Henry opted to govern through a small council and he came to rely on an élite group of councillors who met him regularly. For the most part this group was composed of men with whom Henry had spent time in exile and in whom he placed a great deal of trust. They included:

- the chief officers of state: the Lord Chancellor, John Morton, the Lord Privy Seal, Richard Fox, the Lord Treasurer, John, Lord Dynham

- those holding minor offices: Sir Reginald Bray, Giles Lord Daubeny, Sir Richard Guildford, Sir Thomas Lovell and Sir John Riseley
- the élite councillors who emerged later in Henry's reign: Sir Richard Empson, Sir Edward Belknap, Sir Edward Poynings and Edmund Dudley.

These men, the cream of the 40 councillors who made up the élite group, provided the new regime with the stability English governments had previously lacked (with the possible exception of Edward IV's government) because Henry kept them in power for so long. For example, Morton served as Lord Chancellor for 14 years until his death in 1500, while Fox served as Lord Privy Seal for 22 years until the king's death in 1509.

Occasionally, Henry called together the great council which met at court and included every member of the nobility, senior clerics in the Church and others such as the most prominent gentry. These men, totalling over 200, would be invited to meet with the king to offer advice on any matter that he deemed fit to discuss but usually connected with war, taxes and rebellion.

However, the real power lay with the élite group of councillors who met the king in a room in the Palace of Westminster with stars painted on the ceiling. As the burden of work became heavier and more complex Henry was compelled, in 1497, to create a new office Lord President of the Council. The president's task was to oversee the work of the council when the king was away on progress or on some diplomatic mission.

In order to improve the efficiency of central government, Henry followed the example set by his Yorkist predecessors by using smaller committees, formed from within the council, to deal with particular tasks. For example, in 1483 Richard III had established a conciliar committee to deal with legal cases, involving those who could not afford the high costs of the regular court system. Henry revived this idea and in 1495 established the Court of Requests, during which time it earned the nickname of the 'Court for Poor Men's Causes'.

Other committees set up by Henry included one to oversee the implementation of the statute of livery and maintenance of 1487 and, in the same year, one to prevent the intimidation of juries. Because these committees, as offshoots of the king's council, met in a room with a star-painted ceiling, nineteenth-century historians mistakenly thought that they represented the first attempt to set up the 'Court of Star Chamber'. This court became notorious later in the sixteenth and early seventeenth century for its harsh treatment of noblemen and gentlemen brought before it. Many of the committees or tribunals set up by Henry were never intended to become permanent institutions of government, but there were exceptions such as the Court of General Surveyors, which was responsible for auditing the revenues from Crown lands.

Key question
What was the Council Learned in the Law and how effective was it?

Key dates

Council Learned in the Law established: c.1495

Sir Richard Empson appointed head of the Council Learned: 1504

The Council Learned in the Law

The Council Learned in the Law (normally referred to simply as the Council Learned) was a small, professional body of councillors that came into being in 1495 to defend the king's prerogative rights as a feudal landlord. The Council Learned was hated because of its connection with bonds and recognisances (see page 134). It became the instrument of royal extortion – a debt collection agency in the opinion of historian Andrew Pickering – as it supervised the rigorous collection of these financial agreements. The men most associated with the council's financial exactions were Sir Richard Empson, Chancellor of the Duchy, and Edmund Dudley, his able deputy. Empson's promotion to President of the Council Learned in 1504 witnessed a new level of ruthlessness in which bonds and recognisances were increasingly misused to threaten the nobility and gentry. Dudley later confessed that he had acted illegally for the king in more than 80 cases. So hated had the pair become that within three days of Henry's death they were toppled in a palace coup led by the

Henry VII in conference with Sir Richard Empson and Edmund Dudley. What impression of Henry VII is the artist attempting to convey through this painting?

king's other servants. Unfortunately, the names of those responsible for arresting Empson and Dudley have not survived. Ironically, the Council Learned had become, by 1509, the most important and efficient of all Henry's institutions of government.

The personnel of government: clerics, nobles and the 'new men'

Key question
What class of men did Henry VII appoint to serve in his government?

The membership of Henry's council differed very little from its counterpart under the Yorkists. The majority of its members came from the Church and the nobility and, of these, some 29 had sat on the council of one or both of the Yorkist kings. However, it has been argued that the most important members of Henry's council came not from the Church or from the nobility but from a third group, the gentry. Some historians have referred to this group as being 'middle class' because they were lower in degree than the nobility and higher than the masses. Others, such as the historian Steven Gunn, have dubbed them the 'new men' serving a 'new monarchy'.

The membership of Henry's council included the following:

- *Clerics.* The largest social grouping on the council was the clerics, who, between 1485 and 1509, accounted for about half of the total membership. Among the most favoured of them were Archbishop John Morton, who Henry VII appointed his Chancellor or chief minister in 1487, and Bishop Richard Fox, who became the king's principal secretary. Morton was a doctor of civil law who had practised in the Church courts, while Fox had a degree in theology and had studied in Paris. This sort of education and legal expertise proved ideal for administrators, which is why Henry appointed them to his council.
- *Nobles.* That there was a substantial number of nobles represented on the council suggested that Henry did not deliberately seek to oust them from government as was once claimed. Henry was not anti-noble, but he believed that noble blood alone should be no guarantee of appointment to the council. What mattered to him were not title, wealth or breeding but loyalty, usefulness and efficiency. Those nobles who served him well were amply rewarded. Among these was John de Vere, the Earl of Oxford, who had supported Henry since his days in exile; he was given the offices of Great Chamberlain and Lord Admiral. Jasper Tudor received the dukedom of Bedford and the control of Wales. Even former Yorkists were not permanently excluded from serving the king in government. Once they had paid in some way for their 'treachery', they were given opportunities to prove their loyalty to the new regime. The Earl of Lincoln was a member of the council until he joined the Simnel rebellion, while Thomas Howard, Earl of Surrey, became a councillor after his release from the Tower and was appointed Lord Treasurer of England in 1501. Although Henry's council contained numerous representatives of the nobility, only his uncle, the Duke of Bedford, his friend, the Earl of Oxford, and his stepfather,

Sir Reginald Bray depicted in stained glass in a transept window in Great Malvern Priory. Why do you think Bray commissioned and paid for this stained glass image of himself?

Lord Stanley, the Earl of Derby, were really close to the king. It was probably this fact that gave rise to his reputation for being anti-noble.

- *'New men'*. Henry did not rely on a particular nobleman or family as Edward IV and Richard III had done. Instead, Henry's chief advisers and government officials were drawn from the ranks of the gentry, and from the professional classes (especially lawyers), men like Sir Reginald Bray, Edmund Dudley and Sir Edward Poynings. This has led some historians to label them the 'new men' because they were not noble and they did not come from families with a tradition of royal service. Although Henry made less use of the nobility in central government than his predecessors, there was nothing particularly 'new' about his reliance on the gentry rather than on the aristocracy. For example, two of Richard III's most loyal servants, Sir William Catesby and Sir Richard Ratcliffe, were lawyers and came from landowning gentry families. The ancestors of these 'new men' had generations of experience in local government, justice and landowning. As Henry was exploiting his lands through more efficient methods of estate management, he needed servants who understood auditing and property laws and had administrative skills. What mattered to Henry was not social class but ability. Until the creation of the office of President of the Council in 1497, the king was usually present at council meetings so he was very aware of how hard individual councillors worked or how much each contributed.

Regional government

Key question
How was regional government organised under Henry VII?

When Henry became king he faced the difficult task of controlling the individual nobles in the provinces. He dare not strip them of their provincial power for fear of causing a rebellion but he could not afford for them to retain unfettered control of their home regions. Henry acknowledged the fact that he needed them to help him police and govern the kingdom but, wherever possible, he tried to stop individuals building up too much power and he always insisted on their absolute loyalty to the Tudor dynasty.

Three of Henry's strongest supporters were rewarded with estates which brought with them a considerable amount of local control. Significantly, their influence never equalled that of Edward IV's leading nobles:

- Jasper Tudor, Duke of Bedford, became the most influential nobleman in Wales.
- John de Vere, Earl of Oxford, became the most influential nobleman in East Anglia.
- Thomas Stanley, Earl of Derby, became the most influential nobleman in north-west England.

Unless and until they could prove their loyalty, former Yorkists were denied the opportunity to establish or develop regional hegemonies. For example, Henry Percy, Earl of Northumberland, was allowed to continue in his former role of Lord Lieutenant of the North, but his powers were restricted and he gained no more territory. On Percy's death in 1489, Henry ignored the claims of northern noble families by appointing Thomas Howard, Earl of Surrey, as his successor. As a southern landowner, he had neither territory nor influence in the northern counties. His appointment was based purely on ability and not his noble lineage.

The same pattern emerged in Wales after the death of Jasper Tudor in 1495. No great magnate was allowed to succeed him and the power to govern Wales was put in the hands of a council under the presidency of William Smyth, Bishop of Coventry and Lichfield. Thus, by the end of his reign Henry was moving away from the idea of appointing a local magnate to control a particular region. This prevented the growth of magnate power and over-mighty subjects in the provinces and so enabled the links between central and regional government to become stronger.

The Council of the North

The Council of the North differed from the conciliar committees in having a clearly defined function dating from Richard of Gloucester's time as governor (see page 75). To maintain control of the northern council Henry did the following:

- Instructed selected councillors serving on the king's council, such as Sir Reginald Bray, to supervise its activities and to keep a careful watch on its personnel.
- Personally appointed the members of the council to prevent the president from choosing his family, friends and servants to serve under him.
- Required selected members of the northern council, such as William Sever, Bishop of Carlisle, to keep him informed with regular news bulletins.

The Council of Wales and the Marches

Key dates

Council of Wales and the Marches re-established: 1493

Sir Edward Poynings appointed Lord Deputy of Ireland: 1494

Poynings' laws passed: 1494

Unlike his Yorkist predecessors, Henry had less reason to fear rebellion or disorder in Wales because of his Welsh background and the level of support he enjoyed in the country. Nevertheless, Henry was as keen to secure control of Wales as he was of the north of England. He revived the Yorkist-inspired Council of Wales and the Marches in 1493 and appointed his uncle, Jasper Tudor, to oversee its operation. Henry also continued the tradition, begun by Edward I in 1301, of appointing his eldest son and heir as Prince of Wales. Thus his seven-year-old son, Arthur, was installed as its nominal head while the burden of governing the region was entrusted to a president appointed by the king.

Trusted Welshmen were appointed to key positions in Wales: Sir Rhys ap Thomas was appointed to govern south-west Wales while William ap Gruffudd ruled in the north. Henry's control of Wales was helped by the fact that, by 1495, due in part to inheritance, purchase, death and forfeiture, scarcely half a dozen Marcher lordships remained in private hands. Henry, therefore, governed directly, and indirectly, a larger proportion of Wales than any king had done before.

The Council in Ireland

Henry quickly learnt the danger that Ireland could pose when Simnel and Warbeck received considerable support there. In 1492, after the Earl of Kildare had recognised Perkin Warbeck's claim to the throne (see page 122), the king deprived him of his position as Lord Deputy and dismissed his closest supporters from office. Only after they had submitted and sought the king's pardon in person was Henry willing to restore them to some of their titles and offices.

In 1494, Henry set out to secure greater control of Ireland and its government. Sir Edward Poynings, one of his most trusted advisers, was appointed Lord Deputy. Other appointments included that of his infant son, Prince Henry, who was installed as Lord Lieutenant, as a counterpart to the nominal headship exercised by his elder son in Wales. Poynings' main tasks were as follows:

- to bring peace to Ireland, especially Ulster, the most rebellious part of the island
- to control the Irish nobility
- to extend the Crown's authority beyond the Pale
- to discourage support for pretenders and disaffected Yorkists
- to protect Ireland from foreign invasion.

Poynings enjoyed some success – there was no invasion of Ireland and the Irish were less prepared to support pretenders – but he never completely subdued the country outside the Pale and his control of the Irish nobility was tenuous. On the other hand, he did succeed in imposing a constitution on Ireland that would ensure its future obedience to the English Crown. At a meeting of the Irish parliament in 1494, Poynings pushed through a series of decrees that stated the King of England alone had the power:

- to summon and dismiss parliament
- to approve the agenda of business that included the right to decide what legislation and laws could and could not be discussed and enacted
- to ensure that any law made in England would automatically apply to Ireland.

Poynings' laws also:

- established the Court of the Castle Chamber in Dublin to govern the country under the presidency of the Lord Deputy
- passed an act of resumption to include all Crown lands alienated since the end of Edward II's reign (1327)
- imposed a five per cent tax on all imports with the profits going to the king.

In the short term, this gave the king more effective control of Ireland by destroying the independent legislative power of the Irish parliament. However, in the long term the expense of attempting to rule Ireland directly soon proved to be unsustainably high, and the experiment was abandoned.

Henry returned to his earlier policy of ruling through the Irish nobility. Kildare was reinstated as Lord Deputy and, for much of the rest of the reign, Ireland ceased to be a problem for Henry.

Local government

Henry inherited a robust system of local government from his Yorkist predecessors. Edward IV and Richard III had spent a great deal of time and effort restoring the structure and authority of local government after its collapse during the Wars of the Roses. Consequently, Henry was able to focus his attention on controlling the key offices of justice of the peace and sheriff, the backbone of county government.

Henry took a personal interest in the appointment of justices of the peace and sheriffs to ensure that those appointed would govern efficiently and serve the Crown loyally. The key feature of Henry's method of control was supervision from the centre. He and his councillors became the central figures directing operations from London with the aim of bringing royal government and justice closer to the people. In developing the role of the king's council and justices of the peace, Henry hoped:

- to exert his control more effectively over the localities
- to ensure that his instructions were obeyed
- to prevent the local nobility from developing too much power, or from seizing the opportunity to pursue their private feuds.

Although the problem of keeping the peace had not been completely solved, Henry had gone a long way to extending his control of the situation by centralising the system of local government.

Key question
How did Henry VII extend the power of the Crown into the localities?

The sheriffs and justices of the peace

The sheriff and the justice of the peace continued to be the two most important royal officials in each county. As the power of the justice of the peace increased, that of the sheriff continued to decline. Nevertheless, the sheriffs were given a new lease of life in the Tudor period in so far as:

- They became the Crown's representative in every county throughout England. In effect, they became the 'eyes and ears' of the monarch.
- Sheriffs took on greater responsibility for the conduct and management of parliamentary elections.

Unlike the justices of the peace, who were appointed for life, the sheriff was selected annually so that the Crown could exert greater control over these local officials.

After 1485, justices of the peace, like sheriffs, continued to be selected from those with significant amounts of land. However, as did Edward IV, Henry VII frequently chose to rely on the second rank of each county's landowners as it was another way of weakening the power of the greater magnates, which had led to the corruption of justice at the local level so often during the reign of Henry VI.

Henry VII also followed the example of his predecessor in widening the scope of justices of the peace's responsibilities. In 1485 an act of parliament gave them power to arrest and question poachers or hunters in disguise, because this could be a cover for murder or rebellion. Two years later they were given the power to grant bail to those awaiting trial.

Further acts in 1495 dealt with the problem of corrupt or intimidated juries, which had often been used by men of influence as a way of escaping punishment. Justices of the peace were given the power to do the following:

- replace suspect members of juries
- act in cases of non-capital offences without a jury
- reward their informers.

Henry had to rely on the justices' own self-interest as leaders of society for the upholding of law and order. Virtually his only control over them was the threat of removal from the commission if they acted improperly, which would be regarded by most justices of the peace as a considerable social disgrace. The **Court of the King's Bench** could overrule decisions made at the Quarter Session but this did not prove very effective.

There is no doubt that the king was dependent on the goodwill of his officials. What Henry wished to avoid is the fate that befell the Crown on the sudden usurpation of the throne by Richard III when some nobles had seized their opportunity to take authority into their own hands by deliberately choosing to ignore royal commands. A system of paid servants, as existed in France, would have been more efficient but, given the financial constraints on the English Crown, the system adopted by Henry VII worked relatively well by late medieval standards.

Key term

Court of the King's Bench
The highest and most important law court in the kingdom. It had the power to overturn decisions taken in lesser courts.

Parliament

In the 24 years of Henry VII's reign parliament was summoned on only seven occasions, and five of those were in his first decade as king when he was relatively insecure in his possession of the throne. Several reasons have been advanced to explain this:

Key question
Why did Henry VII call so few parliaments?

Henry's first parliament met: 1485

Key date

- He did not need to ask for war taxes very often because his foreign policy was based on avoiding expensive campaigns abroad.
- He did not wish to strain the loyalty of his subjects by making too many demands for grants of money.
- He did not feel the need to initiate legislation on a large scale. The government bills most frequently passed were acts of attainder designed to subdue the more troublesome of his political opponents.
- Parliament's judicial function as the final court of appeal was now being fulfilled by the subsidiary courts of the Royal Council, such as the Council Learned in the Law.

The king might not have summoned parliament frequently but he, like his Yorkist predecessors, used it as an institution to support his policies on law and order. For example, laws were passed against riots and retaining, and 10 per cent of all statutes dealt with the responsibilities of the justices of the peace and the control of the provinces. We also see early signs of what modern sociologists term 'social engineering' when Henry encouraged parliament to enact legislation to deal with social discipline. This is clearly evident in the following acts that:

- laid down rules on wages and hours of work
- instructed vagabonds to be put in the stocks and returned to their original place of residence
- forbade corporations from making any regulations unless they first had the approval of the king.

Parliament was being used by Henry to demonstrate the fact that all power derived from the Crown and that there was only one ruler in England. So, although parliament did not meet on a regular basis during Henry's reign, there was no threat of its ceasing to exist as a political institution (see Table 7.1).

Table 7.1: List of parliamentary meetings under Henry VII. Why did Henry VII call on parliament to meet on the dates listed?

Year	Date of session	Approximate length of session
1485–6	07/11/85–04/03/86	3 months
1487	09/11/87–10/12/87	1 month
1489	13/01/89–23/02/90	1.5 months
1491	17/10/91–04/11/91	0.5 month
1495	14/10/95–22/12/95	2 months
1497	16/01/97–13/03/97	2 months
1504	25/01/04–01/04/04	2.5 months

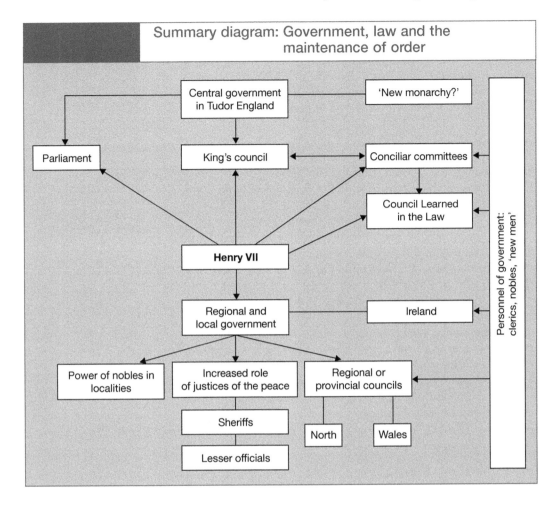

Summary diagram: Government, law and the maintenance of order

2 | Seeking Solvency: Henry's Financial Policy

Key question
How successful was Henry in restoring the financial strength of the monarchy?

Henry VII's financial aims were quite simple: to achieve solvency by increasing royal income, decreasing expenditure and thereby restoring the Crown's financial strength.

Henry VII has been described as 'the best businessman ever to sit upon the English throne', and on his death he was credited with being the 'richest lord that is now known in the world'. However, the truth is Henry lacked experience in government and was untried and untested in the rigours of financial administration and diplomacy.

Nevertheless, in spite of his shortcomings, he was very aware of the importance of strong finances if he was to remain safely on his throne. He told Henry Wyatt, one of his councillors, that 'the kings my predecessors, weakening their treasure, have made themselves servants to their subjects'. His usurpation of the Crown meant there was always the possibility of others putting forward their own claim. The availability of revenue together with financial stability was essential if he was to be able to raise an army to defeat them.

This is why Henry was so keen to reorganise the financial administration, because he believed that a wealthy king was a healthy king, one that was better able to finance his way out of trouble. However, Henry was well aware that his determination to make the collection of revenue more efficient would encounter opposition from those who would be expected to pay.

Financial administration

In the first two years of his reign, Henry VII had neither the experience nor the time to continue the Yorkist practice of using the chamber (see pages 85–6) so the exchequer resumed its control of royal finances. However, as early as 1487, Henry admitted that this might have been a mistake. In focusing so intensely on his own security, he had neglected to take adequate care of his estates and the consensus of contemporary opinion suggested that they had 'fallen into decay'. The accounts bear witness to this. In Edward IV's reign they had brought in between £20,000 and £25,000 per annum, but by 1486 this had declined to a fraction over £12,000.

Key question
How was England's financial administration organised under Henry VII and how efficient was it?

From the end of 1487, Henry gradually began to restore the chamber system to its former position as the most important institution of financial administration. By the late 1490s it was once again at the heart of royal finance, responsible for an annual turnover in excess of £100,000. It dealt with the transfer of all revenue from the following:

- Crown lands
- profits of justice
- feudal dues
- French pension.

In fact, it dealt with all sources of income except custom duties and the accounts of the sheriffs (the officials responsible for the maintenance of law and order in the shires). These remained under the control of the Exchequer because their collection involved detailed information and a complex organisation of officers and records not available to the **Treasurer of the Chamber**.

The Treasurer of the Chamber had become the chief financial officer of the Crown and during Henry's reign the post was held by two men only: Sir Thomas Lovell (1485–92) and Sir John Heron (1492–1521). They were two of Henry's most loyal and efficient servants and he worked very closely with them, checking the accounts himself and leaving his signature on them as proof of their accuracy.

Treasurer of the Chamber
Chief financial official responsible for the king's money.

Key term

The Privy Chamber

Arguably the most important development in the financial administration of the kingdom involved the king's Privy [private] Chamber. This was staffed by his personal household servants, who were entrusted with the task of overseeing the administration of the royal household as well as taking care of Henry's private expenditure. The chief officer of the Privy Chamber, the Groom of the Stool, became second in importance to the Treasurer of the Chamber, and lesser household officials, such as Gentlemen of the Bedchamber, grooms and ushers, found that new opportunities for promotion were open to them.

Financial personnel: Sir Reginald Bray (died 1503)

In order to ensure the smooth running of the Crown's financial administration Henry demanded loyalty, efficiency and integrity from the officials he put in charge. His most trusted adviser in financial matters was Sir Reginald Bray, the Chancellor of the Duchy of Lancaster. Bray's promotion was due to the recommendation of Henry's mother, Margaret, who he had served in her household. His efficiency and administrative skills were amply demonstrated during his time as Chancellor of the Duchy of Lancaster, a position that brought with it responsibility for running the richest and most important groups of royal estates in the country.

Bray had been responsible for successfully restoring the effective methods of estate management at the Duchy, which had been disrupted by the chaos caused by the Wars of the Roses. It was for this reason that Henry entrusted him with the task of introducing new methods of **auditing** the accounts. Although he held no formal office in either the Chamber or Exchequer – he was sometimes described as the 'under-treasurer of England' – Bray became the king's chief financial adviser. Bray was among a select group of royal officials and Henry regarded him as being as much a friend as a servant.

Bray did not work in isolation. He co-operated closely with both Lovell and Heron, and other household officials, making the system more efficient by holding frequent meetings to discuss and examine the Chamber accounts. According to Giovanni de Bebulcho, an Italian merchant, Bray, 'who controls the king's treasure', was the only man who really had any influence over Henry. Bray's death in 1503 hit the king hard but he found in Sir Robert Southwell a worthy successor. Southwell had been one of the king's most efficient auditors and he was promoted by Bray to become his assistant. Like Bray, Southwell's talent lay in offering the king sound advice on financial matters and in devising new and more efficient methods of collecting and accounting for money paid into the royal treasury.

Key term

Auditing
The process whereby financial accounts are checked by senior accountants employed by the king.

The financial resources of the Crown

Ordinary revenue

Ordinary revenue was the regular annual income on which the Crown could rely to finance the costs of monarchy (see pages 83–4).

Crown lands

Henry inherited all the lands which had belonged to the houses of York and Lancaster, including the Earldoms of Richmond, March and Warwick, the Duchy of Lancaster and the Principality of Wales. He also further enriched the Crown through **escheats** and attainders, but, unlike Edward IV, Henry did not grant a large proportion of them to his family and supporters; he thus retained the profits from them for himself.

Henry was clearly pursing a different policy towards his landed estates from that of Edward IV. This was partly due to his personal circumstances. He was lucky in having few relatives who expected to benefit from his seizure of the crown. He had no brothers; his uncle, Jasper Tudor, died in 1495, and his elder son, Arthur, in 1502. This left only Prince Henry requiring financial and territorial support. Henry did not shower honours on his extended family, such as the Stanleys, or over-reward his friends and supporters. Consequently, on his death in 1509, the Crown lands were more extensive than those he had inherited in 1485. A combination of efficient management and good fortune meant that the annual income from Crown lands had increased from £29,000 (£14 million in today's money) in 1485 to £42,000 in 1509 (£20 million today).

> **Key term**
>
> **Escheat**
> The system whereby, in the event of a landholder dying without heirs, his lands passed by right to the king.

Act of resumption

Henry was determined to restore the territorial wealth and strength of the Crown. In his very first parliament in 1486 he instructed its members to pass the act of resumption which recovered for the Crown all properties granted away as far back as 1455. This was a significant declaration by Henry because:

> **Key date**
>
> Act of resumption: 1486

- it expressed his belief that the majority of Crown lands had been wrongly alienated as a result of the civil war
- he was clearly, and legally, laying claim to substantial blocks of valuable territory
- having stated his claim, he did not take back all the estates involved because he did not wish to antagonise the majority of noble families affected by the act.

This last point is equally important because Henry knew that if he was to successfully consolidate the dynasty he must gain the support of the nobility by showing them he was prepared to compromise.

Customs duties

Henry considered the revenue derived from customs duties to be important enough for him to take a personal interest. For example:

- Within 18 months of his accession he introduced a system whereby merchants involved in shipping merchandise from one English port to another were required to produce a certificate from the first port as proof that duties had been paid.
- In 1496 he tried to reduce some of the privileges enjoyed by foreign merchants such as immunity from English customs duties paid on their goods.

- The Book of Rates, the setting of tariffs of customs duties to be paid in London, was twice updated to take account of price inflation and increasing mercantile profits.

Despite Henry's efforts, income from customs did not greatly increase. In fact, by the end of his reign the revenue collected from customs duties had been overtaken by that derived from Crown lands. Nevertheless, customs duties were still providing a third of the Crown's ordinary revenue. The average annual receipts were about £33,000 for the first 10 years of the reign and about £40,000 thereafter.

Feudal dues

Henry was determined to enforce these traditional rights to the full and to extract the maximum income possible from them. Initially the proceeds from wardship and marriage were small, amounting to only £350 in 1487, but after 1503 a special officer (the Master of the King's Wards) was appointed to supervise them, and by 1507 the annual income had risen to £6000.

Key date

Office of Master of the King's Wards established: 1503

Profits of justice

There is no doubt that Henry was rigorous, some have said ruthless, in his running of the judicial system. The income he derived from fines imposed on law-breakers, particularly for serious crimes such as murder, kidnap and arson, made a significant contribution to Henry's income. This policy attracted criticism because it looked as if the king was more concerned with financial gain than properly punishing the criminals. For example, even treason – a capital offence punishable by death – was sometimes commuted to life imprisonment and/or the imposition of a huge fine. Thus many of the rebels found guilty of participating in the Cornish rebellion of 1497 were fined rather than executed (see pages 117–18).

Another type of fine that the king used as punishment against opponents was that of attainder. For example, the attainder imposed on Sir William Stanley in 1495 resulted in the immediate confiscation of his total assets in cash and jewellery of £9000

Table 7.2: The number of attainders passed during the reigns of Edward IV, Richard III and Henry VII. Which king can be charged with the excessive use of attainders?

Attainders	Number
Passed by Edward IV	140
Reversed	42
Passed by Richard III	100
Reversed	1
Reversed by Henry VII directly after Bosworth	99
Passed by Henry VII	138
Reversed	46

Source: John Guy, *Tudor England*, Oxford University Press, 1988.

followed by an annual fine of £1000 charged on the income from his estates. There was only one parliament during the reign which omitted to pass any attainders and the highest number in any session was 51.

Extraordinary revenue
Extraordinary revenue was money which came to the Crown on particular occasions and therefore with no regularity (see pages 84–5).

Parliamentary grants
Henry was cautious in his dealings with parliament. He wished to exploit parliament's capacity to raise huge sums of money but he did want to overburden MPs for fear of provoking disobedience and opposition. He therefore used parliament sparingly, asking for financial assistance on only three occasions:

- 1487 to pay for the battle of Stoke
- 1489 to go to war against the French
- 1496 to defend the throne against attack from the Scots and Perkin Warbeck.

Historians have accused Henry of cheating his subjects by raising money for wars that did not actually took place, as in 1496. Certainly, Henry received the grant from parliament after the initial invasion of the Scots had failed to cross the border, but it could be argued that the money was still needed as the attack might have been renewed at any time. In the event, there was no further trouble from Scotland, but some of the money was used to suppress the Cornish rebellion the following year.

Loans and benevolences
Following precedents set by Edward IV, Henry turned increasingly to exploiting the system of loans and benevolences (see page 85). In times of crisis they proved a useful method of raising large sums quickly. Two such crises arose in 1491 and 1496:

- In 1491 Henry raised a **forced loan** when he intended to take his army across the Channel to protect Brittany from French aggression; this produced £48,500, a reasonable amount when compared with the sums yielded by direct taxation. Royal Commissioners were stringent in its collection.
- In 1496 the pretender Warbeck threatened to invade England at the head of a Scottish army. In order to raise and fund an army to defend the kingdom Henry appealed to his landholding subjects for financial support. This royal request, drawn up in the form of an 'agreement', was virtually impossible to decline because to do so in the face of war, rebellion or invasion was tantamount to committing treason.

Forced loan
Loans demanded by the Crown from the noble and gentry landowners and wealthy merchants. Those who failed to pay risked being labelled as disloyal.

Key term

Henry was aware that such loans and benevolences were controversial and had the capacity to anger those from whom he requested money, mainly well-to-do merchants and landowners. With this in mind he seems to have asked for only modest sums, based, as far as possible, according to an individual's annual income. For example, Sir Henry Vernon of Haddon Hall, Derbyshire, who enjoyed an annual income of over £900, was expected to 'lend' the Crown the sum of £100. On the other hand, if the king's officers suspected someone of trying to avoid payment they were less than sympathetic. One lady, whose name is no longer legible on the contemporary account, offering only £5 of the £20 deemed appropriate for her to contribute was threatened with being summoned before the king's council.

There is no evidence of any resentment leading to rebellion, probably as most of the loans appear to have been repaid, partly in cash but mainly in the form of land or office. In truth, Henry had little choice but to repay them because those subjects who were owed money by the king were more likely to support a rival claimant to the throne.

Clerical taxes

Henry received quite substantial sums from the Church. On several occasions, usually when Parliament made a grant, the Convocations followed suit with their own contributions. In 1489 they voted £25,000 towards the cost of the French war.

Henry also made money from **simony**, charging £300 for the Archdeaconry of Buckingham on one occasion. Like many of his predecessors, the king kept bishoprics vacant for many months before making new appointments so that he could pocket the revenue in the meantime. Owing to a rash of deaths among the bishops in the final years of the reign, Henry received over £6000 per annum in this way. However, he did not exploit this method as much as some of his contemporaries in other countries such as France or Spain who often prolonged vacancies for years. Henry rarely left a diocese without a bishop for more than 12 months.

Key term

Simony
The selling of Church appointments.

The French pension

The Treaty of Étaples of 1492 demonstrated Henry's skill in diplomacy. Threatening war on the French he nonetheless offered to discuss peace. It was a risky strategy that worked since the French wished to avoid war and they were not sure whether Henry was bluffing. In tough negotiations Henry forced the French into making concessions, the most important of which was the grant of a pension. It was a tactic used by Edward IV in 1475 when he negotiated the terms of the Treaty of Picquigny. Henry was promised £159,000 to compensate him for the cost of the war, a sum to be paid in annual amounts of about £5000, only half of what Edward IV managed to force from the French.

Bonds and recognisances

Henry also exploited another source of extraordinary revenue through bonds and recognisances. In general terms this was the practice of subjects paying a sum of money to the Crown as a guarantee of their future good behaviour. However, there was a subtle difference between the two:

- Bonds were written obligations in which people promised to perform some specific task in the service of, or on behalf of, the king. If they failed to carry out the designated task they were subjected to a financial penalty. Bonds had long been used as a condition for the appointment of officials but in the later fifteenth century their use was extended to private individuals as a way of keeping the peace and ensuring loyalty to the Crown. For example, in 1491, 55 people were held liable for the good behaviour of Thomas, Marquis of Dorset. The list included nobles, bishops, knights and merchants, each pledging a sum ranging in size from £1000, demanded of the Earl of Kent, to £50, requested from Thomas Quadryng, a merchant.
- Recognisances were formal acknowledgements of actual debts and they became the normal way of ensuring payment of money owed to the Crown. Henry took a personal interest in such matters in that they were issued only on his explicit instructions. For example, in 1485 he demanded a recognisance of £10,000 from Viscount Beaumont of Powicke and a similar sum from the Earl of Westmorland as guarantees of their future loyalty.

Historians have long debated Henry's use of bonds and recognisances. While some believe he cynically exploited the system, others dispute this, claiming his only 'fault' was his efficiency in its enforcement and collection. In the first decade of his reign, 191 bonds were collected, rising to well over 200 in the later years of his reign. This is evident in the receipts from bonds, which rose from £3000 in 1493 to over £35,000 in 1505. Those who fell behind in these payments were pursued by the king's officials, particularly those from the Council Learned in the Law, which was made responsible for administering bonds and recognisances. The council became greatly feared because of the efficiency of two of its officials, Empson and Dudley, in hounding defaulters.

Professor Lander's research noted that during Henry's reign, 46 out of 62 noble families were at one time or another financially at his mercy: seven were under attainder, 36 were bound by recognisances or obligations, and three by other means. It is from such evidence that historians such as Caroline Rogers have concluded that 'Henry's main aim in using bonds and recognisances was to fill his coffers.' This led to his gaining a reputation for cynicism and greed, particularly in relation to the later years of the reign.

However, some historians such as Neville Williams have risen to Henry's defence by pointing to evidence that suggests his chief concern was to threaten financial ruin in order to maintain his subjects' loyalty rather than merely increasing his income. The evidence most commonly referred to concerns the experiences of Henry Percy, Earl of Northumberland. It seems that Henry intended to make the errant Percy pay only £2000 of the £10,000 he was originally made to promise. Therefore, one might argue that Henry policies of 'financial terror' and humiliation were designed to consolidate the dynasty and bolster his security.

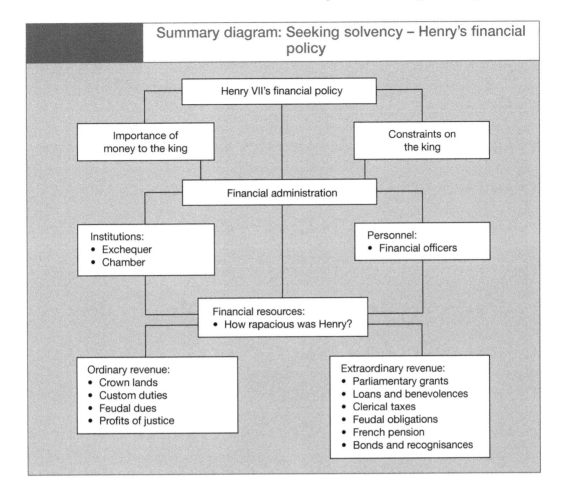

Summary diagram: Seeking solvency – Henry's financial policy

Key question
How far did Henry
achieve his aims in
foreign affairs?

3 | Diplomacy and Alliance: Henry's Foreign Policy

Henry's aims

The principal aims of Henry's foreign policy can be summarised as follows:

- to maintain peace
- to avoid war
- to gain allies.

The reason why he pursued a largely non-interventionist policy was because he had no choice. War was expensive and dangerous; peace was far cheaper and gave him time to consolidate his power in England. Gaining allies offered some guarantee of support and stability. Indeed, it must be remembered that Henry's foreign policy was very much subordinated to his domestic policies of enriching the monarchy and ensuring the obedience of his subjects. In short, Henry's primary aim was to retain control of the Crown and secure the long-term future of his dynasty.

Dynastically, diplomatically and financially Henry was vulnerable. As a usurper, his right to the throne was thought by

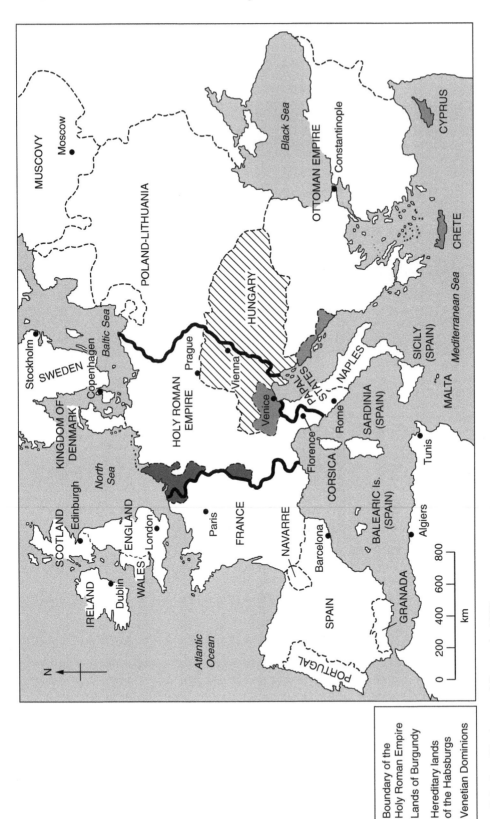

Figure 7.1: A political map of Europe in 1505.

many to be suspect and most of Europe's rulers did not expect him to last long. In addition, Henry was menaced by the claims of pretenders to his throne, two of whom, Simnel and Warbeck, successfully sought aid from foreign powers. Understandably, Henry pursued a more cautious and defensive policy than that of his predecessors because he had to be constantly on his guard against possible invasion. Unsurprisingly, dynastic threats dominated his dealings with foreign rulers, which is why the issue of security lay at the heart of the treaties he concluded with France, Spain, Scotland and Brittany. Of these, Spain alone became a powerful and reliable ally helping to secure international recognition for Henry's kingship of England.

Consolidating support

Key question
How did Henry VII try to consolidate his support in Europe?

In the first three years of his reign (1485–8), Henry's actions in foreign affairs were deliberately designed to give him time to consolidate his position. His preferred policy was the truce because it was temporary, could be extended, and did not tie him down to any long-term promise or commitment:

- Henry's first target was England's traditional enemy, France. The French were willing to negotiate a one-year truce with Henry because they had helped finance his expedition to seize the throne. The French regent, Anne of Beaujeu, believed that Henry was unlikely to survive more than a year but when he did the truce was extended for another three years until 1489.
- Henry next sought peace with his northern neighbour, Scotland, and in July 1486 he succeeded in persuading James III to agree to a three-year truce. The assassination of James III in 1488 and the accession of the 15-year-old James IV disrupted relations but the terms of the truce held firm.
- Henry did not regard Brittany as a threat, more a trading partner, which is why he was prepared to negotiate a long-term treaty rather than a temporary truce. As a consequence, the treaty, signed in July 1486, was more commercial than political and involved favourable trade agreements that benefited England.

Henry had done no more than play for time. He had avoided confrontation and had established important contacts with foreign powers. However, he had failed in his primary aim, which had been to prevent foreign invasion so that he could concentrate on strengthening his power at home. The Simnel rebellion of 1487 had revealed how vulnerable he was because much of the finance for the invasion, together with a sizeable contingent of professional troops, came from a foreign power, Burgundy.

Burgundy

For much of the fifteenth century, and especially during the wars against France, Burgundy had been England's ally. The Burgundian dukes had long opposed French expansionist policies which might lead to the conquest and annexation of the duchy.

Consequently, they sought the aid of France's enemies such as England to protect their independence. Burgundy's ties with England ran deep for, in addition to being political and military allies, they were commercial partners. The duchy was the main outlet for the sale of English cloth, England's biggest industry.

To bring the two nations even closer, Edward IV had arranged for his sister Margaret to marry the Burgundian duke, Charles the Bold. This arrangement worked well until Richard III was killed at Bosworth. However, after Bosworth the relationship between the two former allies naturally faltered. To Margaret, the **Dowager Duchess** of Burgundy (her husband Charles had been killed in battle in 1477), Henry was nothing more than a usurper and she made it her mission to unseat and destroy him. The Burgundian court became a magnet for disaffected Yorkists and pretenders to the English throne such as Simnel and Warbeck. Henry had no chance of sealing a deal with Burgundy so long as Margaret had influence in the duchy.

Dowager Duchess
Title given to the widow of a duke and mother of the heir.

Key term

Brittany and the Treaty of Redon 1489

Brittany, like Burgundy, was threatened by France's riches, power and expansionist plans. Brittany was the only part of the historic kingdom of France that still retained its independence. However, unlike Burgundy, Brittany was small, weak and nowhere near as wealthy. Henry's interest in Brittany was selfish because he saw the duchy as a possible ally in any future conflict with France. To deny France control of Brittany would help England maintain diplomatic and commercial relations with a friendly power on the other side of the Channel. Control of the English Channel was key to Henry's security. With Brittany at one end and England's French colony, Calais, at the other, Henry hoped, with the aid of a rapidly expanding navy, to police the Channel and deter a foreign invasion. However, Henry was not prepared to go to war to protect Brittany's independence. He hoped diplomacy and mediation would be sufficient to prevent armed conflict between Brittany and France: he was wrong.

Key question
Why did Henry VII consider Brittany to be of such vital importance to England?

Henry's plans came unstuck in July 1488 when French troops invaded the duchy and defeated the Bretons at the battle of St Aubin du Cormier. The conflict had arisen over French plans for the future of Brittany. Anne, the French regent, planned to marry her brother, Charles VIII, a minor, to Anne, the daughter and heir of Duke Francis of Brittany. The French were keen to cement this marriage alliance because it would result in the peaceful annexation of Brittany and avoid the need for war. Unfortunately for the French, Duke Francis refused to accept the marriage proposal and sent to Henry for help. Henry faced a dilemma: he did not want to offend either Brittany or France but he felt obliged to do something. His solution was to send an army, unofficially, of several hundred 'volunteers' to support the Bretons while at the same time attempting to act as a mediator between the two courts: it failed.

Duke Francis was forced to sign the Treaty of Sablé:

• He acknowledged the French king to be his feudal overlord.
• He promised that his heiress, Anne, would not marry without the permission of the French king.

Although Henry was not entirely happy with the terms of the treaty, he knew that so long as Francis lived the annexation of Brittany would have to wait. Three weeks later, in September, Francis died (of natural causes) and his 12-year-old daughter became Duchess of Brittany. As feudal lord, the French king immediately claimed custody of Anne and the annexation of Brittany by France seemed imminent.

This fresh crisis caught Henry unawares but again he resisted the temptation to threaten the French with war. He tried to bring pressure to bear on the French by using his diplomatic skills to enlist the help of allies but only Spain offered any realistic prospect of support when they despatched 2000 men to aid England and Brittany. In an effort to convince the French that he would go to war to protect Brittany Henry took a gamble by concluding the Treaty of Redon with the Bretons. According to the terms of the treaty Brittany promised to pay the cost of the 6000 men which Henry sent them in April 1489. Unfortunately, it proved too little too late and when the Spanish troops were withdrawn after serving less than a year, Henry too withdrew. Finally, in December 1491, the Bretons accepted defeat and the Duchess Anne was married to King Charles. Their marriage spelled the end of Brittany's independence.

Key dates
Treaty of Redon: 1489
Treaty of Étaples: 1492

Key question
Who benefited from the treaty of Étaples: England or France?

France and the Treaty of Étaples 1492

Henry's intervention in Brittany had angered the French, who took the opportunity to support the pretender to the English throne, Perkin Warbeck. Henry had no choice but to react to this threat and he did so with a declaration of war against France. He announced his intention to assert his claim to the French crown and sent commissioners to raise funds by collecting a forced loan. He followed this up in October 1491 when he summoned parliament with a request to grant him money to help pay for the army. A year later, in October 1492, a large, well-equipped army of 26,000 men landed in Calais, from where they moved to besiege Boulogne.

Henry did not want war, nor could he afford one, but he needed to convince the French that his warlike intentions were serious. Once again Henry was gambling in the hope that the French too wished to avoid conflict. Fortunately for Henry his bluff worked and nine days after Henry had set foot on French soil, Charles VIII offered to negotiate. A peace treaty was agreed and signed by both parties on 3 November at Étaples. It is likely that Henry's agents had informed him of French intentions to make war in Italy, so that an English army on French soil was a distraction that Charles could do without. Three of the most important concessions Henry wrested from the French at Étaples were the following promises:

- to give no further aid to English rebels, particularly Warbeck
- to pay the cost of transporting Henry's army back to England
- to pay the arrears of the pension agreed with Edward IV at the Treaty of Picquigny back in 1475 (see page 71).

The total cost to the French Crown was in the region of 745,000 gold crowns, payable at the rate of 50,000 crowns a year. In contemporary English currency this equalled about £5000, approximately five per cent of the Henry's annual income.

Henry had scored a significant diplomatic victory. He had shown that his skills as a strategist and tactician were not confined to the battlefield. At Bosworth and Stoke, Henry had proved his courage and had fulfilled the expectations of kingship by his military prowess. At Étaples, Henry had shown himself to be a shrewd and capable negotiator, proving that words could be every bit as effective as the sword.

Spain, Medina del Campo (1489) and the marriage alliance 1501

Next to Étaples the Treaty of Medina del Campo with Spain was the most significant achievement of Henry's foreign policy. Spain emerged as a major power in the late fifteenth century after the unification of the country in 1479. Initially, England and Spain were commercial rivals, but both were willing to sink their differences in a common animosity towards France.

Early in 1488 Henry suggested a marriage between his eldest son, Prince Arthur, and Ferdinand and Isabella's youngest daughter, Catherine of Aragon, when they reached marriageable age. The negotiations were tough and laborious as both sides wanted to secure the best possible terms. Eventually, Ferdinand agreed to Henry's demands:

- Spain would offer no aid to any English rebels or pretenders to the English throne.
- Catherine's dowry would be double that initially offered. The Spanish agreed to pay 100,000 crowns.
- Both nations become trading partners.
- If either country found itself at war with France, the other was to intervene immediately.

War was obviously envisaged in the near future, particularly by Henry, who had become embroiled in the conflict between Brittany and France. The Spanish too were willing to make war on the French in the hope of securing the recapture of the Pyrenean territories of Cerdagne and Rousillon.

By 1493 the Spanish had achieved their aim in the Pyrenees, while doing as little as possible to help Henry in his efforts to secure Brittany's independence. Henry, however, seemed satisfied with his relationship with Spain and he continued his pro-Spanish policy throughout his reign.

Key question
Why was a treaty with Spain so important to Henry VII?

Treaty of Medina del Campo: 1489

Key date

Near contemporary portrait of Prince Arthur. Why was the only surviving portrait of Arthur painted after his death?

In the opinion of historian Caroline Rogers, this was because:

> Henry's triumph lay in the fact that his dynasty had been recognised as an equal by one of the leading royal families of Europe. This was of major importance to a usurper who was desperately keen to secure international recognition of the legitimacy of his position as king.

Key date

Marriage of Catherine of Aragon and Arthur, Prince of Wales: 1501

The alliance with Spain was finally cemented on 14 November 1501 when Catherine and Arthur were married in St Paul's Cathedral. Following Arthur's death in April 1502, Henry and Ferdinand entered into fresh negotiations to keep the alliance alive. In September 1502, after six months of hard bargaining, a new alliance was forged. Under the terms of the new treaty it was agreed that Catherine would marry Prince Henry when he came of age.

The Holy League and *Magnus Intercursus* 1496

The year 1496 proved to be the most successful in Henry's diplomatic career. French military successes in Italy had provoked a violent reaction in the other European rulers who feared that France was becoming too powerful.

To resist French expansionism and drive Charles out of Italy, the Pope, Ferdinand of Spain, the Emperor Maximilian of Burgundy, and the rulers of Venice and Milan formed the League of Venice in 1495. A year later Henry VII of England was invited to join the alliance, which became known as the Holy League. His invitation came from Ferdinand of Spain, who feared an Anglo-French alliance after the French king offered to support Henry in his struggle with Perkin Warbeck.

Henry showed that he was no one's puppet by joining the League only on condition that England was not bound to go to war against France. Ferdinand agreed to this because England's neutrality was preferable to an alliance with France. In fact, Henry managed to outmanoeuvre both ally and potential foe when he concluded a commercial treaty with France while maintaining good relations with his allies in the league.

Arguably his greatest success came with the conclusion of the *Magnus Intercursus*, whereby England and Burgundy agreed to set aside their former enmity and resume trading relations. Henry was fortunate in that Margaret's power and influence were in decline as Maximilian, the new duke and newly elected Emperor of the Holy Roman Empire (1493), took a more active role in the duchy's affairs. Nevertheless, it was still a considerable achievement, especially as Maximilian still had doubts about trusting Henry.

Key dates

Trade agreement, known as the *Magnus Intercursus*, signed: 1496

Truce of Ayton: 1497

Treaty of Ayton: 1502

Scotland and the agreements of Ayton 1497 and 1502

Relations between England and its closest neighbour, Scotland, were always tense. The Scots resented English claims to overlordship of Scotland, a tradition that stretched back to at least the reign of Edward I. In an effort to avoid English political pressure to back their claims, the Scots had established a tradition of their own that involved them in an alliance with France. This 'auld alliance' between Scotland and France was a constant source of tension and worry for English kings. Henry too was wary of Franco-Scottish intentions, which is why he worked hard to conclude truces with both nations within three years of his accession.

However, when Perkin Warbeck sought aid from the Scots their king, James IV, took the opportunity to put pressure on Henry by supporting the pretender. James even went as far as to give Warbeck his cousin in marriage, which must have appeared extremely threatening to Henry. However, Warbeck's invasion of England with Scottish help came to nothing; he gained no support south of the border and, when the Scots heard that Henry was sending an army to oppose them, they took flight.

Key question
Why did Henry consider good relations with Scotland to be important?

Henry felt secure enough to be able to offer terms on which a long-lasting peace treaty with Scotland could be based. The truce of Ayton was concluded in 1497, but it was only after Warbeck had been executed in 1499 that the Scots were prepared to negotiate a full treaty of peace. Warbeck's death left the Scots with little to bargain with, which is why they agreed to the signing of the Treaty of Ayton in 1502.

The Treaty of Ayton was a great achievement for Henry as no such agreement had been reached between the two countries since 1328. The treaty was sealed by the marriage of James to Margaret, Henry's eldest daughter, in August 1503. However, Scotland did not abandon its traditional alliance with France; this meant that the peace depended on the continuation of good relations between England and France, but while Henry lived this did not pose a problem.

Changing diplomacy: Henry's relations with the European powers 1502–9

Key question
How and why did Henry VII's relations with the European powers change after 1502?

Key dates

Death of Prince Arthur: 1502

Death of Queen Elizabeth: 1503

In the opinion of historians Carolyn Towle and Jocelyn Hunt, 'Henry's diplomacy had a tired feel to it.' This is certainly true after 1502 when death and decline conspired to hinder the effective operation of Henry's foreign policy. Following the deaths of his son and heir, Arthur, in April 1502, and his wife, Queen Elizabeth, in February 1503, Henry's health began to decline. His infirmity and inability to cope with the rapidly changing pattern of diplomacy left Henry increasingly vulnerable and isolated. Instead of driving European diplomacy forward, Henry was left reacting to a bewildering number of developments, many of which were beyond his control.

As if to emphasise Henry's vulnerability, Edmund de la Pole chose this time to flee abroad. Pole's intentions were clear, to revive the Yorkist movement and to seek foreign aid against Henry. Although he failed to fulfil his aims the threat he posed added to Henry's worries. These worries were eased somewhat when Spain offered to renew their alliance by agreeing to the marriage of Catherine to Prince Henry.

Nevertheless, Henry remained on alert and his concern to safeguard the dynasty led him to consider the possibility of taking a second wife who might be able to bear him more heirs. Four suitable matches appeared to offer the best prospects of a successful marriage:

- Joan of Naples
- Margaret of Angouleme
- Margaret of Austria and Savoy
- Joanna of Castile and Burgundy.

These were intended to be dynastic marriages where political, diplomatic, financial and strategic considerations far outweighed the bride's ability to produce a healthy child. In each case Henry had mapped out possible benefits of the particular marriage:

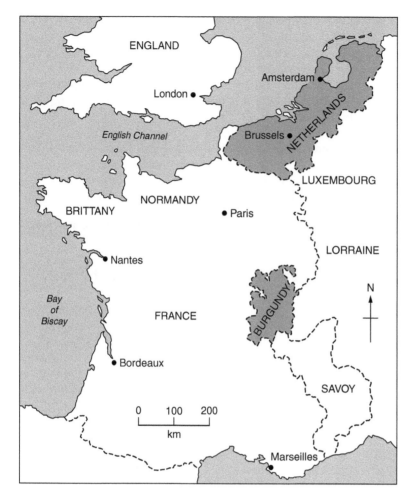

Figure 7.2: Map showing Burgundy and the Netherlands.

- Joan of Naples, was recommended to Henry on two counts: her wealth and the fact that she was the niece of Ferdinand of Spain. This marriage would strengthen England's alliance with Spain and add to Henry's coffers. However, Henry's interest in her cooled when he found she was not as wealthy as he had been led to believe.
- Margaret of Angoulême was the sister of the French king, Louis XII, who hoped to tie Henry into an alliance and thus draw him away from his friendship with Spain. Louis also offered a financial inducement to tempt Henry into marriage but nothing came of the proposal.
- Margaret of Austria, widow of Duke Philibert of Savoy, was the daughter of the Emperor Maximilian. Henry was attracted by the prospect of sharing in her wealth, taking advantage of her position as governor of the Netherlands and forming an alliance with Maximilian. The marriage negotiations dragged on for nearly three years, until 1508, when Margaret eventually declined Henry's proposal.
- Joanna of Castile was the daughter of Ferdinand of Spain. Where Ferdinand had encouraged Henry's proposed marriage to his niece Joan, he opposed any match with his daughter

Joanna. This was due to sudden and unexpected events that changed the diplomatic situation in Europe. In 1504 Ferdinand's wife, Isabella, died, leaving Joanna as heir to the kingdom of Castile. In a legal arrangement drawn up when Ferdinand of Aragon and Isabella of Castile wed, uniting the two kingdoms to form the kingdom of Spain, it was agreed that their eldest daughter Joanna would inherit Castile. Faced with the prospect of losing half his kingdom Ferdinand tried to have the arrangement changed so that he could act as regent and rule Castile on his daughter's behalf. Thus Henry's attempt to marry her and lay claim to half of Spain was viewed most unfavourably. In fact, Ferdinand went so far as to declare that his daughter had gone insane – she became known as Joanna the Mad – which many contemporaries regarded as a bluff to confirm his regency and put off potential suitors.

In the event, Henry never did remarry. Indeed, historians are not entirely convinced that he seriously intended to marry again, believing this to be another of Henry's diplomatic bluffs. By maintaining an apparent interest in remarriage, Henry was able to keep the European powers guessing as to his true intentions. However, all Henry managed to do was create confusion and cause resentment: he alienated Louis of France, angered the Emperor Maximilian and very nearly turned Ferdinand of Spain into an enemy.

The Treaty of Windsor (1506) and League of Cambrai (1508)

Key question
How significant were Windsor and Cambrai?

Key dates

Treaty of Windsor: 1506

League of Cambrai: 1508

In 1506, Philip, Duke of Burgundy, was persuaded by Henry to sign the Treaty of Windsor, which united England and Burgundy in an alliance to resist France. Philip was married to Joanna of Castile and he called on Henry to support his claim to his wife's Spanish kingdom. This angered Ferdinand, who now turned against Henry. Philip's death months later killed the alliance, leaving Henry isolated, and facing the wrath of both Ferdinand and Louis of France. Henry's answer was to stir the matter up further by seeking the hand in marriage of Philip's widow, Joanna. He also succeeded in persuading the French king to join him in an alliance against Ferdinand. Louis did not trust Henry but agreed because he considered Ferdinand a greater threat than Henry.

The League of Cambrai was formed as an anti-Spanish alliance. However, at the eleventh hour the French king, Louis XII, changed his mind and decided not to join with Henry. So when the League of Cambrai was signed in December 1508 it was as an alliance against Venice, between the Pope, Louis XII, Maximilian, the Archduke Charles and Ferdinand. In the end it was Henry, and not his Spanish rival, who was left isolated by this alliance. Fortunately for Henry, the members of the league had their attention focused elsewhere and so did not threaten any of England's vital interests.

In the final analysis, Henry's death came at a time when his foreign policy was in danger of collapse because it was bereft of ideas.

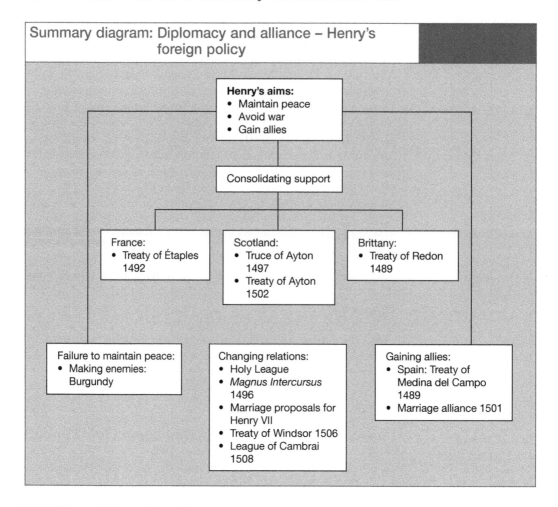

Summary diagram: Diplomacy and alliance – Henry's foreign policy

Henry's aims:
- Maintain peace
- Avoid war
- Gain allies

Consolidating support

France:
- Treaty of Étaples 1492

Scotland:
- Truce of Ayton 1497
- Treaty of Ayton 1502

Brittany:
- Treaty of Redon 1489

Failure to maintain peace:
- Making enemies: Burgundy

Changing relations:
- Holy League
- *Magnus Intercursus* 1496
- Marriage proposals for Henry VII
- Treaty of Windsor 1506
- League of Cambrai 1508

Gaining allies:
- Spain: Treaty of Medina del Campo 1489
- Marriage alliance 1501

4 | The Dynasty Secured

Henry died of a stroke in April 1509. His death did not witness
the collapse of the government, the return to civil war or the end
of the dynasty. His son and heir, Henry, ascended the throne
peacefully and without challenge. The Crown was secure, solvent
and not embroiled in conflict with its European neighbours.
Henry may not have been popular when he died, his reputation
for ruthlessness and greed saw to that, but he had succeeded in
securing the Tudor dynasty. In the final analysis, the majority of
historians would agree that the memorable achievements of
Henry VIII and Elizabeth I would not have been possible without
the secure foundations laid by Henry VII.

Summary diagram: Henry's legacy

BALANCE SHEET

Aims and policies	Success	Failure	Comment
Establishing the dynasty	Henry firmly established the Tudor dynasty. He defeated his rivals and the pretenders, and he secured the throne. The fact that he stayed in power and passed on his throne to his son is an impressive achievement. (First monarch to do so successfully for nearly a century.)	Henry failed to establish a sense of security. His position as king was constantly under threat until at least the last three years of his reign.	It has been argued that this was Henry's only achievement.
Finance	Henry left the Crown solvent. He was the first king to do so in more than a century. The Crown's finances were more stable and secure, and the methods of collection were more efficient.	Henry failed to innovate or improve upon the financial achievements of his Yorkist predecessors. The wealth amassed in his final years was by illegal or highly dubious means. The efficiency of his tax collecting methods made the king unpopular.	It has been argued that solvency was not such an achievement. No other Tudor monarch died solvent yet their reputations have not suffered as a result.
Nobility	Henry re-established the Crown's primacy over the nobility. He kept the nobility in check and largely reduced the threat they posed by such devices as bonds and recognisances.	He bullied the majority of the nobility into subjection. His harsh methods were resented by many and pushed some into rebellion, e.g. Earl of Lincoln.	Had he worked more on a basis of consensus rather than coercion, he might have avoided rebellion and encouraged loyalty.
Foreign policy	He won respect for England abroad and created a stable diplomatic environment. The alliance with Spain was perhaps his greatest achievement.	He failed to play a full part in international relations. His reliance on Spain did little to enhance his dealings with other nations. By 1509 England was largely isolated.	Henry did not take advantage of his wife's death to marry a foreign princess. In human terms this was commendable but in policy terms it was a missed opportunity.
Law and order	He re-established respect for the law and restored confidence in the government after the uncertainties of the Wars of the Roses.	He failed to reduce the tension that existed between rival noble families. He failed to stop rebellions and periodic disorder from breaking out.	England was a more peaceful and stable country under Henry than it had been under the Yorkists.
The economy	Henry encouraged trade and commerce. Royal patronage, peace at home and a more stable international situation promoted economic growth.	Economic advantages were often sacrificed for gains in foreign policy.	England had become a richer country under Henry.

Study Guide: AS Questions

In the style of AQA

1. **(a)** Explain why Henry VII issued many bonds and recognisances during his reign.
   (b) How far was Henry VII's control of the throne dependent on strong finances?
2. **(a)** Explain why Henry VII established diplomatic marriages for his children. (12 marks)
   (b) How important was the need for security to Henry's foreign policy between 1485 and 1509? (24 marks)

Exam tips

The cross-references are intended to take you straight to the material that will help you to answer the questions.

1. **(a)** Obviously you will need to show that you understand what is meant by bonds and recognisances (pages 159–60). You will need to consider their financial implications (the acknowledgement of a debt to the Crown) and their use as a means of controlling the nobility (binding members of the nobility and important officials to the king to ensure they remained loyal and did not rebel). You might also see them, more generally, as a way of extending the king's power and increasing security as well as breeding loyalty. Try to offer a range of inter-linked reasons and provide an overall summary that shows some judgement in the conclusion.

   (b) The main focus of this question should be on the contribution of strong finances to Henry's position as king (pages 154–61 and 173). How important was it for Henry VII to have a steady income and financial security? To provide a balanced answer you will also need to consider other factors which contributed to Henry's control of the throne. Some of these have been dealt with in earlier chapters, for example his control of the nobility, his concern with law and order, his use of institutions such as the Council Learned in Law and his employment of loyal and efficient officials. Decide how you will apportion the credit for Henry's control between these and develop an argument in your answer which leads to a well-supported conclusion.

2. **(a)** In this question you will need to explain why the marriage of Henry's children strengthened England's diplomatic links, for example:

   - The marriage between Arthur and Catherine of Aragon strengthened England's trade and political links with Spain (pages 166–7).
   - The marriage between Margaret and James IV of Scotland secured England's northern border and prevented Scottish aid for the pretender Warbeck (pages 168–9).
   - The marriages with foreign powers added to the prestige and stability of the Tudor dynasty.

(b) You will need to evaluate the extent to which the need for security dominated Henry's foreign policy and balance this against other factors such as trade and prestige. You should also show how Henry's priorities shifted between security and other factors throughout his reign, for example:

- Henry's treaties with Spain and Scotland show that security was a very important part of his foreign policy (pages 166–9).
- Henry's treaties with Burgundy and France show how important trade and prestige were to a newly crowned king (pages 163–4).

In the style of Edexcel

1. How far did Henry VII achieve his aims in foreign affairs?

2. How far do you agree that Henry VII obtained internal security for his realm mainly through his financial policy?

Exam tips

The cross-references are intended to take you straight to the material that will help you to answer the questions.

1. This question is asking you for an assessment of Henry's success in relation to what he was trying to achieve. You should first identify his aims clearly, and then explore the extent to which the evidence suggests he did achieve them.

You could establish that his aims were to:

- enhance and protect his dynasty, cutting off support for challengers
- preserve England's finances
- promote trade.

Sometimes one aim was in conflict with another, and you can show that defending the dynasty was paramount, even at the expense of damaging trading interests (for example, in breaking off trade with Flanders in 1493, Chapter 6, page 123).

With these aims in mind, you can then examine relations with France, Scotland and Burgundy. The Treaty of Étaples indicates that Henry was prepared to pursue limited aims and to subordinate England's traditional rivalry with France to his greater other priorities of preservation from challengers and financial stability (pages 165–6). You could show that, in spite of periods when they gave support to challengers to his throne, Henry ultimately succeeded in establishing peaceful relations with Burgundy, and achieved the marriage alliance with Scotland (pages 163–9).

You should examine the strengths and limitation of Henry's relations with Spain. The Treaty of Medina del Campo can be seen as a major achievement in establishing the dynasty and in opening up the possibility of an anti-French partnership (pages 166–7). You should, however, acknowledge Henry's lack of control of events and the problems of relations with Ferdinand of Aragon after 1504 and his isolation from the League of Cambrai in 1508 (page 171).

Your overall assessment of Henry's success should be in relation to his broad aims. If, in your view, these were substantially achieved, then you can give less weight to setbacks and failures – but you must also acknowledge these when coming to your conclusion.

2. The key words to think about when planning your answer to this question are 'internal security' and 'mainly though his financial policy'. You will need to be clear about the significance of financial policy in contributing to the strength and security of Henry VII's throne, but the word 'mainly' implies that you will need to show the contribution of other factors too. You should plan to devote between one-third and one-half of your answer to 'financial policy', allowing yourself time to deal convincingly with other policies – in foreign affairs and in controlling the nobility, for example – which also contributed to a level of internal security which he did not have at the beginning of his reign (pages 143–72).

There will be no need to describe in detail Henry's actions or policies. Plan to show the link between financial policies and the strength of the regime making clear points and then supporting those points with evidence related to financial policies. Then show the importance of Henry's other policies before coming to an overall conclusion.

In support of the argument that financial policies were significant you could: show that his policies did succeed in building up the royal finances and weakening noble challenge in the process (pages 153–61); show that these healthy finances also enabled him to secure loyalty (pages 159–60) and defeat challenges to the throne (pages 156–9).

In support of the significance of other factors you could show that his foreign policy (pages 161–72) and his measures to strengthen the powers of central government (pages 143–51) also strengthened the internal security of his realm.

You should round off your answer by offering your judgement: do you agree or disagree with the statement in the question? In this case you could argue that financial policies were the most important, or that other factors were. One possibility might be to argue that control of the nobility was key to internal security and that that was achieved by an effective combination of policies, including financial policies, which enabled Henry to assert his personal control and increase his power.

In the style of OCR

1. Why, and with what success, did Henry VII strengthen the royal finances?
2. To what extent was Henry VII's foreign policy motivated by financial considerations?
3. 'Henry VII built his foreign policy around keeping the Tudors on the English throne.' To what extent do you agree with this assessment?

Exam tips

The cross-references are intended to take you straight to the material that will help you to answer the questions.

1. In this question you should explain why the royal finances needed strengthening and why sound finances were important to Henry and evaluate his success in strengthening the royal finances. Two-thirds of your answer should concentrate on evaluating the success of Henry's financial policies. For example:

   - The royal accounting system and revenue collection were still inefficient in spite of the improvements made under Edward IV and Richard III (pages 153–61).
   - Sound finances would enable Henry to be independent and strong (pages 153–61).
   - Henry needed to repay the debts that had been incurred in his bid for the throne (pages 153–4).
   - Henry needed money to reward loyalty and to defeat any rival claimants to the throne (pages 154–5).
   - You need also to evaluate Henry's success in strengthening the finances, for example the king's financial methods became more efficient, which resulted in a corresponding rise in revenue. Henry's success in finance is often hailed to be among his greatest achievements. On the other hand, his methods were too rigorous and his determination to collect all available sources of revenue led to resentment and uprisings.

2. In this question you must compare and evaluate the reason mentioned (financial considerations) in the question with other equally relevant reasons rather than simply offer a descriptive list of causes. Therefore, you should consider the extent to which Henry VII's foreign policy was motivated by other factors aside from finance, for example, although the French pension and the financial settlement received from the King of Spain on the marriage of Arthur and Catherine of Aragon suggest that financial gain was at the heart of Henry's foreign policy (pages 166–7), other equally important motivating factors need to be considered:

   - to secure the throne and dynasty (pages 161–3)
   - to enhance Henry's status and prestige (page 163).

3. This question asks you to judge Henry's foreign policy aims and the quotation gives you an angle around which to discuss what

was his prime motive. There is plenty of evidence to draw on to show links between his foreign policies and securing the Tudor dynasty, whether looking at Henry's agreements with Scotland, the Empire or Castille/Aragon. You can examine ways in which Henry used his foreign policies both positively and negatively in this respect: marriage alliances to build the new Tudor dynasty and clauses in a variety of treaties to shut off foreign support for Yorkists.

Henry VII was a usurper and he worked hard to secure international recognition both for his own kingship and for the new dynasty he was founding. This was difficult since foreign relations were far from stable and this international recognition was thus never secure, especially in the period from 1502 with the deaths of Prince Arthur, Queen Elizabeth, Queen Isabella and Philip of Burgundy (see pages 169–70).

Against the claim in the quotation, you can produce evidence that the prime direction of Henry's aims abroad geared his foreign policies, as was required of every king of England, to protect and strengthen the interests of England. The defence of the Scottish border was essential for any king in London. To go one stage further and try to change the relationship with Edinburgh through alliance and marriage was not just far-sighted but astute, especially when in James IV the Scots had a child king. In his relationship with Brittany to 1491–2, Henry's complex manoeuvres show consistent attempts to secure the interest of England. So too do one of the major trade treaties of his reign: *Magnus Intercursus* (see page 168).

What does Henry's inclination to peace rather than war show us? The evidence points in more than one direction, as do the specific details of his foreign policies. How well worked out were Henry's aims? By definition, foreign policy had to adapt as circumstances developed. Successful foreign policy must be flexible, as in Henry abandoning Brittany when it became too weak or abandoning Ferdinand of Aragon in 1504 and working hard to create an anti-Ferdinand League of Cambrai in 1508 (see page 171). Henry often failed (for example, he failed to defend Brittany; he failed to isolate Ferdinand after 1507) and he made expensive mistakes (signing *Malus Intercursus*; the massive loans to Emperor Maximilian), but England was held in much higher regard in 1509 than it had been in 1485.

Glossary

Act of accord   An act of parliament responsible for determining the line of succession to the throne.

Act of resumption   An act of parliament intended to recover Crown lands given away as reward for service.

Artillery   Wheeled cannons of various sizes.

Attainted   The process by which nobles who broke the law were condemned and then punished. This law enabled the king to seize the law-breaker's estates so that he could benefit from the profits.

Auditing   The process whereby financial accounts are checked by senior accountants employed by the king.

Auditors   Officials who counted and wrote down the figures in an account book.

Benevolence   A type of forced loan which would not normally be repaid to the loanee.

Black Death   Plague that spread across the British Isles between 1347 and 1351 killing up to half of the population.

Bloody flux   Dysentery, an inflammatory disorder of the intestine, that results in severe diarrhoea accompanied by fever and abdominal pain.

Boroughs   Towns with a royal charter granting privileges for services rendered, usually dating well back into the Middle Ages.

Chivalry   The medieval institution of knighthood. It is usually associated with ideals of knightly virtues, honour and fair play.

Clientship   Relationship based on service and support. The majority of the most-powerful nobles led large numbers of followers who served them and who, in turn, were protected by them.

Commissioners of 'oyer et terminer'   Literally meaning to 'hear and determine', these commissions were given the power to investigate any crime or disturbance thought serious enough for the Crown to become involved.

Commons   One of the two houses of parliament staffed by elected representatives, mainly gentry landowners, to assist in the business of government.

Commonweal   The common good or common wealth of the people and the nation.

Convocation   The clerical equivalent of parliament in which the upper house of bishops and lower house of ordinary clergy met to discuss Church business.

Council Learned   Council staffed by legally trained officials entrusted with the task of defending the king's rights and imposing financial penalties on law-breakers.

Counties   The key units of administration in England. The kingdom was divided up into counties, very much like today, to make the government of England easier. Each county elected representatives to sit in parliament.

Coup d'état   A French term used to describe the overthrow of a monarch or government.

Court of the King's Bench   The highest and most important law court in the kingdom. It had the power to overturn decisions taken in lesser courts.

Crowland Chronicle   Also known as the *Croyland Chronicle*, this important chronicle was written by a well-informed monk from the Benedictine Abbey of Croyland in Lincolnshire. The most significant part of the chronicle, covering the years 1459–86, was written sometime in April 1486.

Depose To rid the kingdom of its reigning monarch by forcing him to abdicate or resign.

Divine right Belief that monarchs were chosen by God to rule the kingdom and that their word was law. To challenge their right to rule was the same as challenging God's.

Doctrine Rules, principles and teachings of the Church.

Dowager Duchess Title given to the widow of a duke and mother of the heir.

Dowry The sum of money or property a father provided to his daughter to give to her husband on marriage.

Eisteddfod An annual Welsh cultural festival in which prizes are offered to competitors in poetry and music.

Escheat The system whereby, in the event of a landholder dying without heirs, his lands passed by right to the king.

Evil councillors A useful and often-used contemporary label to brand those around the king as the enemies of sound advice and good government.

Excommunicating Expelling from the Church.

Feudal The medieval social and political system by which lords were given land in return for serving the king in time of war.

Feudatories Territories with feudal lords who owed allegiance to the King of France.

Field guns Small cannons mounted on wheels.

Fool of God A contemporary term used to describe someone who is far too religious for his own good.

Forced loan Loans demanded by the Crown from the noble and gentry landowners and wealthy merchants. Those who failed to pay risked being labelled as disloyal.

French pox An outbreak of syphilis, a sexually transmitted disease, which spread through the ranks of the French army and also infected the English.

Gentry Class of landowners below the nobility. They were divided into three strata: knight, esquire and gentleman.

Great Chain of Being The belief that God has ordained that everybody was born into a specific place in the strict hierarchy of society and had a duty to remain there.

Hanseatic League Merchants from the mainly German city ports on the Baltic and North Sea who came together to form a trading union and thus dominate trade in northern Europe.

Heretic A Christian who denies the authority of the Church and accepts or rejects some of its teachings.

Hog Refers to Richard's emblem of the white boar.

Hundred Years War Historical term used to describe the intermittent conflict between the kings of England and France for possession or control of the French crown and kingdom of France.

Indenture Agreement or contract between a master and his servant.

Indicted Charged with a crime.

Infection resistant Constant exposure to an infection enabled some people to develop a natural immunity.

Inquisitions post mortem Local enquiries into the lands held by people of some status and wealth, in order to discover whatever income and rights were due to the Crown. Such inquisitions were only held when people were thought or known to have held lands of the Crown.

Justice of the peace Local law officer and magistrate at county level. He also governed the county by enforcing acts of parliament and acting on decisions taken by the Crown and central government.

Justices of assize Senior judges who dealt with serious crimes and dispensed justice in the king's courts, which were held twice a year in each county.

King's council Élite body of councillors, drawn mainly from the nobility, who met the king regularly to frame policy and govern the country.

King's peace   The idea that, as the king was appointed by God, his law was the highest authority which brought order and protection to the people.

Laity   Laypeople; those who are not members of the clergy.

Live of their own   A contemporary term meaning monarchs should pay their own way using money from their own pockets rather than burden the state with taxes.

Livery   The giving of a uniform or badge to a follower.

Lollardy   A heretical movement that supported the translation of the Bible into English.

Lord Deputy   The effective ruler of Ireland invested with the power and authority to govern the Irish on behalf of the Crown.

Lord Lieutenant   In times of peace the office had no function beyond the ceremonial, such as the state opening of the Irish parliament, but in times of war it was responsible for raising and leading the Crown's forces in Ireland. Between 1472 and 1478 Ireland was at peace so Clarence played no effective part in Irish affairs.

Magnate   A greater or more powerful nobleman.

Maintenance   The protection of a follower's interests.

Marcher counties   English counties bordering Wales that were originally intended to defend England from Welsh attack.

Marriage   The royal right to arrange the marriage, for a fee, of heirs and heiresses.

Muster of the militia   The muster was a method by which local representatives of the Crown called up fit and able men to serve in the army. The militia was an army of conscripts raised to serve the king for a set period.

National assessment   A country-wide system of assessing people's wealth for purposes of taxation.

National debt   Money owed by the Crown to members of the English nobility and continental bankers and financiers. The Crown borrowed the money to help pay for the costs of the court, the royal household and the government.

Northern affinity   Used to describe the noble and gentry supporters of Richard III who came from northern England.

Order of the Garter   Founded in 1348, this honour was bestowed on the most important knights, who then became the senior rank of knighthood.

Orthodox   Accepting without question the doctrine of the Church.

Over-mighty subject   A strong noble who was very wealthy, powerful and often over-ambitious.

Palatine   A territory ruled by a person invested with princely or royal authority.

The Pale   Territory in eastern Ireland occupied and ruled by English kings since the thirteenth century. The capital of this English-controlled region was Dublin.

Parliament   Institution of government representing English landowners consisting of the Houses of Lords and Commons. It had the power to grant taxes and to pass laws.

Patronage   The award and distribution of royal favours.

Pluralism   The holding of more than one parish by a clergyman.

Privy seal   The king's personal seal was a substitute for his signature and was used to authenticate documents.

Propaganda   The method by which ideas are spread to support a particular point of view.

Protector   Another word for regent.

Readeption   In this sense, the restoration of Henry VI as king.

Receivers   Officials who collected and stored money on behalf of the king.

Re-endowment   Reinvestment, or finding other ways of raising money for the Crown.

Regent   Someone who governs the kingdom on behalf of a king.

Regular clergy   Monks and nuns who devoted their lives to prayer and study in monasteries, sheltered from the outside world.

Relief   A payment the king received on the transfer of lands through inheritance.

Retaining   Employing or maintaining armed servants and/or private armies.

Retrenchment   Cutting down on expenditure.

Revisionist historians   Historians who revisit historical events and revise earlier historical interpretations.

Robin of Redesdale and Robin of Holderness   Pseudonyms used to mask the true identities of the rebel leaders.

Royal court   The court acted as a public place for people to come and meet the king. The court was attached to whichever palace the king happened to be living in.

Royal household   The retinue and servants who looked after the monarch's personal needs and his financial and political affairs.

Royal patronage   Rewards given by the Crown for faithful service. The rewards were often given in the form of property, money, title or office.

Royal proclamations   Royal commands that had the same authority in law as acts of parliament.

Sanctuary   A place of safety within the walls of a religious institution such as a monastery or church.

Secular clergy   Parish priests, chaplains and bishops who lived in the outside world. They performed tasks such as marriage, baptism and burial.

Semi-regal princes   Nobles exercising the powers of a monarch in a particular lordship or locality.

Service nobility   Nobles whose power and promotion rested on serving the king in government office.

Sheriff   Chief law officer in the county who arrested and detained criminals, some of whom were dealt with in the sheriff's court or passed on to the justices of the peace. The sheriff also supervised parliamentary elections.

Simony   The selling of Church appointments.

Subsidy   Voluntary grants of money to the king by his subjects.

Sweating sickness   A virulent form of influenza.

Treason   Betrayal of one's country and its ruler.

Treasurer of the Chamber   Chief financial official responsible for the king's money.

Under-mighty monarch   A weak king.

Usurpation   The seizure of the throne without authority or in opposition to the rightful line of succession.

Viceroy   A title given to a nobleman entrusted with royal authority to rule as the king's deputy in some part of the realm.

Wardship   The practice whereby the king took control of the estates of minors (those who were too young to be legally responsible for their inheritance) and received most of the profits from their estates.

Yorkist invasion   Used by historians to describe the return of armed Yorkists to England from exile abroad.

Index